Unwin Critical Library
GENERAL EDITOR: CLAUDE RAWSON

MIDDLEMARCH

Unwin Critical Library

GENERAL EDITOR: CLAUDE RAWSON

Middlemarch

KERRY McSWEENEY
Professor of English,
Queen's University, Kingston, Canada

London
GEORGE ALLEN & UNWIN
Boston   Sydney

George Allen & Unwin (Publishers) Ltd,
40 Museum Street, London WC1A 1LU, UK

George Allen & Unwin (Publishers) Ltd,
Park Lane, Hemel Hempstead, Herts HP2 4TE, UK

Allen & Unwin Inc.,
9 Winchester Terrace, Winchester, Mass. 01890, USA

George Allen & Unwin Australia Pty Ltd,
8 Napier Street, North Sydney, NSW 2060, Australia

First published in 1984

British Library Cataloguing in Publication Data

McSweeney, Kerry
    Middlemarch.—(Unwin critical library)
    1. Eliot, George. Middlemarch
    I. Title
    823'.8   PR4662
    ISBN 0-04-800031-0
    ISBN 0-04-800032-9 Pbk

Library of Congress Cataloging in Publication Data

McSweeney, Kerry, 1941–
    Middlemarch.
    (Unwin critical library)
    Bibliography: p.
    Includes index.
    1. Eliot, George, 1819–1880. Middlemarch. I. Title.
    II. Series.
    PR4662.M39 1984   823'.8   84–2982
    ISBN 0-04-800031-0
    ISBN 0-04-800032-9 (pbk.)

Set in 10 on 12 point Plantin by
V & M Graphics Ltd, Aylesbury, Bucks
and printed in Great Britain
by Biddles Ltd, Guildford, Surrey

GENERAL EDITOR'S PREFACE

Each volume in this series is devoted to a single major text. It is intended for serious students and teachers of literature, and for knowledgeable non-academic readers. It aims to provide a scholarly introduction and a stimulus to critical thought and discussion.

Individual volumes will naturally differ from one another in arrangement and emphasis, but each will normally begin with information on a work's literary and intellectual background, and other guidance designed to help the reader to an informed understanding. This is followed by an extended critical discussion of the work itself, and each contributor in the series has been encouraged to present in these sections his own reading of the work, whether or not this is controversial, rather than to attempt a mere consensus. Some volumes, including those on *Paradise Lost* and *Ulysses*, vary somewhat from the more usual pattern by entering into substantive critical discussion at the outset, and allowing the necessary background material to emerge at the points where it is felt to arise from the argument in the most useful and relevant way. Each volume also contains a historical survey of the work's critical reputation, including an account of the principal lines of approach and areas of controversy, and a selective (but detailed) bibliography.

The hope is that the volumes in this series will be among those which a university teacher would normally recommend for any serious study of a particular text, and that they will also be among the essential secondary texts to be consulted in some scholarly investigations. But the experienced and informed non-academic reader has also been in our minds, and one of our aims has been to provide him with reliable and stimulating works of reference and guidance, embodying the present state of knowledge and opinion in a conveniently accessible form.

C.J.R.
University of Warwick
December 1979

PREFACE

George Eliot once observed that 'it is often good to consider an old subject as if nothing had yet been said about it; to suspend one's attention even to revered authorities'. This was the procedure followed by David Daiches in his fine little book on *Middlemarch* of twenty years ago; but it has not been my procedure. The novel has been the subject of informed critical commentary ever since the copious reviews that followed its publication in 1871-2; and in the past two decades it has received an enormous amount of attention. There was far too much of value in this material to make its neglect appropriate, though it is fair to say that I am less indebted to revered authorities than to the excellent work of a number of less eminent commentators, which I hope my study will make better known.

I am grateful to Professor Claude Rawson of the University of Warwick for the opportunity to contribute to the discussion of one of the greatest English novels. It is a pleasure to acknowledge once again the support of the Social Sciences and Humanities Research Council of Canada, this time for the award of a leave fellowship during 1982-3. I am also grateful to Baroness Faithfull of Wolvercote, Dr Roy Park of University College, Oxford, Mr Paul Turner of Linacre College, Oxford, and my daughters Lucy and Kendra. All of them helped to make the circumstances in which this book was written most pleasant. My greatest debt is to my wife Susanne for her good-humour and expert assistance.

Quotations from *Middlemarch* are from the Riverside edition by Gordon S. Haight (Boston, Mass.: Houghton Mifflin, 1956). For quotations from Eliot's other works of fiction I have used the editions in the Penguin English Library.

Oxford
April 1983

CONTENTS

In memory of my uncle
John McSweeney

CHAPTER 1

Preliminary

I shudder a little to think what a long book it will be.
George Eliot, letter of 4 August 1872

Middlemarch is an extraordinarily rich novel. It depicts the life of a segment of English provincial society in the second quarter of the nineteenth century with an abundance of circumstantial detail that includes over one hundred characters. The novel's four major plots connect at innumerable points both with each other and with the rest of the novel's world; the central characters are presented with a wealth of moral and psychological notation; and the thematic complex of which they are part includes the relation of the individual to society and of character to circumstance, the problem of vocation, the possibilities for heroic action in the modern world, the search for the 'minute processes which prepare human misery and joy' (ch. 16), and the importance of fellow-feeling rather than ideas or doctrines as the basis of a post-Christian religion of humanity. Its comprehensive examinations of character in its social and historical setting and of society itself in its manifold interconnections make *Middlemarch* one of the classic texts of nineteenth-century realistic fiction. Its thematic richness and intellectual sweep make it even more than that. In one of his digressions, the novel's narrator pays tribute to his great predecessor Henry Fielding, contrasting Fielding's 'copious remarks' and leisurely expansiveness with the belated diminution of the narrator's concentration on a 'particular web' rather than 'that tempting range of relevancies called the universe' (ch. 15). The modesty is engaging, but false: in its breadth of moral and philosophical vision *Middlemarch* is unsurpassed not only by *Tom Jones* but also by any other English novel.

The achievement of *Middlemarch* was apparent even to contemporaries. Henry James, for example, spoke of the contrasting histories of the two central characters having 'that supreme sense of the vastness and variety of human life, under aspects apparently similar, which it belongs only to the greatest novels to produce';[1] and Emily Dickinson answered the question 'What do I think of *Middlemarch*?' with 'What do I think of glory ... The mysteries of human nature surpass the "mysteries of redemption".'[2] For Edith Silcox, a woman of letters, social reformer, and passionate admirer of George Eliot:

Middlemarch marks an epoch in the history of fiction in so far as its
incidents are taken from the inner life, as the action is developed by the
direct influence of mind on mind and character on character, as the
material circumstances of the outer world are made subordinate and
accessory to the artistic presentation of a definite passage of mental
experience, but chiefly as giving a background of perfect realistic truth
to a profoundly imaginative psychological study. The effect is as new as
if we could suppose a *Wilhelm Meister* written by Balzac.[3]

And, in trying to account for 'why I rate *Middlemarch* so high', Lord
Acton, the great historian, came to this conclusion:

> My life is spent in endless striving to make out the inner point of view,
> the *raison d'être*, the secret of fascination for powerful minds, of
> systems of religion and philosophy, and of politics, the offspring of the
> others, and one finds that the deepest historians know how to display
> their origin and their defects, but do not know how to think or to feel as
> men do who live in the grasp of the various systems. And if they
> sometimes do, it is from a sort of sympathy with the one or the other,
> which creates partiality and exclusiveness and antipathies ... George
> Eliot seemed to me capable not only of reading the diverse hearts of
> men, but of creeping into their skin, watching the world through their
> eyes, feeling their latent background of conviction, discerning theory
> and habit, influences of thought and knowledge, of life and of descent,
> and having obtained this experience, recovering her independence,
> stripping off the borrowed shell, and exposing scientifically and
> indifferently the soul of [her characters] without attraction, preference,
> or caricature. And each of them should say that she displayed him in his
> strength, that she gave rational form to motives he had imperfectly
> analysed, that she laid bare features in his character he had never
> realised.[4]

One of the reviewers of *Middlemarch* predicted that future critics
would point back to the novel 'as registering the low-tide mark of spiritual
belief among the literary class of the nineteenth-century'.[5] This has not
turned out to be the case, of course: it is in the novels of Thomas Hardy,
only one of which had been published when *Middlemarch* began to
appear, that future critics have found this low-tide mark. The reviewer
was right enough, however, in sensing that *Middlemarch* was an exemplary
text and an important piece of evidence in the case of the disappearance of
God in the nineteenth century. The major precipitates of the Victorian

crisis of belief were the Higher Criticism of the Bible and the demythologised version of Christianity that had grown up in Germany, and the rise of modern evolutionary modes of thought and investigation in the earth sciences, the life sciences and the social sciences. It is hardly surprising to find that these currents of thought circulate in *Middlemarch*, for in the decades before she came to write her great novel George Eliot had translated into English both David Friedrich Strauss's *Leben Jesu* and Ludwig Feuerbach's *Wesen des Christenthums*, and been closely associated with some of the most advanced British thinkers of the day, including Herbert Spencer and George Henry Lewes, with both of whom she was at different times in love. This intellectual side of George Eliot is most directly reflected in her essays, the bulk of which were written during the 1850s for the *Leader* and the *Westminster Review*. The rest of her work before *Middlemarch* consists of a long poem and the six works of prose fiction, beginning with *Scenes of Clerical Life* in 1857, that established her as one of the leading novelists of the day. Since the greatest influence on any mature writer is always his own past work (as John Fowles has remarked), the following chapters contain numerous references to both George Eliot's essays and her other novels.

In contrast, there will be no later opportunity to discuss the experiences and relationships in Eliot's private life that have a bearing on *Middlemarch*. The world of the novel is that of north-east Warwickshire where her childhood, adolescence and youth were spent, and the profusion of social notation in the novel is principally owing to her formidable memory. Like Adam Bede, the title character of her first novel, Caleb Garth in *Middlemarch* is modelled on George Eliot's beloved father Robert Evans. The religious intensities of the adolescent Dorothea Brooke, who behaved 'as if she thought herself living in the time of the Apostles' (ch. 1), have their source in the Evangelical excesses of Mary Ann Evans during her own late teens. And perhaps, as Richard Ellmann has interestingly speculated, Casaubon's 'sexual inadequacy was a version of her struggles with adolescent sexuality'. If so, this would add a poignancy to the report of F. W. H. Myers that, when asked about the original of Casaubon, 'with a humorous solemnity, which was quite in earnest, nevertheless, she pointed to her own heart'. And Ellmann has also argued that Will Ladislaw, whom he calls 'the first character of either sex in her novels to be irresistibly handsome and at the same time good', is a reflection of Eliot's romanticised response to John Walter Cross, the young American whom she met in Rome a few months before she began *Middlemarch*, and who later became her second husband.[6]

Other connections between specific episodes and persons in

Middlemarch and those in Eliot's life can and have been made, but the tracing out of such point-for-point correspondences quickly becomes both dubious and unprofitable, and does not take one far towards understanding the novel and accounting for its power. It is of more value to investigate its genesis and gestation. A good deal of information on these subjects is contained in Eliot's letters and journals, in the notebooks into which she copied extracts from the many books she read just before and during the novel's composition, in another notebook that she called the 'Quarry for *Middlemarch*', and in the manuscript of the novel. A survey of this material will no more uncover a genetic key or an originating principle in the light of which the whole of *Middlemarch* can be understood than any of several characters in the novel can find the true beginning for which they are searching. But the chips from the workshop (to use Tennyson's phrase) can nevertheless tell one a good deal about the finished product.

In March 1867, with *Felix Holt* behind her and *The Spanish Gypsy*, a book-length dramatic narrative in verse, beginning to take shape, Eliot mentioned in passing to her publisher John Blackwood that 'I also have my private projects about an English novel, but I am afraid of speaking as if I could depend on myself'.[7] Nothing more was heard of this new 'English novel' for over a year and a half, until, on New Year's Day 1869, Eliot recorded in her journal as one of her 'tasks for the year – I wonder how many will be accomplished? – A Novel called Middlemarch'. Minimal progress had been made on the new novel by 19 February when she told Blackwood: 'I mean to begin my novel at once, having already sketched the plan. But between the beginning and the middle of a book I am like the lazy Scheldt; between the middle and the end I am like the arrowy Rhone ... The various elements of the story have been soliciting my mind for years – asking for a complete embodiment.'[8]
  But by late summer she had completed only an introduction and three chapters. What this material consisted of can be inferred from detailed study of the manuscript, particularly of chapters 11–16. The introduction was apparently a background account of Lydgate's intellectual awakening, vocational choice, education, and professional ambitions. The three chapters appear to have been mainly concerned with Fred Vincy, including a breakfast scene in his family's home and a visit to Stone Court, where Fred's sister Rosamond meets Lydgate while Featherstone capriciously demands that Fred obtain a note from Bulstrode saying he does not believe certain rumours concerning the young man's conduct of his financial affairs.[9] All this material appears,

mutatis mutandis, in the finished novel, but it seems clear that at this point, despite the plan she had sketched, Eliot still did not know how the narrative should develop. Between September 1869 and May 1870 she made little progress, and for almost half a year after that there is no mention of 'Middlemarch' in her letters or journals.

Composition may have been stalled, but Eliot's prodigious background reading continued unchecked. Between the beginning of 1868 and the end of 1871 she read over 290 works, ranging from single poems and articles to multi-volume works of literature, biography, philosophy and history.[10] From this vast body of material Eliot copied into two notebooks passages that she felt might be of use in connection with her novel. A good deal of verse was transcribed, as well as information on medical subjects. But the great majority of the notes come from historical works – biographies, studies of mythology and philology, historical fiction, literary history, social and political history, classical history. These many entries show George Eliot to be – in the words of the first sentence of *Middlemarch* – one of those 'who cares much to know the history of man, and how the mysterious mixture behaves under the varying experiments of Time'.

The editors of these notebooks consider the works most important to the evolution of *Middlemarch* to be Thomas Warton's *History of English Literature* (where Eliot probably found the name Lydgate), Lucretius' *De Rerum Natura* (read in the original), George Grote's *History of Greece*, John Thomson's *Life, Lectures, and Writings of William Cullen, MD*, W. E. H. Lecky's *History of European Morals*, Maine's *Ancient Law: Its Connection with the Early History of Society, and Its Relation to Modern Ideas*, John Lubbock's *The Origin of Civilization and the Primitive Condition of Man*, John Mayor's essay on 'Latin–English Lexicography', and Max Müller's *Lectures on the Science of Language*. The editors further observe that the passages Eliot transcribed show that she was 'repeatedly impressed ... with the relativity of so-called truths and definitive statements' and that she 'became increasingly preoccupied with the question of how human behavior was determined and how change in the human condition was effected. Did great men and "noble natures" really affect the course of history? How free was any man to shape his own destiny and that of others?'[11]

All this note-taking, however, seems to have done little to kindle Eliot's creative fires. One may even suspect that the labour of transcription was in part a surrogate for the task of original composition, for there seems something Casaubon-like in her accumulation of learned data, a connection Eliot herself hinted at in an 1872 letter to Harriet Beecher

Stowe when she remarked that 'the Casaubon-tints [in *Middlemarch*] are
not quite foreign to my own mental complexion'.[12] Certainly Casaubon has
a point when he observes in chapter 9 of the novel that 'for the
achievement of any work regarded as an end there must be a prior exercise
of many energies or acquired faculties of a secondary order, demanding
patience'. Unlike Ladislaw, to whom Casaubon is referring, George Eliot
had no difficulty in making these ancillary exertions; but they proved no
substitute for creative ardour and apparently no stimulus to it.

The state of the 'Middlemarch' manuscript had not improved by the
end of 1870 and, in early December, Eliot turned to other creative work:
'I am experimenting in a story', she recorded in her journal, 'which I
began without any very serious intention of carrying it out lengthily. It is a
subject which has been recorded among my possible themes ever since I
began to write fiction, but will probably take new shapes in the
development. I am today at p. 44.' This piece of fiction went very well and
by the last day of the year she had a hundred pages of manuscript and a
title – 'Miss Brooke'.[13] There is no difficulty in discovering from the
manuscript of *Middlemarch* of what 'Miss Brooke' consisted: it forms the
first nine and a half chapters of the finished novel, during which the story
of Dorothea Brooke unfolds in a crisp and straightforward manner that
bespeaks the relative ease and fluency with which it was composed. Nor
were any notebook transcriptions needed as background to the
introduction of Dorothea, the development of her relation to Casaubon,
the mention of Mr Brooke's political ambitions, the brief appearance of
Ladislaw, and the other narrated events prior to the departure of
Dorothea and her new husband on their wedding journey to Rome.

What happened next is that, sometime between the beginning of 1871
and the middle of March, George Eliot decided to fuse the 'Miss Brooke'
manuscript, which was going so well, with the 'Middlemarch'
manuscript that had lain more or less dormant for so long. On 19 March
she noted in her journal that 'I have written about 236 pages ... of my
Novel ... My present fear is that I have too much matter, too many
"momenti".'[14] By 'my Novel' she now means the combined manuscripts
of 'Middlemarch' and 'Miss Brooke', and by 'too many "momenti" ' she
means that she now has the problem of abundance, not of scarcity. From
this point until its completion in September 1872, Eliot worked on the
novel steadily and with a clear sense of direction. The 'arrowy Rhone'
sometimes threatened to overflow its banks. 'However it will not be
longer than Thackeray's books, if so long,' she reassured Blackwood.
'And I don't see how the sort of thing I want to do could have been done
briefly.'[15]

It would be of great interest to know the precise circumstances and reasons that led George Eliot to fuse the two stories into one. Unfortunately, she left no comment on the linkage, and the only basis for conjecture is the manuscript. The person most qualified to give an opinion is the one who has studied the manuscript most carefully. Jerome Beaty points to the similarity between the careers of Lydgate and Dorothea, as well as to the similarity of 'the time element and scene' in the two stories, and reasonably suggests that 'the two separate works were joined when it became apparent to the author that their themes were similar'. He is perhaps less reasonable when he speaks of 'a flash of inspiration' and 'the sudden flash of insight'; for what is inspiration to one critical eye may be cold-blooded carpentry to another.[16] The join that remains most visible occurs in the middle of chapter 10 – the place where the narrative for the first time shifts from the 'Miss Brooke' material to the 'Middlemarch' material. One paragraph ends in a supernal glow as Dorothea is likened to 'a picture of Santa Barbara looking out from her tower into the clear air'; the next paragraph begins a description of a dinner party at which a number of Middlemarchers – all distinctly sublunar – are introduced to the reader. This is followed by two awkward intrusions by the narrator, who goes out of his way to alert the reader to the fact that Lydgate, who is one of the dinner guests, will figure prominently in what is to follow and that his and Dorothea's stories will become intertwined. It is excellent that our first glimpse of the two central characters together should be out of the corner of Lady Chettam's eye and that as Lydgate leaves the party he reflects that it would have been 'altogether tedious but for the novelty of certain introductions, especially the introduction to Miss Brooke', who none the less seems to him 'a little too earnest' and not to look at things in an appropriately feminine way. What is not excellent is the heavy underlining in the narrator's too knowing comment that Lydgate 'might possibly have experience before him which would modify his opinion as to the most excellent things in woman' and the portentous comment at the beginning of the following chapter that, although at present nothing could seem 'much less important to Lydgate than the turn of Miss Brooke's mind, or to Miss Brooke than the qualities of the woman [Rosamond Vincy] who had attracted this young surgeon', the 'stealthy convergence of human lots', nay, 'Destiny' herself, would prove both of them wrong.

Eliot worked very hard to weave the different strands of her novel together effectively. A record of her labours is contained in the 'Quarry for *Middlemarch*', another notebook that she kept during the novel's composition. The first of this notebook's two parts consists of entries on medical and scientific subjects that relate only to the Lydgate story and show how thoroughly Eliot went into the questions of the state of medical knowledge and practice and the status of its practitioners during the time the novel is set. (There are also lists of quotations for possible use as chapter epigraphs.) It is the entries in the second half of the 'Quarry' that show Eliot trying to shape and blend together the different parts of her story. There are lists of public and private dates, outlines of certain scenes and a detailed 'sketch' of the Bulstrode–Raffles–Ladislaw connection, lists of 'motives', of 'relations to be developed', of 'elements', of 'scenes' and 'conditions' to be included, and of 'how to end the parts'.[17] On the whole these labours were notably successful, as were Eliot's attempts to work into the text certain parallels and contrasts between the various story-lines (Featherstone's and Casaubon's manipulative wills are one example). By the third book of *Middlemarch* Eliot was firmly in control of the alternating story-lines; and by the novel's climax in the seventh and eighth books she had become something of a virtuoso at interweaving the principal story-lines. Particularly impressive is the way in which the circumstances and repercussions of Bulstrode's disgrace are made to involve other characters and the way in which the private lives of Dorothea and Lydgate are drawn together through the brilliant stroke of developing a connection between the beloved of one and the wife of the other.

But one is here speaking of successful interweaving only at the level of narrative. That the story in the main flows smoothly does not necessarily imply that *Middlemarch* is a unified work of art in any significant way. And it is quite another question whether or not at the level of characterisation and theme the novel's central plots have genetic characteristics that make them incompatible. To take one example: there is evidence to suggest that when 'Middlemarch' and 'Miss Brooke' were initially linked the common thematic thread was the need for Fred, Lydgate and Dorothea to discover and realise their vocations. It has been argued that as *Middlemarch* grew the theme of high aspiration versus domestic reality replaced vocation as the dominant link and that in consequence Fred Vincy, the principal character in 'Middlemarch', became a distinctly subordinate character in *Middlemarch*, as Lydgate 'began to emerge as a major character moving in tandem with Dorothea Brooke'.[18] But does not this evidence imply that in *Middlemarch* Fred Vincy is to a degree a vestigial character and that the flash of inspiration was not hot enough, or the carpentry cold-blooded enough, to make his story as quantitatively subordinate in the novel as it is thematically or qualitatively subordinate?

Even before the manuscript of *Middlemarch* was finished the question of the best way to present the novel to the reading public of the early 1870s was being considered. Eliot's husband George Henry Lewes was also her agent and business manager. In May of 1871 he wrote to Blackwood with a bold proposal:

> Mrs. Lewes finds that she will require 4 volumes for her story, not 3. I winced at the idea at first, but the story must not be spoiled for want of space, and as you have more than once spoken of the desirability of inventing some mode of circumventing the Libraries and making the public *buy* instead of borrowing I have devised the following scheme, suggested by the plan Victor Hugo followed with his long *Misérables* – namely to publish it in *half-volume parts* either at intervals of one, or as I think better, two months. The eight parts at 5/- could yield the 2£ for the four volumes, and at two month intervals would not be dearer than Maga. Each part would have a certain unity and completeness in itself with separate title. Thus the work is called *Middlemarch*. Part I will be *Miss Brooke*.
>
> If in a stiff paper cover – attractive but not bookstallish – (I have one in my eye) this part ought to seduce purchasers, especially if Mudie were scant in supplies. It would be enough to furnish the town with talk for some time, and each part thus keep up and swell the general interest. *Tristram Shandy* you may remember was published at irregular intervals; and great was the desire for the continuation. Considering how slowly the public mind is brought into motion, this spreading of the publication over 16 months would be a decided advantage to the sale – especially as each part would contain as much as one ought to read at a time.
>
> Ponder this: or suggest a better plan![19]

Lewes's proposal was commercially shrewd, and Blackwood could not suggest a better plan. Four-volume novels had not proved popular with the public, and circulating libraries like Mudie's had been demanding what Blackwood regarded as unacceptably high discounts. In addition, the comparatively poor sales of Eliot's previous novel, *Felix Holt* (which had first appeared in three volumes), meant that the libraries could not be expected to place large orders for the author's next novel. For her part, Eliot was anxious for aesthetic reasons not to have her work appear serially in a magazine – a common publication format for a lengthy novel.

The eight-part publication proved a commercial success. Eliot must have thought it an aesthetic success as well, for when *Middlemarch* was republished in volume form she let the eight-book division stand. As J. A.

Sutherland remarks: 'to keep the physical divisions of the serial in this way was extremely unusual, if not unique. Dickens, Thackeray, Trollope, and others would always dissolve then regroup the parts of their serials into new wholes when they reprinted in volumes.'[20] Was anything gained by the retention of the eight-part book division? I would say not and would have preferred it if at least the titles of the books were dropped, for they either suggest a more naïve kind of novel ('Waiting for Death', 'Three Love Problems', 'The Dead Hand') or else seem factitious ('Old and Young', 'The Widow and the Wife', 'Sunset and Sunrise').

This is, however, a minor matter compared with the question of the chapter mottoes or epigraphs, which for Henry James indicated 'a want of tact' on the author's part.[21] These epigraphs are present in the text not because of the conventional expectations of Victorian readers. Scott had established the practice in his Waverley novels, but Dickens and Thackeray had done without them, as had George Eliot herself in her first four novels. The epigraphs are of two kinds: quotations from the works of past writers, the sources of which are indicated; and unattributed mottoes written by Eliot herself. More than occasionally the epigraphs taken from the works of others have a witty or ironic aptness, a pithiness that encapsulates the implications of the chapters they precede, or a resonance that amplifies them. The epigraph of the second chapter, for example, is from Cervantes: to Sancho Panza an approaching rider seems 'nothing but a man on a grey ass like my own, who carries something shiny on his head'. But Don Quixote sees on a dapple-grey steed a cavalier wearing the golden helmet of Mambrino (*Don Quixote*, I, iii, 7). This epigraph transposes into a wry key the Brooke sisters' different perceptions of Mr Casaubon, qualifies the implications of the prelude's association of Dorothea and the heroic St Theresa of Avila by suggesting a parallel with a very different Spanish quester, and adumbrates the novel's serious epistemological concern with the relativity of truth to point of view. The epigraph to chapter 74 is from the Book of Tobit's 'Marriage Prayer': 'Mercifully grant that we may grow aged together.' This underlines the deep seriousness of the chapter's content, which ends with Harriet Bulstrode uniting herself in sorrow with her disgraced husband as she prepares to share his wretched exile from the one place on earth where she would like to grow old. The quotation from Wordsworth's 'Ode to Duty' at the beginning of chapter 80, which includes the climax of Dorothea's spiritual development, may seem unduly portentous. But the poem – epitome of the moral imperative of renunciation that became a characteristic feature of Victorian literature – is the perfect literary-historical gloss for Dorothea's dark night of the soul.

On the other hand, the epigraphs from other writers are equally likely to be related to the chapters they precede only in an abstract, generalised way that is not suggestive or telling, and frequently overstates the chapter's implications – 'more pretentious than really pregnant' in Henry James's phrase.[22] This, alas, is almost invariably true of the unascribed epigraphs – all but one of the twenty-eight in metrical form – that Eliot supplied when nothing appropriate from her reading came to mind to fill in the blank space between chapter number and text. Eliot was a barely competent writer of verse and there is nothing stylistically felicitous in the great majority of these epigraphs to mitigate their overtly and tendentiously moralising tone. These metrical dicta compete unnecessarily, and compare very unfavourably, with many of the in-the-text aphorisms of the narrator of *Middlemarch* – a subject to be discussed in a later chapter. The auto-epigraphs are a recurrent eyesore in *Middlemarch*, and one is hard put to think of a good reason why readers should not be dissuaded from skipping them.[23]

In 1873, the year after the eight-part publication of *Middlemarch* had been completed, Eliot noted in her journal that 'No former book of mine has been received with more enthusiasm – not even *Adam Bede*'. A short time later, however, she returned to the subject of the contemporary reception of her novel in a mood more typical of her hypersensitive and hypercritical response to criticism of her work: 'Though *Middlemarch* seems to have made a deep impression in our own country, and though the critics are as polite and benevolent as possible to me, there has not, I believe, been one really able review of the book in our newspapers and periodicals.'[24] Both remarks are overstatements. The numerous reviews – well over twenty – had been on the whole enthusiastic but they had hardly been uncritical. And a number of them had been very able indeed – had in fact both accurately gauged the magnitude of Eliot's achievement and called attention to most of the places in the novel that pose critical problems.

Of course, as with all contemporary reviews of Victorian novels, the primary emphasis was on character and characterisation. *Middlemarch* proved most satisfying in this regard: 'The book is like a portrait gallery,' one reviewer exclaimed; 'all are photographed from life ... what a ceaselessly busy observation, what nicety of penetration'. There was much to savour and applaud, from the humour characters and the amusing sketches of ordinary people that readers always looked forward to from the pen of the creator of Mrs Poyser in *Adam Bede*, to the major figures in the novel that displayed the full range of Eliot's talents. 'For no writer', as another reviewer observed, 'uses so many instruments in riveting the interest of the cultivated reader about her characters, and springs of character, which she is exhibiting.'[25]

A number of reviewers, however, were confused by the novel's depiction of the relation of the individual to society and of character to circumstance. As A. V. Dicey observed at the beginning of his review in the *Nation*: 'There is a well-known remark of Novalis that character is destiny, which George Eliot criticises severely in *The Mill on the Floss*, on the ground that destiny depends rather on circumstances than on disposition. *Middlemarch* might well have been written to illustrate at once the truth of the dictum and of the criticism.'[26] Several reviewers took particular exception to the concluding generalisation about Dorothea Brooke's destiny in the novel's penultimate paragraph:

> Certainly those determining acts of her life were not ideally beautiful. They were the mixed result of young and noble impulse struggling under prosaic conditions. Among the many remarks passed on her mistakes, it was never said in the neighbourhood of Middlemarch that such mistakes could not have happened if the society into which she was born had not smiled on propositions of marriage from a sickly man to a girl less than half his own age – on modes of education which make a woman's knowledge another name for motley ignorance – on rules of conduct which are in flat contradiction with its own loudly-asserted beliefs. While this is the social air in which mortals begin to breathe, there will be collisions such as those in Dorothea's life ...

R. H. Hutton was one of the reviewers who found in this passage a discontinuity between the teller and the tale. He observed that it 'really has no foundation at all in the tale itself ... We hardly see how Dorothea could have been better protected against her first mistake ... we find in this passage a trace that George Eliot is ... a little dissatisfied with her own picture of the "prosaic conditions" to which she ascribes Dorothea's misadventures, and that she tries to persuade herself that they were actually more oppressive and paralyzing than they really were.'[27] Eliot wisely came to agree with her commentators on this important point; in the 1874 edition of *Middlemarch* she removed this reductive and misleading passage and replaced it with a generalised and unexceptionable comment on the perennial situation of 'young and noble impulse struggling amidst the conditions of an imperfect social state'.

Another point on which there was wide agreement among reviewers may surprise readers today. Rightly noting that *Middlemarch* was more

philosophical than Eliot's early novels, they went on to observe with
regret that the novel was informed by a melancholy vision of human
existence which emphasised failure and disillusionment. Unhappiness
was detected in the narrator's commentary, which at times was said to
intensify into sarcasm. Most important, there seemed to be no spiritual or
religious dimension to the characters' existence or the author's vision. To
quote R. H. Hutton again:

> The whole tone of the story is so thoroughly noble, both morally and
> intellectually, that the care with which George Eliot excludes all real
> faith in God from the religious side of her religious characters, conveys
> the same sort of shock with which, during the early days of eclipses,
> men must have seen the rays of light converging towards a centre of
> darkness ... in all these cases the province chosen for the religious
> temperament is solely the discharge of moral duty, and the side of these
> minds turned towards the divine centre of life, is conspicuous only by
> its absence, especially in Dorothea's case. In reading the description of
> the night of Dorothea's darkest trial one feels a positive sense of
> vacancy; so dramatic a picture of such a one as she is, going through such
> a struggle without a thought of God, is really unnatural.[23]

Fine as many of the reviews of *Middlemarch* were, one of them stands
out above the others for its insight, authority, rigorous sympathy, and
shrewd identification of almost all of the fundamental critical points. The
early years of the writing career of Henry James coincided with the time
during which Eliot's pre-*Middlemarch* novels appeared and they were an
important influence on the young American, who when he reviewed
Middlemarch at the age of thirty still had before him his illustrious career
as the principal founder and principal theoretician of the modern novel in
English. James's major reservation concerning the novel is announced at
the opening of his review: while a 'treasure-house of details',
Middlemarch was 'an indifferent whole' – more a 'chain of episodes,
broken into accidental lengths', than 'an organized, moulded, balanced
composition'. The novel was diffuse because the natural manner of its
creator was 'discursive and expansive'. Eliot's aim was to be a 'generous
rural historian' and she succeeded splendidly. The novel was 'not
compact, doubtless; but when was a panorama compact?' Indeed, 'this
very redundancy of touch, born of abundant reminiscence', was one of its
'greatest charms'.

Yet nominally *Middlemarch* had a definite subject: the depiction of 'an
obscure St Theresa'. Dorothea Brooke was 'certainly the great

achievement of the book'. But her career was only one of its episodes and she was 'of more consequence than the action of which she [was] the nominal centre'. Unfortunately, too much time was devoted to the 'relatively trivial' question of whether she would marry Ladislaw, whose characterisation was 'the only eminent failure in- the book'. He did not have 'the concentrated fervor essential in the man chosen by so nobly strenuous a heroine. The impression once given that he is a *dilettante* is never properly removed.' Lydgate was the real hero of the story, and 'the balanced contrast' of his history and Dorothea's was the novel's finest compositional felicity. Its most 'perfectly successful passages' were perhaps the scenes between Lydgate and 'his miserable little wife'. There was 'nothing more powerfully real than these scenes in all English fiction, and nothing certainly more *intelligent*'. The novel's secondary characters offered ample evidence of 'the superabundance of the author's creative instinct'. The only infelicity among them was Mr Bulstrode. His story and its complex ramifications had 'a slightly artificial cast, a melodramatic tinge, unfriendly to the richly natural coloring of the whole'.

In conclusion, James praised the 'deeply human' world of the novel and located its particular distinction in the fusion of realism and intelligence. George Eliot had 'commissioned herself to be real, her native tendency being that of an idealist, and the intellectual result is a very fertilizing mixture. The constant presence of thought, of generalizing instinct, of *brain*, in a word, behind her observation, gives the latter its great value and her whole manner its high superiority.' But at times there was perhaps an excessive amount of brain, for *Middlemarch* was 'too often an echo of Messrs Darwin and Huxley'. Its panoramic richness also seemed to border on excess, for 'if we write novels so, how shall we write history?' These were the reasons for James's thinking that *Middlemarch* set 'a limit ... to the development of the old-fashioned English novel' even as it made a contribution of the first importance to the rich imaginative department of our literature'.[29] We must now begin to consider in detail the nature and the possible limitations of this splendid contribution.

CHAPTER 2
Art, Ideas, Aesthetics

Art ... is a mode of amplifying experience and extending our contact with our fellow-men beyond the bounds of our personal lot.
'The Natural History of German Life'

George Eliot came late to the writing of fiction. She was over 35 when she began work on *Scenes of Clerical Life*, having spent most of the previous decade engaged in activities – translating, editing, reviewing – that would today be called those of a left-of-centre literary intellectual. It is therefore not surprising that even before she became a novelist Eliot had clear and distinct views on the role of the artist and the nature and purpose of art. These views first found extended expression in a series of review essays written for the *Westminster Review* in the mid-1850s. One of them was on the third volume of *Modern Painters* and contained an emphatic endorsement of the central tenet of Ruskin's aesthetic: 'The truth of infinite value that he teaches is *realism* – the doctrine that all truth and beauty are to be obtained by a humble and faithful study of nature, and not by substituting vague forms, bred by imagination on the mists of feeling, in place of definite substantial reality. The thorough acceptance of this doctrine would remould our life.'[1]

This same insistence on truth to nature – this time to human nature and man's social existence – runs through Eliot's excoriation of 'Silly Novels by Lady Novelists'. These genteel writers were strictly limited in both knowledge of society and intellectual competence – 'inexperienced in every form of poverty except poverty of brains'. In their religious novels, for example, they ignore 'the real drama of Evangelicalism [which] lies among the middle and lower classes' and instead 'nauseate us with novels which remind us of what we sometimes see in a worldly woman recently "converted"; – she is as fond of a fine dinner table as before, but she invites clergymen instead of beaux; she thinks as much of her dress as before, but she adopts a more sober choice of colours and patterns; her conversation is as trivial as before, but the triviality is flavoured with gospel instead of gossip'. As for ideas, these ladies apparently thought 'that an amazing ignorance, both of science and of life, [was] the best possible qualification for forming an opinion on the knottiest moral and speculative questions'. But perhaps their most serious deficiency was 'the want of those moral qualities that contribute to literary excellence –

patient diligence, a sense of the responsibility involved in publication, and an appreciation of the sacredness of the writer's art'.[2] An even more acid attack on artistic insincerity is found in the essay on 'Worldliness and Otherworldliness: The Poet Young'. The cause of the *'radical insincerity'* of the author of *Night Thoughts* was that

> he habitually treats of abstractions, and not of concrete objects or specific emotions ... Now, emotion links itself with particulars, and only in a faint and secondary manner with abstractions ... The most untheoretic persons are aware of this relation between true emotion and particular facts, as opposed to general terms, and implicitly recognise it in the repulsion they feel towards any one who professes strong feeling about abstractions ... In Young we have the type of that deficient human sympathy, that impiety towards the present and the visible, which flies for its motives, its sanctities, and its religion, to the remote, the vague, and the unknown.[3]

It was not only minor writers who furnished examples of unrealistic and insincere art. In the finest of the *Westminster Review* essays – 'The Natural History of German Life' – Eliot turned her attention at one point to the work of Dickens, 'the one great novelist' of the mid-Victorian period who was 'gifted with the utmost power of rendering the external traits of our town population'. If Dickens could render the psychological side of his characters – 'their conceptions of life, and their emotions – with the same truth as their idiom and manners, his books would be the greatest contribution Art has ever made to the awakening of social sympathies'. But Dickens rarely passed from the external to the internal 'without becoming as transcendent in his unreality as he was a moment before in his artistic truthfulness'.

In the same essay George Eliot makes her most forceful and succinct statement of the positive value of art:

> The greatest benefit we owe to the artist, whether painter, poet, or novelist, is the extension of our sympathies. Appeals founded on generalizations and statistics require a sympathy ready-made, a moral sentiment already in activity; but a picture of human life such as a great artist can give, surprises even the trivial and the selfish into that attention to what is apart from themselves, which may be called the raw material of moral sentiment.[4]

Three years later, having herself become an artist, Eliot was to restate this belief with explicit reference to her own work:

If Art does not enlarge man's sympathies, it does nothing morally ...
opinions are a poor cement between human souls; and the only effect I
ardently long to produce by my writings, is that those who read them
should be better able to *imagine* and to *feel* the pains and joys of those
who differ from themselves in everything but the broad fact of being
struggling erring human creatures.[5]

Exactly the same passionately expressed views on realism, sincerity
and sympathy, together with an insistence on the superior moral and
pathetic potential of low subject-matter, are heard in the reflexive
comments of the narrators of Eliot's first three works of fiction. At the
beginning of the fifth chapter of 'The Sad Fortunes of the Rev. Amos
Barton', the first of the three *Scenes of Clerical Life*, the narrator pauses to
point out that Barton is 'in no respect an ideal or exceptional character';
he is, rather, 'palpably and unmistakably commonplace ... Yet these
commonplace people – many of them – bear a conscience, and have felt
the sublime prompting to do the painful right'; there is 'a pathos in their
very insignificance'. The reader is assured that 'you would gain
unspeakably if you would learn with me to see some of the poetry and the
pathos, the tragedy and the comedy, lying in the experience of a human
soul that looks out through dull grey eyes, and that speaks in a voice of
quite ordinary tones'. Another example is the famous seventeenth
chapter of *Adam Bede*, 'In Which the Story Pauses a Little'. Again the
narrator is at pains to explain what he is doing in the novel, and why. His
task is 'the faithful representing of commonplace things', the purpose of
which is to deepen the reader's capacity for fellow-feeling by making him
recognise that the common people of his story are 'fellow-mortals' whom
'it is needful you should tolerate, pity, and love'. The 'quality of
truthfulness' he aspires to is like that of many Dutch paintings with their
faithful renditions of 'a monotonous homely existence' despised by 'lofty-
minded people'.

Finally, in Eliot's second novel, *The Mill on the Floss*, the narrator on
several occasions points out that his story is realistic, not romantic. Like
the ruined villages along the Rhone described in the thirtieth chapter,
which are so different from the picturesque ruins on the castled Rhine,
the story oppresses 'with the feeling that human life – very much of it – is
a narrow ugly, grovelling existence, which even calamity does not
elevate'. But in other passages, in the fifth and fourteenth chapters, the
narrator holds out the hope that the ugliness and calamities of life can be
mitigated, even transcended, and the affections nourished by an
experience common to all men: the perceptual freshness and richness of

childhood, when 'the outer world seemed only an extension of our own personality'. This 'home-scene' of the childhood past becomes 'the mother tongue of our imagination' and the 'loves and sanctities' of childhood can continue to sustain us in later life when they have 'deep immovable roots in memory'.

In both the review essays of the mid-1850s and her first three works of fiction, the dominant influence on Eliot's ideas about art was that of Wordsworth (both directly and through the mediation of Ruskin, another Victorian disciple of the poet). Wordsworth was George Eliot's favourite poet at least from her twenty-first year when she reported in a letter that 'I never before met with so many of my own feelings, expressed just as I could like them'.[6] The passages in 'Amos Barton' and *Adam Bede* on the results of close observation of common humanity, for example, read like a prose rescoring of a passage in book 13 of the 1850 *Prelude* (the last three of the quoted lines were in fact underlined in Eliot's copy of the poem):

> When I began to enquire,
> To watch and question those I met, and speak
> Without reserve to them ...
> There saw into the depth of human souls,
> Souls that appear to have no depth at all
> To careless eyes.

Similarly, the emphasis on human sympathy and the superiority of fellow-feeling to abstractions repeats Wordsworth's insistence on the primacy of 'the human heart by which we live'. And the stress on the fundamental importance of childhood experiences and the later memory of them is of course quintessentially Wordsworthian.

From the point of view of *Middlemarch*, what is most striking about Eliot's early aesthetic is how small a part it plays in the novel, which began to appear more than a decade after the publication of *The Mill on the Floss*. Memory and the special perceptual intensities of childhood, for example, are the subject of only two brief passages in the entire novel. One is the sonnet that supplies the epigraph for chapter 57. It describes the 'wonder, love, belief' with which Sir Walter Scott's novels enhance 'the little world [of] childhood'. Childhood – of whom? Presumably Mary Ann Evans and her brother Isaac; for the poem was almost certainly written at the same time as, and was probably intended to be a part of, the suite of 'Brother and Sister' sonnets which celebrate the intensities of the childhood sibling bond, through which are developed a 'root of piety' and a 'primal passionate store,/Whose shaping impulses make manhood whole'. The sonnets were composed in July 1867, when *Middlemarch* was germinating

and (as Gordon Haight, Eliot's biographer, suggests) 'intensive
meditation on the Warwickshire of 1830 revived poignant memories of
her childhood with Isaac'.[7] Only one other poignant early memory has
found its way into the novel, however. This splendid passage – the
opening paragraph of chapter 12 – is more sharply focused, less abstract
and, because its emotion is linked to concrete particulars, much more
evocative and affecting than the sonnet. (The difference epitomises the
superiority of Eliot's prose to her verse.) With a nostalgic intensity that
recalls comparable passages in *The Mill on the Floss*, the narrator
describes

> a pretty bit of midland landscape, almost all meadows and pastures,
> with hedgerows still allowed to grow in bushy beauty and to spread out
> coral fruit for the birds. Little details gave each field a particular
> physiognomy, dear to the eyes that have looked on them from
> childhood: the pool in the corner where the grasses were dank and trees
> leaned whisperingly; the great oak shadowing a bare place in mid-
> pasture; the high bank where the ash-trees grew; the sudden slope of
> the old marl-pit making a red background for the burdock; the huddled
> roofs and ricks of the homestead without a traceable way of approach;
> the grey gate and fences against the depths of the bordering wood; and
> the stray hovel, its old, old thatch full of mossy hills and valleys with
> wondrous modulations of light and shadow such as we travel far to see
> in later life, and see larger, but not more beautiful. These are the things
> that make the gamut of joy in landscape to midland-bred souls – the
> things they toddled among, or perhaps learned by heart standing
> between their father's knees while he drove leisurely.

It is not fortuitous that this passage introduces the episode in which
Fred Vincy rides into the country to visit Mary Garth, or that the
epigraph to chapter 57 introduces a pleasant family scene in the Garths'
garden, for the other parts of *Middlemarch* that recall Eliot's early novels
and their Wordsworthian preoccupations are the Fred–Mary relationship and the presentation of the Garths, particularly Caleb and his
daughter Mary. The father is not only painted in the warmest of colours;
in chapter 23 the narrator echoes the gauche intrusions of the early fiction
when he cannot forbear to exclaim parenthetically, 'pardon these details
for once – you would have learned to love them if you had known Caleb
Garth'. And the conventions of the 'solid Dutch sort of realism'[8] used in
the early novels are re-employed in the depiction of Mary. At one point

the reader is told to go down into the street, find an unexceptional-looking young woman and 'take that ordinary but not disagreeable person for a portrait of Mary Garth' (ch. 40). Lest he fail to grasp what kind of portraiture the narrator has in mind, the reader is told in another place that 'Rembrandt would have painted her with pleasure, and would have made her broad features look out of the canvas with intelligent honesty' (ch. 12). In the love of Fred and Mary their shared childhood past and its 'root of piety' are dominant. When they were little, 'the children drank tea together out of their toy tea-cups, and spent whole days together in play. Mary was a little hoyden, and Fred at six years old thought her the nicest girl in the world, making her his wife with a brass ring which he had cut from an umbrella' (ch. 23). To the suggestion that he may come to outgrow his love for her, Fred answers: 'I have never been without loving Mary. If I had to give her up, it would be like beginning to live on wooden legs' (ch. 52). For Mary's part, her feeling for Fred has 'taken such deep root' in her that she 'cannot imagine any new feeling coming to make that weaker' (ch. 52). For them to give each other up, says Mary, 'would make too great a difference ... like seeing all the old places altered, and changing the name for everything' (ch. 86). As the narrator observes: 'When a tender affection has been storing itself in us through many of our years, the idea that we could accept any exchange for it seems to be a cheapening of our lives' (ch. 57). In the novel's penultimate chapter Mary is made to reaffirm the childhood bond that unites her and Fred; and at the end of the scene Fred's recollection of their first engagement with the umbrella ring is interrupted when Mary's young brother Ben and his dog bound into the room. While this scene has an undeniable charm, there is no greater emotional charge to be got from it or from any other part of the story of Fred and Mary. Their relationship is a good deal thinner and less weighty than the other principal relationships in the novel, and a little out of phase with them. Like the wholly lovable Caleb Garth and his immaculate honesty, Fred and Mary's early love seems to belong to a different world from that of the other characters in *Middlemarch*, a world in which George Eliot seems to be no longer passionately interested. This is why it is so hard to regard Mary and/or Caleb Garth as the moral centre of the novel that they have been taken to be by some commentators.[9] It is true that the father is a leading spokesman for his creator's belief in the importance of fellow-feeling and of work. But both are too peripheral to the central concerns of *Middlemarch* to be regarded as in any important way the novel's centre. They belong to a different and less complex world – the world of Eliot's early novels.

We must now consider the ways in which the aesthetic concerns informing *Middlemarch* differ from those of the *Westminster Review* essays and the early novels. The differences, however, must not be thought to suggest that the values and aims of the later novel are opposed to those of the earlier ones. They are different more in degree than in kind and represent an extension and maturation of Eliot's earlier artistic concerns, not their supersession. The end remains the same: to depict human life in a way that will amplify the reader's experience and extend his sympathies. What changes are the means by which this is to be achieved. One important difference is that in *Middlemarch* Eliot is less interested in the *past* – in traditional values and the roots of personal and social piety – and more interested in *history*, in the processes of social change. The focus of interest is the relation of the individual to society. This relationship had of course already been memorably explored in *The Mill on the Floss*, but in *Middlemarch* the question is not tied to the claims of the past and is examined in a much wider context. Since the relationship of private to public life is dominant, a landscape of opinion replaces a natural landscape and makes exceptional a passage like the one that opens chapter 12. For the same reason the principal characters in *Middlemarch* are defined by their present circumstances and their longings and aspirations (that is, by their vision of the future) rather than by their pasts. Unlike Maggie Tulliver in *The Mill on the Floss*, for example, Dorothea Brooke, the central female character in *Middlemarch*, has no parents and no past.

It also follows that the two central characters of *Middlemarch*, Lydgate and Dorothea, are not 'commonplace things' but persons of unusual potential whose gifts set them apart from society. For these individuals, the presentational devices of Dutch realism will not do. They were appropriate to the depiction of Amos Barton, who looked out at the world through dull grey eyes, and spoke in a voice of quite ordinary tones. But through his eyes and his microscope Lydgate looks deeply into the secret processes of living organisms, and Dorothea's voice, which reminds one character of 'bits in the "Messiah"' (ch. 56), is the aural correlative of her exalted spiritual nature, which is 'enamoured of intensity and greatness' (ch. 1). It is not the art of Teniers or Rembrandt that is used in her depiction but the idealising art of the Italian Renaissance. At the opening of the first chapter Dorothea's sleeve is said to recall those 'in which the Blessed Virgin appeared to Italian painters'; later she is compared by the narrator to Palma Vecchio's picture of Santa Barbara (ch. 10); and later still her face after a sleepless night is said to have the 'pale cheeks and pink eyelids of a *mater dolorosa*' (ch. 80). And Naumann, an artist who specialises in 'the idealistic in the real', wants to paint her as Santa Clara (ch. 22).

The ideal aspects of Dorothea and the intellectual distinction of Lydgate both point to the most significant difference between Eliot's early novels and *Middlemarch*: the increased importance of ideas. During the 1860s Eliot had become interested in poetry as a medium of artistic expression precisely because it could accommodate ideas and abstractions more directly than realistic prose fiction could. She had become less interested in the 'faithful representing of commonplace things' and more interested in what in a letter of 1866 she calls 'aesthetic teaching [which] is the highest of all teaching because it deals with life in its highest complexity'.[10] For the later Eliot, as for the later Wordsworth, the years were bringing a 'philosophic mind'. If the arousal of sympathy still remains her goal as an artist, the reader will be stirred in a more reflective and intellectual, and a less intense and emotional, way than he was in the early novels.

What were these ideas? The 1866 letter quoted above was addressed to Frederic Harrison, one of the leading British exponents of Positivism, that is, of the teachings of the nineteenth-century French thinker Auguste Comte, who was an important influence on the thought of many liberal Victorian intellectuals, including John Stuart Mill, Herbert Spencer, George Henry Lewes and George Eliot. Indeed, during the last three decades of her life 'it is no exaggeration to say that [Eliot's] intellectual life was lived in an atmosphere saturated with Comte's influence through her own study and through her close association with the most prominent of Comte's admirers in England'. On the intellectual level it is Comte's religion of humanity that more than anything else is responsible for making recessive the Wordsworthian strain in Eliot's fiction.[11] There are two principal doctrines in Comte's thought. The first is that the history of human societies passes through three stages: the theological, the metaphysical, and the positivist or scientific. In the first, events are thought to be governed by the volitions of superior beings of some sort – a single God in the case of traditional Christian theology. In the second phase, abstractions or what Bentham called fictitious entities, like the Ideas of Plato or the essences and quiddities of Aristotelians, are thought to explain all phenomena. In the third stage, the Positivist, it is recognised that man has no knowledge of anything but phenomena, that the knowledge is relative and not absolute and is derived solely from experience. The other major Comtean idea is that, like human history, the sciences pass through the same three stages and that once this is recognised and they are placed on a proper empirical foundation the highest of the sciences, the social science, can begin to yield authoritative, verifiable information about man in society.[12]

There is no doubt that the author of *Middlemarch* was deeply influenced by Positivist ideas concerning the scientific study of man in society. The novel's narrator may even be described as a social biologist studying the structure of a society, investigating the relationship of an individual organism to its surrounding environment (or medium). For this study a 'careful telescopic watch' would be of no avail; what is needed, as the narrator puts it in chapter 6, is a microscope with a strong lens that will show the 'play of minute causes'. In this investigation vocabulary drawn from biology is often employed: 'living substance', 'organ', 'fibres', 'nerves', 'muscular movement', 'pulse', 'throbs', 'shock', 'laceration', 'bruise', 'medium', 'assimilation', 'nourishment'. Even the intrusion of the narrator into the action can be seen as scientific – as a reflection of the increased awareness of the importance of the witness's participation in empirical observation.[13] Finally, the goal of the narrator's investigation into the structure of society may be seen as analogous to those of several real-life scientists mentioned in *Middlemarch* who sought through the systematic observation of particulars to discover interconnections and reveal an underlying unity: Sir Humphry Davy, whose *Elements of Agricultural Chemistry* (discussed at a dinner party in chapter 2) attempted to create a regular and systematic form for its subject; Robert Brown, whose *Microscopic Observations on the Particles Contained in the Pollen of Plants* (offered to Farebrother by Lydgate in chapter 17) is concerned to illuminate the structure of pollen; Vesalius, one of Lydgate's heroes, who in the sixteenth century began a new era in anatomy through the close examination of bodies; Pierre-Charles Louis, whom Lydgate is said to have known in Paris, and whose researches into typhoid led – as Eliot noted in the 'Quarry for *Middlemarch*' – to a complete and connected view of the disease; and finally Marie-François Bichat, of whose conception of the 'intimate relations of living structure' (ch. 15) Lydgate was enamoured.[14]

Comte's other major doctrine – the three historical states – figures less centrally in *Middlemarch*, though it is true that there are interesting similarities between the novel and the specific suggestions Frederic Harrison made to Eliot in 1866 concerning a work he hoped she would write that would dramatise the Positivist conception of historical change. (His advice was to take as her subject a rural society in France surrounding 'a secluded manufacturing village', in which 'strictly dogmatic religion' had declined. A capitalist from the village and a new type of leader, preferably a 'physician ... a man of the new world with complete scientific and moral cultivation', would enter into alliance, gradually pushing 'the actual church . . . into the background'.)[15] Of much more importance to *Middlemarch* than specific Positivist doctrines is the general similarity that the author of *Middlemarch* has with Comte and a number of other nineteenth-century writers who could no longer accept traditional Christian beliefs and assurances and sought some this-worldly equivalent for lost supernatural absolutes.

The pattern of George Eliot's religious development is, in fact, typical of the period: 'the whole predicament she represents', as Basil Willey put it, 'was that of the religious temperament cut off by the *Zeitgeist* from the traditional objects of veneration, and the traditional intellectual formulations'.[16] The religion of Eliot's father Robert Evans had been practical, undogmatic Anglicanism of a traditional sort, one suspicious of any emotional excess. But through two of her teachers the young Mary Ann Evans was exposed to Evangelical Christianity, which became the dominant influence in her life between her sixteenth and twenty-third years. Piety, good works, a keen eye for opportunities for renunciation, rigorous introspection, the sense that life was a pilgrimage, and the longing for spiritual exaltation were the hallmarks of her existence. During a visit to London in 1838 she refused to go to the theatre with her brother and spent her evenings reading Josephus' *History of the Jews*. Her comment on a musical programme that included Haydn's *Creation* and Handel's *Jephtha* was that it was 'not consistent with millennial holiness': 'nothing can justify the using of an intensely interesting and solemn passage of Scripture as a rope dancer uses her rope'.[17] As her nineteenth birthday approached she prayed that 'the Lord give me such an insight into what is truly good, and such realizing views of an approaching eternity, that I may not rest contented with making Christianity a mere addendum to my pursuits, or with tacking it as a fringe to my garments. May I seek to be sanctified wholly.'[18] And her first publication was a poem in the January 1840 *Christian Observer*, in which the speaker, in the evening of her life, says goodbye to all the things of this world except her Bible; and from her 'dear kindred, whom the Lord to me has given', she parts '*only* till we meet in heaven'.[19]

By 1842, however, George Eliot had rejected Christian belief so emphatically that even though it deeply hurt her father she refused to attend church. The turning-point had been her reading during the previous year of a work by one of a small circle of gifted friends she came to know after she and her father had moved to Coventry. It was Charles Hennell's *Inquiry Concerning the Origin of Christianity* (1838), which offered a historical, psychological and literary explanation of the supposed supernatural and miraculous events recounted in scripture.

The devastating effect of Hennell's arguments on George Eliot was comparable to the effect that the *Leben Jesu* of the great German scholar David Friedrich Strauss (who admired Hennell's work and arranged for its translation into German) was to have on many British readers when an English translation was published in 1846. The translator was Mary Ann Evans, who eight years later turned into English another key work of German religious thought, Ludwig Feuerbach's *Wesen des Christenthums*. In it, Feuerbach passionately argued that all of the enormous positive value of traditional Christianity could be recovered for the modern age once it was recognised that what earlier ages had regarded 'as objective, is now recognized as subjective; that is, what was formerly contemplated and worshipped as God is now perceived to be something *human* ... The divine being is nothing else than the human being, or rather the human nature purified, freed from the limits of the individual man [and] contemplated and revered as another, a distinct being. All the attributes of divine nature are, therefore, attributes of human nature.'[20]

Feuerbach's subjective, humanised Christianity powerfully appealed to Eliot because it offered a way of healing the split between her intellect, which could no longer accept the existence of a supernatural god, and her deepest emotions, which were inextricably linked with the religious culture of her early life. Furthermore, it widened the channels of sympathy and fellow-feeling between the agnostic intellectual and ordinary humanity. 'I begin to feel for other people's wants and sorrows', Eliot wrote in 1853, 'a little more than I used to do. Heaven help us! said the old religions – the new one, from its very lack of that faith, will teach us all the more to help one another.'[21] Far from being anti-religious, Eliot (as she explained in a letter of 1859) had come to have no antagonism

> towards any faith in which human sorrow and human longing for purity have expressed themselves; on the contrary, I have a sympathy with it that predominates over all argumentative tendencies. I have not returned to dogmatic Christianity – to the acceptance of any set of doctrines as a creed, and a superhuman revelation of the Unseen – but I see in it the highest expression of the religious sentiment that has yet found its place in the history of mankind, and I have the profoundest interest in the inward life of sincere Christians in all ages.[22]

For George Eliot, then, the replacement for traditional Christianity was to be a religion of humanity. Like all her books, *Middlemarch* has as its 'main bearing a conclusion ... without which I could not have cared to write any representation of human life – namely, that the fellowship between man and man which has been the principle of development, social and moral, is not dependent on conceptions of what is not man: and that the idea of God, so far as it has been a high spiritual influence, is the ideal of a goodness entirely human (i.e., an exaltation of the human).' [23] In *Middlemarch*, Eliot presents a non-theological and non-metaphysical body of beliefs that she believes capable of providing a basis for non-egotistic values and other-regarding actions, and of performing for gifted members of the modern social organism the same ennobling function that traditional religious ideals had performed for St Theresa of Avila, who lived in a society still in its theological phase. These beliefs form the doctrinal core of *Middlemarch*; since they are directly articulated by the narrator, as well as reflected in character and action, it is not difficult to extrapolate them from the text. The fundamental epistemological tenet in *Middlemarch* is the relativity of truth to point of view, and the subjectivity, partiality and fallibility of human perception. It is frequently expounded and exemplified: 'Signs are small measurable things, but interpretations are illimitable' (ch. 3); 'Probabilities are as various as the faces to be seen at will in fretwork or paperhangings: every form is there, from Jupiter to Judy, if you only look with creative inclination' (ch. 32); changing the lens in a microscope will lead to a different interpretation of exactly the same observed phenomenon (ch. 6); 'In watching effects, if only of an electric battery, it is often necessary to change our place and examine a particular mixture' from more than one perspective (ch. 40); 'who can represent himself just as he is, even in his own reflections?' (ch. 70). Sir James Chettam naturally interprets a change in Dorothea's complexion 'in the way most gratifying to himself' (ch. 3); when Dorothea looks into Casaubon's mind, she sees 'reflected there in vague labyrinthine extension every quality she herself brought' (ch. 3); her sister Celia has a 'marvellous quickness in observing a certain order of signs generally preparing her to expect such outward events as she had an interest in' (ch. 5); and Fred Vincy 'fancied that he saw to the bottom of his uncle Featherstone's soul, though in reality half of what he saw there was no more than the reflex of his own inclinations' (ch. 12). In short, we all belong to 'the fellowship of illusion' (ch. 34).

Egotism is the moral correlative of the subjectivity of all perception. A 'pier-glass or extensive surface of polished steel [may be] multitudinously and randomly scratched in all directions; but place now against it a lighted candle as a centre of illumination, and lo! the scratches will seem to arrange themselves in a fine series of concentric circles around that little sun'. This is a 'parable', as the narrator explains at the beginning of chapter 27: 'the scratches are events, and the candle is the egoism of any person now absent'. The comparison is ingenious and elegant, but calls attention to the universality of egotism less tellingly than does the narrator's raw and abrupt exclamation at the end of chapter 21: 'We are all of us born in moral stupidity, taking the world as an udder to feed our supreme selves.' This inherited stupidity has the same importance in Eliot's religion of humanity as does the doctrine of original sin in traditional Christian belief. The antidote to this primal taint is strong feeling, particularly fellow-feeling, the only certain stimulus to non-egotistical action. As early as 1843, Eliot had realised what other Victorian writers – Tennyson in *In Memoriam* is one example – were also discovering: 'Speculative truth begins to appear but a shadow of individual minds, agreement between intellects seems unattainable, and we turn to the *truth of feeling* as the only universal bond of union.'[24]

This quality is often referred to in *Middlemarch*: Dorothea's ardent feelings are repeatedly called attention to; Caleb Garth is a person who knows his duty because of 'a clear feeling inside me' (ch. 56); the narrator's final comment on Bulstrode's appalling inhumanity is that 'there is no general doctrine which is not capable of eating out our morality if unchecked by the deep-seated habit of direct fellow-feeling with individual fellow-men' (ch. 61). (This is a more abstract and generalised restatement of the principle that the title character of *Adam Bede* enunciates in simpler and more pragmatic terms in his novel's seventeenth chapter: 'It isn't notions sets people doing the right thing – it's feelings.') And, finally, the narrator remarks of Casaubon that his wounded egotism and withdrawal from life 'is only to be overcome by a sense of fellowship deep enough to make all efforts at isolation seem mean and petty instead of exalting' (ch. 42).It is not that any person's egotism can be fully eradicated, any more than subjectivity can be removed from human perception. If elimination of egotism were the goal, then Farebrother, Caleb Garth and Mary Garth would be the moral exemplars of *Middlemarch*. It is, rather, the case that an individual's egotism should be modified by the awareness of 'an equivalent centre of self' (ch. 21) in others and of the 'involuntary, palpitating life' (ch. 80) of ordinary humanity.

For George Eliot, then, ardent feeling and a sense of human fellowship are the humanistic equivalents of, and replacement for, the Christian conception of grace. But if 'our good depends on the quality and breadth of our emotion', as the narrator of *Middlemarch* insists in chapter 47, how does a person come to possess this saving capacity? Depending on how it is put, this question can be a difficult, even embarrassing, one to ask of *Middlemarch*, for in some cases the answer would seem to be that either

you have it or you don't. Take the cases of Ladislaw and Lydgate, who by
the climax of the novel have both arrived at a 'perilous margin' (ch. 79) in
their life-journeys, but whose lots turn out to be quite different. Ladislaw
finds private and public fulfilment, while Lydgate, 'pitifully' carrying the
'burthen' (ch. 81) of his appalling wife, ends as a failure in both his private
and professional life. A contemporary reviewer was among the first to
find it difficult to see the appropriateness of these contrasting fates:

> [Ladislaw] does what he likes, whether right or wrong, to the end of the
> story; he makes no sacrifices; even his devotion to Dorothea does not
> preserve him from an unworthy flirtation with his friend Lydgate's
> wife. He is happy by luck, not desert ... while poor Lydgate – ten times
> the better man – suffers not only in happiness, but in his noblest
> ambitions, and sinks to the lower level of a good practice and a good
> income because he marries and is faithful to the vain selfish creature
> whom Ladislaw merely flirts with.[25]

In terms of Eliot's humanistic religion, the reason for their different lots
would seem to be that intense feeling and emotional depth are naturally
present in Ladislaw (though they need Dorothea's nurture in order to
flourish) and naturally absent in Lydgate, the outward sign of which is his
socially nurtured 'spots of commonness' (ch. 15). But, if neither is
responsible for the presence or absence in himself of these saving
qualities, how can it be morally appropriate that one is rewarded and the
other punished? The answer is that their lots are not morally appropriate;
but they are necessary to the exposition of Eliot's doctrine which, like any
general doctrine, is 'capable of eating out our morality'.

This difficult question and its subversive implications can be
sidestepped if one follows Eliot's own practice in *Middlemarch* and
focuses attention not on the origin of the secular grace of intense feeling
but on the beneficent effect that one human being who possesses it can
have on the egotism of another. As the narrator puts it in one of the
novel's most florid passages: 'There are natures in which, if they love us,
we are conscious of having a sort of baptism and consecration: they bind
us over to rectitude and purity by their pure belief about us; and our sins
become the worst kind of sacrilege which tears down the invisible altar of
trust' (ch. 77). This central tenet of George Eliot's faith, which might in
less sentimental terms be called the humanistic economy of salvation, is
not only asserted by the narrator. It is also shown in operation in the
climactic sections of *Middlemarch*, when it becomes an important part of
the resolution of the novel's principal plots. The turning-point in Fred

Vincy's love for Mary, for instance, comes when Farebrother lays down his own possible happiness for another's and warns Fred that he is once again slipping into a way of living that may cost him Mary's love. This fine act – Farebrother himself, despite his habitual self depreciation, calls it 'a very good imitation of heroism' – has a powerful effect on Fred, producing 'a sort of regenerating shudder through the frame' and making him 'feel ready to begin a new life' (ch. 66). Dorothea has a similar effect on Lydgate when she comes to his assistance in his hour of greatest need. He feels 'something very new and strange' entering his life and tells Dorothea that 'you have made a great difference in my courage by believing in me'. The narrator underlines the doctrinal point: 'The presence of a noble nature, generous in its wishes, ardent in its charity, changes the lights for us: we begin to see things again in their larger, quieter masses, and to believe that we too can be seen and judged in the wholeness of our character' (ch. 76).

This same 'saving influence of a noble nature, the divine efficacy of rescue that may lie in a self subduing act of fellowship' (ch. 82), is also seen in operation in Dorothea's meeting with Rosamond in chapter 81, a crucial scene in which the two central female characters in the novel talk together for the first time. Indeed, so powerful is Dorothea's outward-flowing fellow-feeling that it moves Rosamond, the novel's most complete egotist, to the performance of her first unselfish act when she tells Dorothea what had actually transpired during her interrupted conversation with Ladislaw and thereby makes possible the final coming together of Dorothea and Will. Rosamond is said to be 'taken hold of by an emotion stronger than her own', to be urged by 'a mysterious necessity', and to deliver 'her soul under impulses which she had not known before'. Rosamond's unselfish act has been called a moral surprise; but it is better placed in a religious rather than an ethical perspective. The 'mysterious necessity' is the amazing grace of intense fellow-feeling, and Rosamond's act is a secular version of the Christian *etiam peccata* paradox: even the most self-centred character in *Middlemarch* is shown to be capable of contributing to the humanistic economy of salvation. It is these acts that ultimately provide Eliot's secular religion of humanity with a certain eschatological dimension. They contribute to what in the last paragraph of *Middlemarch* is called 'the growing good of the world' that makes the noble spirits who have gone before parts of the mystical body of evolving humanity, and, if their deeds have made them widely known, members of what in her Positivist hymn Eliot calls

> the choir invisible
> Of those immortal dead who live again
> In minds made better by their presence.

No wonder that Emily Dickinson could say of *Middlemarch* that 'the mysteries of human nature surpass the "mysteries of redemption"'.

In the 1866 letter in which Eliot speaks of 'aesthetic teaching' she also speaks of her continuing effort to make 'certain ideas thoroughly incarnate, as if they had revealed themselves to me first in the flesh and not in the spirit'. She insists that if aesthetic teaching 'ceases to be purely aesthetic – if it lapses anywhere from the picture to the diagram – it becomes the most offensive of all teaching'. The presentation of ideas has to 'lay hold on the emotions as human experience'; the aim of the work of art devoted to aesthetic teaching is not to showcase ideas, however attractively, but to ' "flash" conviction on the world by means of aroused sympathy'.[26] Ardent emotion and strong feeling could not simply be described or dramatised; they had to be communicated to the reader – otherwise the teaching was pointless. As Dorothea tells Celia in explaining her refusal to describe how her union with Ladislaw came about: 'you would have to feel with me, else you would never know' (ch. 84).

George Eliot did not restrict her thinking about aesthetic teaching to her correspondence; it is also reflected in the text of *Middlemarch* to a degree sufficient to make the reflexive concern with its own intentions and meanings a subsidiary theme of the novel. These concerns find expression in three different ways: in comments about art and aesthetics made by certain characters; in the reflexive comments of the intrusive omniscient narrator; and in places where something in the text may be taken to refer at another level to the creative process or aesthetic goals of the author.

Part of Dorothea Brooke's development in the first two-fifths of *Middlemarch* involves her aesthetic sense. At the beginning of the novel she knows little about art; the aesthetic part of her education has been as neglected as the other parts, and has left her, as the narrator wryly observes, with 'a slight regard for domestic music and feminine fine art [that] must be forgiven her, considering the small tinkling and smearing in which they chiefly consisted at that dark period' (ch. 7). She can appreciate the fineness of a miniature portrait, and the sound of the great organ at Freiberg makes her sob; but she is not responsive to very much in between. Certainly not to the pictures and casts that her uncle had brought back from his Continental travels, for Dorothea cannot see a relationship between them and her own existence. To her 'these severe classical nudities and smirking Renaissance-Correggiosities were painfully inexplicable, staring into the midst of her Puritanic conceptions: she had never been taught how she could bring them into any sort of relevance with her life' (ch. 9). Landscape sketches are similarly blank to her: 'They are in a language I do not understand. I suppose there is some relation between pictures and nature which I am too ignorant to feel' (ch. 9).

The sketch that has prompted Dorothea's comment is by Will Ladislaw and it is he who begins to improve her aesthetic understanding during their meetings in Rome. In the first of them (in chapter 21) she confesses that when she enters a room full of pictures she first feels herself 'in the presence of some higher life than my own. But when I begin to examine the pictures one by one, the life goes out of them ... It must be my own dulness ... It is painful to be told that anything is very fine and not be able to feel that it is very fine.' Ladislaw answers by pointing out that 'Art is an old language with a great many artificial affected styles' and that it is helpful to know the conventions. But Dorothea seems less interested in learning these languages than in learning more about Ladislaw; and she ends their conversation by observing with a degree of 'Puritanic' severity that in Rome, the squalor and human degradation of which have deeply affected her, there are 'so many things ... more wanted ... than pictures'. She begins to learn something of the conventions of art when Ladislaw takes her to visit the studio of his German painter friend, Naumann: 'some things which had seemed monstrous to her were gathering intelligibility and even a natural meaning' (ch. 22). What the reader learns from this visit, and from an earlier discussion between Ladislaw and Naumann at which Dorothea was not present, is that language is a finer medium than painting or the plastic arts because it can give a fuller and more suggestive image of what it represents, and that a work of art can suffer from an excess of meaning likely to occur when the representation is made subservient to the symbolic expression of the creator's ideas or ideals (that is, when the art work lapses from the picture to the diagram). Their last interview in Rome in chapter 22 shows that Dorothea is still preoccupied with the question of the relation of art to common humanity. Art should make 'everybody's life' beautiful; but it seemed to 'lie outside life' and her enjoyment of it was spoiled when she reflected 'that most people are shut out from it'. And later she will again sound like an early-Victorian anti-Romantic when she makes the same point more bluntly to her uncle: 'I used to come from the village with all that dirt and coarse ugliness like a pain within me, and the simpering pictures in the drawing-room seemed to me like a wicked attempt to find delight in what is false, while we don't mind how hard the truth is for the neighbours outside our walls' (ch. 39).

Dorothea's spiritual and emotional maturation is just beginning during her stay in Rome. But her aesthetic development ends there, for after her return to England the subject of her learning the language of art is dropped. At the same time Ladislaw, who during their final meeting in Rome had been more interested in Dorothea's dismal future than in her views on art, turns his attention from the arts to public affairs. This change of direction is disappointing, for in themselves the discussions of art in Rome throw less light on the aesthetic principles of *Middlemarch* than, say, the Italian scenes in *Anna Karenina* throw on those of Tolstoy's novel. It is regrettably difficult to agree with critics who point to these chapters as evidence that the novel contains its own aesthetic theory.[27] One does note the preference for a realistic art that is not distorted by excessive idealising and the imposition of symbolic meanings; and for an art that takes into account the unpleasant facts of ordinary life. The implication is equally clear: the realistic depiction of ordinary life – including its sordidness – is the key to the sympathetic involvement of the reader, which is the *sine qua non* for the communication of emotion and the arousal of feeling.

These same matters are gone into more penetratingly by the narrator in some of his reflective comments. It is here more than anywhere else that the aesthetics of *Middlemarch* are adumbrated. One of the first things one notices about the narrator is his concern with the transmission and control of meaning: 'signs are small measurable things', he observes early on, 'but interpretations are illimitable' (ch. 3); and two chapters later the reader is warned that 'the text, whether of prophet or of poet, expands for whatever we can put into it'. Both of these remarks are instances of the novel's pervasive epistemological concern with the relativity of truth to point of view. But they also have a particular application to what the author is trying to achieve in *Middlemarch*. The novel's major characters are concerned to find a significance in their lives and actions, though quotidian reality often seems to deny the possibility of any resonant action or radiant meaning.[28] His reflexive comments suggest that the narrator is in the similar position of trying to find meaning and a *bona fide* significance in the mundane reality of his subject-matter without imposing arbitrary interpretations or symbolic meanings. To do so successfully would heal the breach between art and life 'outside the walls'. Living in the nineteenth century, Dorothea cannot lead a heroic life as could St Theresa of Avila in the sixteenth century. But the narrator of *Middlemarch*, who also lives in the nineteenth century, may be able to avoid the lot of Dorothea through the heroic act of writing a major work of literature that would adapt to a modern prose idiom and a realistic subject-matter the two traditionally highest literary genres, epic and tragedy. This attempt is the subject of most of the narrator's comments on the work he is presenting.

The possibility of writing an epic work in the nineteenth century – a subject of consuming interest to most of the major creative artists of the Romantic and Victorian periods – is raised at the very beginning of *Middlemarch*. In the' sixteenth century, St Theresa's 'passionate, ideal nature' demanded, and found, 'an epic life'. But 'many Theresas' born into the modern world have found 'no epic life wherein there was a constant unfolding of far-resonant action'; their 'spiritual grandeur [was] ill-matched with the meanness of opportunity' (prelude). The point is again underlined in the finale: 'A new Theresa will hardly have the opportunity of reforming a conventual life, any more than a new Antigone will spend her heroic piety in daring all for the sake of a brother's burial: the medium in which their ardent deeds took shape is for ever gone.' Since the necessary subject-matter is lacking, *Middlemarch* cannot be an epic work in the traditional sense. For Dorothea Brooke, the central female character, there proves no way to 'lead a grand life here – now – in England' (ch. 3). There is, however, a modern equivalent to epic action that the narrator calls 'the home epic'; he explains in the finale that its 'great beginning' is marriage, which leads to 'the gradual conquest or irremediable loss of that complete union which makes the advancing years a climax, and age the harvest of sweet memories in common'. This definition is incomplete, however, for it makes no mention of what might be called the home-epic prelude of attraction and desire that figures prominently in the novel's story of several young lives. When Rosamond meets Lydgate in chapter 12, the attraction is mutual and she is perfectly correct in thinking that 'the great epoch of her life' is beginning.

As a literary subject, the home epic has the advantage of freshness. Even though marriage has been 'the bourne of so many narratives' (finale), Lydgate is never more victimised by his spots of commonness than when he thinks that 'the complexities of love and marriage' are subjects on which he has been 'amply informed by literature, and that traditional wisdom which is handed down in the genial conversation of men' (ch. 16). The literature from which Lydgate has picked up his information has presumably included poetry and romance, but for the subject of modern love and marriage the appropriate literary vehicle is realistic prose fiction – or so the narrator seems to imply in a cryptic aside in chapter 37 concerning Will Ladislaw's impatience to see Dorothea

alone: 'However slight the terrestrial intercourse between Dante and
Beatrice or Petrarch and Laura, time changes the proportion of things,
and in later days it is preferable to have fewer sonnets and more
conversation.' Furthermore, the home epic requires no epic machinery or
supernatural causation: 'the cloud of good or bad angels' that fill the air in
chapter 37 is simply a simile for Dorothea Brooke's memories of the
'spiritual struggles [and] spiritual falls' of her inner life that have been
brought on by her marriage to Casaubon. Such struggles have an
intensity, a profundity and a perilousness that make marriage and its
prelude a uniquely testing human experience: 'Marriage is so unlike
anything else,' says Dorothea. 'There is something even awful in the
nearness it brings' (ch. 81). Mr Brooke puts it more bluntly: Marriage '*is* a
noose' (ch. 4). The narrator speaks more dispassionately when he
observes that its conditions 'demand self-suppression and tolerance' (ch.
75). That is to say, they demand a movement away from egotistic self-
absorption and towards fellow-feeling. As such, marriage is for the author
of *Middlemarch* what the university was for her older contemporary
Newman – a great but ordinary means to a great but ordinary end; the end
in this case being the mitigation of the moral stupidity into which we are
all born.

Just as there is a modern form of epic, so the narrator argues that there
is also a viable modern form of tragedy. Not everyone in the nineteenth
century thought so. Some Victorian critics felt that there were
insuperable difficulties in extracting tragic effects from contemporary
life, and that tragedy was incompatible with the dominant literary form of
the day, the realistic novel. For the tragic emotions of pity and fear to
become operative, so the arguments ran, a certain distance was needed
between the audience and the hero, who should be elevated, larger than
life, and involved in undertakings of high moral seriousness. If the hero
were not exalted, he could not be a representative figure, his fall could
have no wide significance, and the end of his story could not convey a
sense of finality. As R. H. Hutton remarked of Thomas Hardy's *The
Return of the Native*, it treated 'tragedy itself as hardly more than a deeper
tinge of the common leaden-colour of the human lot, and so [made] it
seem less than tragedy – dreariness, rather than tragedy'.[29] One of the
critics who felt differently was George Henry Lewes. As early as 1842 he
had made a strong case for there being 'stuff for tragedy in the age of
civilization':

The [modern] tragedy, in its treatment, must be different from that of
one placed in a distant era. Instead of being poetical, it must be prose

... it must not endeavour to thrust this age into a poetical region which stands in contradiction to it, but diving deep down into the realities of this present time, reproduce it in its truth and passion, instead of idealizing it by beauty and dignity. It must not blink any mean or ludicrous associations which may be inseparable from its subject, but make them necessary, though subordinate to its effect. To take an instance, no one doubts that the life of an author affords materials for a very deep tragedy – his blighted hopes – his misunderstood aspirations – his wrung heart – the contrast of his faith and earnestness with the scepticism and despair around him – these afford tragic materials ... But in such a work, if correctly conceived, all that is petty, mean, or ludicrous, instead of marring its effect, would but conduce to its vivid reality, and feather the arrow of its pathos. On the other hand, should the author attempt to make it poetical ... he must fail, because he would thereby deprive it of its real strength, its truth, and could not succeed in giving it beauty and dignity, owing to the tyranny of that law of association which cannot be eluded; the very facts of hats, coats, gloves, and general habits, would contradict the poetical language.[30]

In reading this passage, it is hard not to think of *Middlemarch* and to substitute Eliot's aspiring medical researcher for Lewes's author. Eliot certainly agreed that the essence of modern tragedy lay not in the exceptional nature of the action or the idealisation of its participants but in its very commonness, even sordidness. One justification for her belief was Wordsworthian: 'a common tale/An ordinary sorrow of man's life' (as its narrator describes the story of Margaret in the first book of *The Excursion*) had an affective power which could touch the quick of fellow-feeling. A second justification was provided not by Wordsworth but by science, not by the emotions but by the intellect. As the narrator of *The Mill on the Floss* explains in that novel's thirtieth chapter: 'does not science tell us that its highest striving is after the ascertainment of a unity which shall bind the smallest things with the greatest? In natural science, I have understood, there is nothing petty to the mind that has a large vision of relations, and to which every single object suggests a vast sum of conditions. It is surely the same with the observation of human life.' In this perspective, Eliot's humanistic economy of salvation and her aesthetic theory become one. Just as modern science gives to each aspect of the visible world, however common, a function and a dignity similar to that with which they were formerly endowed by the Christian cosmology, so, too, in the historical advance of mankind every human struggle, however prosaic, acquires a significance that makes no longer tenable the traditional aesthetic distinctions between high and low subject-matter and the prescription that tragedy must involve exalted persons.

In *Middlemarch*, it is Lydgate, the scientist who aspires to discover a unity binding the smallest things with the highest, who is the protagonist of the modern tragedy. The narrator is at pains to have the reader recognise this. In order to do so, he must learn to overcome aesthetic spots of commonness similar to Lydgate's social ones that might cause him to find 'beneath his consideration' details like the cost of keeping two horses and of supplying a dinner table without stint, the price paid for life insurance, and the high rent for house and garden (ch. 58). Since the 'element of tragedy which lies in the very fact of frequency, has not yet wrought itself into the coarse emotion of mankind', as the narrator puts it at one point (ch. 20), he is at pains in several places in the novel to help the reader to recognise the tragic dimension in Lydgate's ordinary history. A 'commoner', and therefore more realistic, 'history of perdition than any single momentous bargain' is the 'pleasureless yielding to the small solicitations of circumstance' (ch. 79). Other protagonists

> have made an amazing figure in literature by general discontent with the universe as a trap of dullness into which their great souls have fallen by mistake; but the sense of a stupendous self and an insignificant world may have its consolations. Lydgate's discontent was much harder to bear: it was the sense that there was a grand existence in thought and effective action lying around him, while his self was being narrowed into the miserable isolation of egoistic fears, and vulgar anxieties for events that might allay such fears. His troubles will perhaps appear miserably sordid, and beneath the attention of lofty persons who can know nothing of debt except on a magnificent scale. Doubtless they were sordid; and for the majority, who are not lofty, there is no escape from sordidness but by being free from money-craving, with all its base hopes and temptations, its watching for death, its hinted requests, its horse-dealer's desire to make bad work pass for good, its seeking for function which ought to be another's, its compulsion often to long for Luck in the shape of a wide calamity. (ch. 64)

These reflections of the narrator do not perhaps go very much beyond the familiar lofty-ordinary, Rhine-Rhone contrasts made by the narrators of Eliot's early novels. But in the most important of the passages in which the narrator reflects on the nature of Lydgate's history a more distinctive note is struck. The passage occurs in chapter 15 when we are first given an inside view of Lydgate:

> Is it due to excess of poetry or of stupidity that we are never weary of describing what King James called a woman's 'makdom and her fairnesse', never weary of listening to the twanging of the old Troubadour strings, and are comparatively uninterested in that other kind of 'makdom and fairnesse' which must be wooed with industrious thought and patient renunciation of small desires? In the story of this passion, too, the development varies: sometimes it is the glorious marriage, sometimes frustration and final parting. And not seldom the catastrophe is bound up with the other passion, sung by the Troubadours. For in the multitude of middle-aged men who go about their vocations in a daily course determined for them much in the same way as the tie of their cravats, there is always a good number who once meant to shape their own deeds and alter the world a little. The story of their coming to be shapen after the average and fit to be packed by the gross, is hardly ever told even in their consciousness; for perhaps their ardour in generous unpaid toil cooled as imperceptibly as the ardour of other youthful loves, till one day their earlier self walked like a ghost in its old home and made the new furniture ghastly. Nothing in the world more subtle than the process of their gradual change.

Lydgate's great passion and its gradual frustration is not like the ennobling but unrequited love sung of by the troubadours during the Middle Ages. Like St Theresa of Avila's epic life or Faustian bargains with the devil, this kind of literary subject-matter belongs to an earlier stage of historical evolution. Lydgate's story belongs to the modern age and can only be properly told by using empirical techniques that are closely similar to the ones Lydgate brings to his own scientific investigations and that will enable the artist to bring into focus the subtle process of gradual change. The appropriate instrument for this revelation is not a telescope scanning the tempting 'range of relevencies called the universe' but a microscope concentrated on 'this particular web'.

The similarity between Lydgate's scientific method of investigation and the creative method of the author of *Middlemarch* is memorably expressed in the splendid description in chapter 16 of the arduous invention that enamours the young doctor, which is at the same time a celebration of the imaginative power of his creator:

> Fever had obscure conditions, and gave him that delightful labour of

the imagination which is not mere arbitrariness, but the exercise of
disciplined power – combining and constructing with the clearest eye
for probabilities and the fullest obedience to knowledge; and then, in
yet more energetic alliance with impartial Nature, standing aloof to
invent tests by which to try its own work.

Many men have been praised as vividly imaginative on the strength
of their profuseness in indifferent drawing or cheap narration: –
reports of very poor talk going on in distant orbs; or portraits of Lucifer
coming down on his bad errands as a large ugly man with bat's wings
and spurts of phosphorescence; or exaggerations of wantonness that
seem to reflect life in a diseased dream. But these kinds of inspiration
Lydgate regarded as rather vulgar and vinous compared with the
imagination that reveals subtle actions inaccessible by any sort of lens,
but tracked in that outer darkness through long pathways of necessary
sequence by the inward light which is the last refinement of Energy,
capable of bathing even the ethereal atoms in its ideally illuminated
space. He for his part had tossed away all cheap inventions where
ignorance finds itself able· and at ease: he was enamoured of that
arduous invention which is the very eye of research, provisionally
framing its object and correcting it to more and more exactness of
relation; he wanted to pierce the obscurity of those minute processes
which prepare human misery and joy, those invisible thoroughfares
which are the first lurking-places of anguish, mania, and crime, that
delicate poise and transition which determine the growth of happy or
unhappy consciousness.

The reference to the tawdry and exaggerated effects of inferior artists,
rather than to the work of inferior medical researchers, signals that this
account is as much about the narrator of *Middlemarch* as about Lydgate;
so does the removal of the normal distance that is kept between the
narrator and his protagonist. Indeed, the ambition to discover the sources
of human misery and joy and of the growth of happy or unhappy
consciousness is not – as it has sometimes been taken to be – an indication
of Lydgate's superbia and his flawed knowledge of human beings. It is,
rather, the one expression in all of *Middlemarch* of the confident ambition
that, together with the passion and excitement that the passage also
communicates, must have sustained George Eliot during the composition
of her great novel of provincial life. But the passage also exemplifies the
same quality of 'patient diligence' that fifteen years before in 'Silly
Novels by Lady Novelists' Eliot had identified as one of the 'moral
qualities that contribute to literary excellence'. It is this combination of

high ambition and patient diligence that makes for the disciplined power
with which in *Middlemarch* George Eliot penetrates beneath the surface
of her subject-matter – not in order to implant symbolic meanings that
will inflate it to lofty dimensions but in order to reveal the 'minute
processes' that are the source of tragic misery to some and of home-epic
happiness for others.

CHAPTER 3
A Study of Provincial Life

but there is no private life which has not been determined by a wider public life.

Felix Holt, ch. 3

In the previous chapter's discussion of the influence of Positivist ideas on *Middlemarch*, the narrator was compared to a social scientist. Since the society being studied is removed in time, and since he is concerned not only to understand its 'minute processes' but also to re-create and represent them to the reader, the narrator may equally well be considered a social historian. At one point he refers to his work as 'provincial history' and several times in the novel speaks of himself as a 'historian'. This was of course a common self-designation for the narrators of nineteenth-century novels from Sir Walter Scott on – as the reader of *Middlemarch* is reminded in chapter 32 when Borthrop Trumbull picks up a copy of Scott's *Anne of Geierstein* and intones its opening sentence: 'The course of four centuries has well-nigh elapsed since the series of events which are related in the following chapters took place on the Continent.'

One reason for the novelist calling his work a history was to suggest that his representation was worthy of more serious consideration than that implied in Rosamond Vincy's comment on her brother's reading-matter: 'Fred's studies are not very deep, he is only reading a novel' (ch. 11). The point was forcefully made by Henry James in his essay on Trollope: 'It is impossible to imagine what a novelist takes himself to be unless he regards himself as an historian and his narrative as a history. It is only as an historian that he has the smallest *locus standi*. As a narrator of fictitious events he is nowhere; to insert into his attempt a backbone of logic, he must relate events that are assumed to be real.'[1] In the case of *Middlemarch*, the claim of the narrator to be a historian is more than a rhetorical strategy. The novel really is what its subtitle calls it: 'a study of provincial life'. The setting is Middlemarch (that is, Coventry) and the surrounding country in the north-east corner of Loamshire (that is, of Warwickshire) around the time of the First Reform Bill – to be more precise, the period between 30 September 1829 and May 1832.[2]

The historical re-creation is richly detailed, and its accuracy and usefulness to social historians have been attested by professionals.[3] But its verifiable accuracy (with only the place-names changed) is much less important to the experience of reading *Middlemarch* than the felt, self-authenticating sense the novel everywhere conveys of the way it was in a particular time and place. As one of a large number of possible examples, take the description in chapter 39 of the dilapidated farmhouse in which the Dagley family lives:

> It is true that an observer, under that softening influence of the fine arts which makes other people's hardships picturesque, might have been delighted with this homestead called Freeman's End: the old house had dormer-windows in the dark-red roof, two of the chimneys were choked with ivy, the large porch was blocked up with bundles of sticks, and half the windows were closed with grey worm-eaten shutters about which the jasmine-boughs grew in wild luxuriance; the mouldering garden wall with hollyhocks peeping over it was a perfect study of highly-mingled subdued colour, and there was an aged goat (kept doubtless on interesting superstitious grounds) lying against the open back-kitchen door. The mossy thatch of the cow-shed, the broken grey barn-doors, the pauper labourers in ragged breeches who had nearly finished unloading a waggon of corn into the barn ready for early thrashing; the scanty dairy of cows being tethered for milking and leaving one half of the shed in brown emptiness; the very pigs and white ducks seeming to wander about the uneven neglected yard as if in low spirits from feeding on a too meagre quality of rinsings – all these objects under the quiet light of a sky marbled with high clouds would have made a sort of picture which we have all paused over as a 'charming bit', touching other sensibilities than those which are stirred by the depression of the agricultural interest, with the sad lack of farming capital, as seen constantly in the newspapers of that time.

A sense of verisimilitude and the sympathetic involvement of the reader is nicely achieved through the rhetorical device of having the narrator distinguish between a distanced, aesthetic view of the scene and his own first-hand, close-up view. This sense is intensified by the easy fullness of specific visual detail and the quiet display of a working knowledge of farm life – the corn being readied for early thrashing, the cows being tethered for milking, the insufficiency of the pigs' and ducks' diet. The appeal to a verifiable source at the end of the passage is included because newspapers are on Mr Brooke's mind as he arrives at the farmhouse to visit his tenant. Their citation is hardly needed to authenticate the passage. Similarly, it may be true that the description has a meaning beyond itself because of its association with the romantic-realist contrast that is so important in the aesthetics of *Middlemarch*. But it is the description itself, not the thematic overlay, that gives the passage its sparkle and its principal interest.

This 'amplification of experience', as George Eliot called it in 'The Natural History of German Life', is one of the great satisfactions that nineteenth-century realistic fiction has to offer, and few novels satisfy as fully as *Middlemarch*. But since the provincial England of over a century and a half ago was a far different place from the advanced capitalist democracies of the last quarter of the twentieth century some sorting out of the social-historical world represented in the novel is helpful for a full understanding of its principal characters and themes.

The most important social division in *Middlemarch* is that between country and town. In the former there are clear distinctions of rank based on birth. They and their corresponding emoluments have traditional sanctions and justifications; one of the gentry calls them 'providential arrangements' (ch. 37), while the views of someone at the other end of the rural social spectrum are guided by his 'farming conservatism, which consisted in holding that whatever is, is bad, and any change is likely to be worse' (ch. 39). The principal country characters belong to the small group of landed gentry, a social rank just below the lower fringes of the aristocracy (which is unrepresented in the novel). Those who live in this 'rarefied social air' (ch. 34) include Mr Brooke of Tipton Grange, whose connections, if 'not exactly aristocratic, were unquestionably good' (ch. 1) and whose estate is worth around £3,000 a year – a considerable sum at the time, as the narrator explains. Mr Brooke has the additional social distinction of being a magistrate with responsibility for the preservation of law and order in his district. This position involves him in two cases mentioned in passing: that of Trapping Bass, the poacher, and of Bunch, the sheep-stealer, who is to be hanged despite Mr Brooke's intercession.

With Mr Brooke live his two orphaned nieces, who have been privately educated, first with an English, then with a Swiss family. Each marries as she is expected to: into another family of the gentry. Celia weds the young baronet who is the heir of Freshitt, the Chettam estate; Dorothea marries Mr Edward Casaubon, who is both the rector of Lowick (though a curate lives in the parsonage and does all the duty except preaching the morning sermon) and the owner of the prosperous estate where 'not a cottager in those double cottages at a low rent but kept a pig, and the strips of garden at the back were well tended. The small boys wore excellent corduroy, and the girls went out as tidy servants, or did a little straw plaiting at home: no looms here, no Dissent' (ch. 9). This social circle is completed by the Cadwalladers. He is the rector of Tipton and Freshitt and has a study filled with fishing tackle. She is of aristocratic background and exceptionally keen on distinctions of rank, though her impecuniousness and companionable manner give a neighbourliness to both rank and religion, and mitigate 'the bitterness of [the] uncommunicated tithe' that provides her husband's income (ch. 6).

The lower social orders of the country are less fully represented. They include Mr Featherstone of Stone Court in Lowick parish, 'a gentleman farmer' (ch. 12) who belongs to the inferior county society who fill the gap between the landed gentry and their tenants, as does Mr Tucker, Casaubon's curate, who is one of the 'inferior clergy' (ch. 9). The tenants include the agricultural labourers who live in the hamlet of Frick on the Lowick estate. One of them is old Timothy Cooper, 'a type lingering in those times – who had his savings in a stocking-foot and lived in a lone cottage' (ch. 56). He is as set in his ways as Dagley, the hereditary farmer who lives at Freeman's End and whose immemorial ignorance is disturbed neither by the gentry who live nearby, nor by proximity to the town of Middlemarch, only three miles away.

The society of Middlemarch is much more variegated and fluid than that of the country and far more characters and social types are represented. Near the lower end of the spectrum is the salty Mrs Dollop, landlady of the Tankard in Slaughter Lane, and her customers – Mr Limp, the shoemaker; Mr Crabbe, the glazier; Mr Dill, the barber; Mr Baldwin, the tax-gatherer; and Mr Jonas, a dyer with crimson hands. Higher up the social scale are Borthrop Trumbull, a 'prosperous provincial auctioneer keenly alive to his own jokes and sensible of his encyclopaedic knowledge' (ch. 60); Mr Mawnsey, a grocer in the Top Market and 'a chief representative in Middlemarch of that great social power, the retail trader' (ch. 51); Caleb Garth, estate agent and failed contractor, who lives with his family 'a little way outside the town [in] a homely place with an orchard in front of it, a rambling, old-fashioned, half-timbered building, which before the town had spread had been a farmhouse, but was now surrounded with the private gardens of the townsmen' (ch. 24); and the patrons of the Green Dragon, who include Mr Horrock, the vet, and Mr Bambridge, the horse-dealer. The vivid character sketch of the latter in chapter 23 is a good example of the quantity and quality of the social notation given to even minor town characters:

Mr Bambridge had more open manners, and appeared to give forth his ideas without economy. He was loud, robust, and was sometimes spoken of as being 'given to indulgence' – chiefly in swearing, drinking, and beating his wife. Some people who had lost by him called him a vicious man; but he regarded horse-dealing as the finest of the arts, and might have argued plausibly that it had nothing to do with morality. He was undeniably a prosperous man, bore his drinking better than others bore their moderation, and, on the whole, flourished like the green bay-tree. But his range of conversation was limited, and like the fine old tune, 'Drops of brandy', gave you after a while a sense of returning upon itself in a way that might make weak heads dizzy. But a slight infusion of Mr Bambridge was felt to give tone and character to several circles in Middlemarch; and he was a distinguished figure in the bar and billiard-room at the Green Dragon. He knew some anecdotes about the heroes of the turf, and various clever tricks of Marquesses and Viscounts which seemed to prove that blood asserted its pre-eminence even among blacklegs; but the minute retentiveness of his memory was chiefly shown about the horses he had himself bought and sold; the number of miles they would trot you in no time without turning a hair being, after the lapse of years, still a subject of passionate asseveration, in which he would assist the imagination of his hearers by solemnly swearing that they never saw anything like it. In short, Mr Bambridge was a man of pleasure and a gay companion.

Since the central male character in the novel is a young doctor who has settled in Middlemarch, the reader learns a good deal about the town's other medical practitioners. The least fully presented is Mr Gambit, who is also the lowest in social standing; he has little education, though 'he made none the worse accoucheur for calling the breathing apparatus "longs"' (ch. 45). Mr Toller and Mr Wrench are surgeon-apothecaries, a category of medical practitioner socially lower than that of physician. Both are long established, but while the former keeps a good house and belongs to an old Middlemarch family the latter – 'a small neat bilious man, with a well-dressed wig ... a laborious practice, an irascible temper, a lymphatic wife and seven children' (ch. 26) – lives in a house with 'the doors all open, the oil-cloth worn, the children in soiled pinafores, and lunch lingering in the form of bones, black-handled knives and willow-pattern' (ch. 36). The two physicians are Dr Sprague and Dr Minchin. They may be called 'Dr' because they are graduates of Oxford or Cambridge, where the curriculum was primarily designed to produce educated gentlemen, not competent practitioners. Dr Minchin, for example, can quote from Pope's *Essay on Man*, but he diagnoses a cramp as a tumour.[4]

The town inhabitants with whom the novel is principally concerned belong to the 'Middlemarch gentry' (ch. 27). Although town society is more fluid than that of the country, there are nevertheless 'nice distinctions of rank', which are 'defined with great nicety in practice, though hardly expressible theoretically' (ch. 23). These distinctions are, however, at least partially based on income rather than on birth, which means that there is the possibility, as there is the desire, of rising socially. For this reason readers today would tend to call the social distinctions in Middlemarch ones of class rather than of rank. One example of the importance of money is the relations between the Vincys and the Garths. The slight connection between the two families through Mr Feather-stone's two marriages (first to Mr Garth's sister, then to Mr Vincy's) had led to an acquaintance and to Fred Vincy and Mary Garth becoming intimate during childhood. But the Garths have come down in the world owing to the father's business failure, and social intercourse between the families has ceased. Mr Garth may be noted for his probity, 'but in no part of the world is genteel visiting founded on esteem, in the absence of suitable furniture and complete dinner-service' (ch. 23). Although she herself is an innkeeper's daughter with 'a tinge of unpretentious, inoffensive vulgarity' (ch. 16), Mrs Vincy now feels no longer at ease with the better-educated Mrs Garth, 'and frequently spoke of her as a woman who had to work for her bread – meaning that Mrs Garth had been a teacher before her marriage' (ch. 23). Even Mr Farebrother, an exemplary clergyman, gives witness to the difference income makes to the social lives of the two families: 'He used to the full the clergyman's privilege of disregarding the Middlemarch discrimination of ranks, and always told his mother that Mrs Garth was more of a lady than any matron in the town. Still, you see, he spent his evenings at the Vincys, where the matron, though less of a lady, presided over a well-lit drawing-room and whist' (ch. 40).

Another example of the importance of money in Middlemarch is the dominant position of Mr Bulstrode, the philanthropic banker, which he has achieved despite the handicaps of being both an outsider – 'a man not born in the town, and altogether of dimly known origin' (ch. 11) – and a religious zealot of a particularly unpleasant type. The latter quality also makes Bulstrode a conspicuous example of the importance of religion in the socio-historical picture painted in *Middlemarch*. Almost all of the characters in the novel are Anglicans, that is, members of the Established Church. There are some Roman Catholics in the Middlemarch area, as one learns from a passing reference to an acre of land Mr Brooke has sold 'the Papists' for a chapel; but none is introduced to the reader. Methodists and other dissenting groups are similarly unrepresented, though one is aware of their existence, as in Mr Brooke's droll story about Flavell, the Methodist preacher, and the hare that came across his path when he and his wife were out walking. It is true that as a young man Bulstrode had belonged to a Calvinistic dissenting church in the London area, but before settling in Middlemarch he had already taken the major social step of joining the Established Church. As Raffles, the nemesis from his past, observes: 'You've taken to being a nob, buying land, being a country bashaw. Still in the Dissenting line, eh? Still godly? Or taken to the Church as more genteel?' (ch. 53) And as Bulstrode's wife implicitly believes: 'true religion was everywhere saving [but] to be saved in the Church was more respectable' (ch. 61).

The wing of the Established Church to which Bulstrode belongs is the Evangelical. Like George Eliot herself during her late teens, he embodies in exaggerated form certain Evangelical characteristics, including the view of the world as a battleground between flesh and spirit, the sense of sacred accountableness for the smallest acts, and an intense preoccupation with personal spiritual hygiene. The other wing of the Established Church was that of traditional undogmatic, plain-speaking Anglicanism, which was more interested in conduct than in faith, in community rather than in intense spiritual struggle. (It must be remembered that *Middlemarch* is set in provincial England in the early nineteenth century; there is no evidence in the social world of the novel of the tripartite division of High (Tractarian or Anglo-Catholic), Broad (liberal) and Low (Evangelical) that became a marked feature of the Anglican Church during the Victorian period.) Traditional Anglicanism has a number of representatives in the novel, who come from both town and country. Mr Vincy is one of them. 'I'm a plain Churchman now', he insists in chapter 13, 'just as I used to be before doctrines came up. I take the world as I find it, in trade and everything else. I'm contented to be no worse than my neighbours.' Mrs Farebrother is another. In chapter 17 she proudly recalls that in her youth 'there never was any question about right and wrong. We knew our catechism, and that was enough: we learned our creed and our duty. Every respectable Church person had the same opinions.' Her father, a clergyman, had preached 'plain moral sermons without arguments, and was a good man ... When you get me a good man out of arguments, I will get you a good dinner with reading you the cookery-book.' Two other representatives provide glimpses of an unattractive side of plain-church Anglicanism. One of them is Mr Crowse, a clergyman whose 'empty face and neat umbrella, and mincing little speeches' are recalled with scorn by Mary Garth in chapter 52. 'What right', she asks, 'have such men to represent Christianity – as if it were an institution for getting up idiots genteelly.' The other is Mr Cadwallader, whose conscience does 'only what it could do without any trouble'. As his wife remarks of him: 'as long as the fish rise to his bait, everybody is what he ought to be' (ch. 8).

A final example of traditional Anglicanism is found in the warm description in chapter 47 of 'the group of rural faces which made the congregation from year to year within the white-washed walls and dark old pews' of the little church at Lowick. With the passing of time they show hardly 'more change than we see in the boughs of a tree which breaks here and there with age, but yet has young shoots'. One of the names put forward to be the new rector of Lowick is Mr Tyke, a fervent Evangelical who wants to use Dissenting hymn-books in his church (ch. 74), and whose sermons are all doctrine, a good deal of which, according to Lydgate, 'is a sort of pinching hard to make people uncomfortably aware of him' (ch. 50). The office is in the gift of Dorothea Brooke, and her reflections on the matter provide the clearest indication in *Middlemarch* of on which side of the Anglican divide the sympathies of the author lie. In Dorothea's view, the doctrinal preoccupations of Tyke, who gives sermons about 'imputed righteousness and the prophecies in the Apocalypse', would be of no use to the farmers, labourers and village artisans of Lowick: 'I have always been thinking of the different ways in which Christianity is taught, and whenever I find one way that makes it a wider blessing than any other, I cling to that as the truest – I mean that which takes in the most good of all kinds, and brings in the most people as sharers in it. It is surely better to pardon too much than to condemn too much' (ch. 50). The appointment goes instead to Mr Farebrother, whose character is known to be less than spotless, but who gives plain moral sermons without arguments (like his grandfather before him), has a deep, undoctrinal concern for the welfare of his flock, and regards the group to which Tyke and Bulstrode belong as 'a narrow ignorant set [who] do more to make their neighbours uncomfortable than to make them better. Their system is a sort of worldly-spiritual cliqueism: they really look on the rest of mankind as a doomed carcass which is to nourish them for heaven' (ch. 17).

Let us come back to Middlemarch society. The Vincys are the principal town family in the novel. They are 'old manufacturers, and had kept a good house for three generations' (ch. 11). They live 'in an easy profuse way, not with any new ostentation, but according to the family habits and traditions ... Mr Vincy himself had expensive Middlemarch habits – spent money on coursing, on his cellar, and on dinner-giving, while [Mrs Vincy] had those running accounts with trades-people, which give [their children] a cheerful sense of getting everything one wants without any question of payment' (ch. 23). The family business is the manufacture of silk ribbons, for which is needed the handlooms of the cottagers in Tipton and Freshitt, who do the work because they are less well off than the pig-keeping cottagers of Lowick. Mr Vincy is not only mayor of Middlemarch; his worldly success is also indicated by his having the means to realise what he calls 'a good British feeling [:] to try and raise your family a little' (ch. 13). He has sent his son Fred to university – Omnibus College would have been at either Oxford or Cambridge – where the young man has acquired the manners, speech, habits and debts of a gentleman. His father intends Fred to be a clergyman, one of the three established professions (law and medicine were the other two) that conferred gentility as well as offering opportunities for material advance.

Mr Vincy's daughter Rosamond has also been given a genteel education. It has served to make her dissatisfied with Middlemarch society, whose two most eligible young men 'had not a notion of French, and could speak on no subject with striking knowledge, except perhaps the dyeing and carrying trades, which of course they were ashamed to mention; they were Middlemarch gentry, elated with their silver-headed whips and satin stocks, but embarrassed in their manners, and timidly jocose' (ch. 27). She has even come to feel that 'she might have been happier if she had not been the daughter of a Middlemarch manufacturer' (ch. 15), and she dislikes anything that reminds her that her maternal grandfather had been an innkeeper. Rosamond's interest in the newcomer Lydgate is whetted by the fact that his family connections with the gentry of another county give him 'rank', which is Rosamond's 'middle-class' ideal of 'heaven' (ch. 12), a state where 'she would have nothing to do with vulgar people' (ch. 16). When she had once seen Mr Brooke's nieces seated among the aristocracy at the county assizes her reaction had been envy; and when she and Dorothea Brooke first meet in chapter 43 the contrast in their dress and demeanour – Dorothea's 'plain dressing', which bespeaks the 'well-bred economy' of good birth (ch. 2), versus Rosamond's 'infantine blondness and wondrous crown of hair-plaits … her pale blue dress of a [perfect] fit and fashion … and that controlled self-consciousness of manner which is the expensive substitute for simplicity' – has important moral overtones. But it is first and foremost a social contrast of a sort 'not infrequent' in provincial life 'when the habits of the different ranks were less blent than now'.

As the rarity of their meeting suggests, there is little social intercourse between the two enclaves. To further his political aims, Mr Brooke does

invite some Middlemarchers to his dinner parties, but Rosamond is not
among them, for he 'would not have chosen that his nieces should meet
the daughter of a Middlemarch manufacturer, unless it were on a public
occasion' (ch. 10). There is even a certain antagonism between the two
groups. Mr Hawley, a town lawyer, is not alone in resenting the attempt
of Mr Brooke, 'an old county man' (ch. 37), to curry favour with the
electors of Middlemarch; Featherstone's dislike of Bulstrode is owing in
part to the fact that he is 'a speckilating fellow' whose wealth comes from
business, not from land (ch. 12); and Mrs Cadwallader believes that 'the
people in manufacturing towns are always disreputable' (ch. 62), finds
'their accent an affliction to the ears' (ch. 6), and prefers joining 'the
farmers at the tithe dinner, who drank her health unpretentiously, and
were not ashamed of their grandfathers' furniture' (ch. 10). There is none
the less a certain amount of social mixing, for the society of north-east
Loamshire is not static, as the narrator makes clear in a colourful
generalisation in chapter 11:

> Old provincial society had its share of this subtle movement: had not
> only its striking downfalls, its brilliant young professional dandies who
> ended by living up an entry with a drab and six children for their
> establishment, but also those less marked vicissitudes which are
> constantly shifting the boundaries of social intercourse, and begetting
> new consciousness of interdependence. Some slipped a little
> downward, some got higher footing: people denied aspirates, gained
> wealth, and fastidious gentlemen stood for boroughs; some were
> caught in political currents, some in ecclesiastical, and perhaps found
> themselves surprisingly grouped in consequence; while a few
> personages or families that stood with rocky firmness amid all this
> fluctuation, were slowly presenting new aspects in spite of solidity, and
> altering with the double change of self and beholder. Municipal town
> and rural parish gradually made fresh threads of connection –
> gradually, as the old stocking gave way to the savings-bank, and the
> worship of the solar guinea became extinct; while squires and baronets,
> and even lords who had once lived blamelessly afar from the civic
> mind, gathered the faultiness of closer acquaintanceship. Settlers, too,
> came from distant counties, some with an alarming novelty of skill,
> others with an offensive advantage in cunning.

Historical change is the name for the long-term results of these subtle
movements, political and ecclesiastical currents, and fresh threads of
connection. It is this process that is the principal interest of the historian-

narrator of *Middlemarch*. In studying the subject the narrator is not, on the one hand, simply a collector of miscellaneous information and documents casually arranged, like Mr Brooke. On the other hand, he is not a taxonomist like Farebrother, whose interests in natural history led him to make an exhaustive classification of the entomology of north-east Loamshire. And he is hardly like Casaubon, who studied certain historical phenomena with a view to demonstrating their supernatural origin. The narrator is much more like the modern professional historian described by J. H. Plumb, who is ultimately concerned with a detailed study of a salient portion of man's past because of what it can tell him about the present:

> The aim of [the historian] is to understand men both as individuals and in their social relationships in time. Social embraces all of man's activities – economic, religious, political, artistic, legal, military, scientific – everything, indeed, that affects the life of mankind. And this, of course, is not a static study but a study of movement and change. It is not only necessary to discover, as accurately as the most sophisticated use of evidence will allow, things as they actually were, but also why they were so, and why they changed; for no human societies, not one, have ever stood still ... The historian's purpose, therefore, is to deepen understanding about men and society, not merely for its own sake, but in the hope that a profounder knowledge, a profounder awareness will help to mould human attitudes and human actions.[5]

As Eliot herself remarked in a late note on the 'historic imagination': 'the exercise of a veracious imagination in historical picturing ... might help the judgement greatly with regard to present or future events ... For want of such real, minute vision of how changes come about in the past, we fall into ridiculously inconsistent estimates of actual movements.'[6]

It does not take much knowledge of nineteenth-century British history to see that the external precipitates of change in the Middlemarch world are microcosmic reflections of some of the principal forces that shaped the century's history. The 'infant struggles of the railway system', which when full-grown would transform the social and commercial life of Victorian Britain, help to determine 'the course of this history' with regard to two of the novel's principal characters. In and around Middlemarch railways were as exciting a topic as the Reform Bill or 'the imminent horrors of Cholera' (ch. 56) – that is, as two other important historical forces: the movement for political reform and the complex of related movements during 'that unsanitary period' (ch. 23) that led to the reform of the medical profession, the better understanding of disease, and the improvement of public health.

It is important, however, not to overestimate the role that the infant stages of these forces for change play in the novel. This is particularly true of political reform. Jerome Beaty has shown that there are numerous references in the novel to events and personalities involved in the struggle for the passage of the First Reform Bill, but that they are all obliquely introduced and never call attention to themselves.[7] These allusions add to the historical verisimilitude of *Middlemarch*, but the events themselves impinge very little on the society of the novel or even on the consciousness of its characters. This is underlined in several places: 'even in 1831 Lowick was at peace, not more agitated by Reform than by the solemn tenor of the Sunday sermon' (ch. 47); 'even the rumour of Reform had not yet excited any millennial expectations in Frick, as of gratuitous grains to fatten Hiram Ford's pigs, or of a publican at the "Weights and Scales" who would brew beer for nothing' (ch. 56); the scandal concerning Bulstrode and Lydgate gives to 'all public conviviality' in Middlemarch 'a zest which could not be won from the question whether the Lords would throw out the Reform Bill' (ch. 71); and even among the landed gentry interest in the action of the Lords runs a poor second to interest in Dorothea's impending second marriage.

Middlemarch, then, can hardly be taken to be what Frank Kermode thinks it is – 'a novel of ... crisis', set in 'earlier crisis-years' when civilisation seemed 'on the brink of radical change'; 'a novel concerned with the end of a world'.[8] There is no sense of historical crisis to be found in the commentary of the novel's narrator, who is, like George Eliot herself, a gradualist and a uniformitarian, not a catastrophist or a believer in apocalypse.[9] Change is seen as a process occurring slowly over a long period of time, the result of innumerable small causes which it takes a real, minute vision to discern. There is nothing in *Middlemarch* to gainsay Eliot's own description of its design: 'to show the gradual action of ordinary causes rather than exceptional'.[10]

What does preoccupy the historian-narrator of *Middlemarch* is not the end of a world but the relationship of the individual to society. As he remarks in the finale: 'there is no creature whose inward being is so strong that it is not greatly determined by what lies outside it'. That this relationship was a matter of particular concern to liberal Victorian intellectuals is clear from John Stuart Mill's *On Liberty*, which was published in the same year (1859) as Eliot's first novel. The subject of Mill's classic monograph is 'the nature and limits of the power which can be legitimately exercised by society over the individual'. The tendency of modern society was 'to impose, by other means than civil penalties, its own ideas and practices as rules of conduct on those who dissent from them; to fetter the development and, if possible, prevent the formation of any individuality not in harmony with its ways, and compel all characters to fashion themselves upon the model of its own'. For Mill, when tradition or custom dictated conduct there was wanting 'one of the principal ingredients of human happiness, and quite the chief ingredient of individual and social progress'. Human advancement depended on the 'disposition to aim at something better than customary'; for it was only from the 'strong natures' of individuals that 'the initiation of all wise or noble things' would come.[11] This encapsulation of the central argument of *On Liberty* could serve almost equally well for the social-historical analysis of *Middlemarch*. But what Mill argues logically, the narrator of Eliot's novel attempts to show through his real, minute vision of characters living in the early 1830s, whose struggles help to bring into being the world that his readers in the 1870s inhabit.

The struggle is most clearly seen in the case of Lydgate. *Middlemarch* is not quite the first Victorian novel to have a practising medical doctor in an important role. As Q. D. Leavis pointed out, there are earlier examples in Dickens's *Bleak House* (1852), Charles Kingsley's *Two Years Ago* (1857) and Mrs Oliphant's *Miss Majoribanks* (1865).[12] But Eliot's protagonist differs from these predecessors in that his professional life is an essential aspect of his story and that he is put back in time into 'a dark period', 'the heroic time of copious bleeding and blistering' (ch. 15), when provincial society was untouched by modern scientific notions of medical practice. As Lady Chettam observes: 'I like a medical man more on a footing with the servants. [Hicks] was coarse and butcher-like, but he knew my constitution' (ch. 10). With his superior scientific training and informed interest in both public health and medical research, Lydgate had almost nothing professionally in common with his fellow medical practitioners and is in fact out of place in early nineteenth-century society. He belongs to the future and is in the vanguard of modern medical practice (an early example of what came to be called the general practitioner) and of 'the better understanding of disease' which George Eliot regarded as a leading example in the lifetime of her contemporaries of the 'mutual determination of each other's life'.[13] The details of Lydgate's practice would certainly have had this resonance for the first readers of *Middlemarch*: his correct diagnosis and/or treatment of cholera, erysipelas, cramp, pneumonia, delirium tremens, the pink-skinned stage of typhoid fever, and fatty degeneration of the heart; his prescribing drugs rather than dispensing them; his views on post-mortem examinations and the appointment of coroners; his use of the stethoscope and microscope; and his avoidance of bleeding, patching and blistering. Lydgate, then, exemplifies George Eliot's belief that the application of the principles of science was the only way of increasing man's store of knowledge and happiness. But what *Middlemarch* shows in detail is how destructive of this potential is the petty medium in which Lydgate must realise his ideals. When he arrives in Middlemarch, Lydgate is full of confidence in his powers and integrity; but he has yet to realise what it is like to live and practise medicine in a community where 'sane people did what their neighbours did' (ch. 1), and where 'it was dangerous to insist on knowledge as a qualification for any salaried office' (ch. 16). Lydgate is made to run a gauntlet beginning with the business of the appointment of a chaplain to the new hospital, in which he first feels the grasp of petty alternatives, through the conspiracy of the other medical practitioners to undermine the new hospital's work, the spectrum of contrary public opinion in which every social shade in the town is represented, the financial pressures that leave him without the energy for research or speculative thought, to the 'malignant effect' (ch. 71) on his reputation of his rumoured involvement in the Bulstrode–Raffles affair, which leads to a 'general black-balling' (ch. 73).

It is all a sorry business; but one might reflect that at least Lydgate had a vocation – 'something particular in life ... to do for its own sake and not because [one's father] did it' (ch. 15) – through which he is able to actualise his talents and do good work in the world. The problem of vocation is an important aspect of the relation of the individual to society not only in *Middlemarch* in particular but also in nineteenth- and twentieth-century literature in general. The appearance of the concern is itself a reflection of historical change, for as society becomes more shifting and fluid and comes to be increasingly based on class distinctions rather than on traditional distinctions of inherited rank the choice of a career becomes increasingly important for the many young men of ability 'whose only capital was in their brains' (ch. 30). The classic statement of the problem is found in the second book of Carlyle's *Sartor Resartus* (1834), one of the seminal works of Victorian literature: 'To each is given a certain inward Talent, a certain outward Environment of Fortune; to each, by wisest combination of these two, a certain maximum of Capability. But the hardest problem were ever this first: To find by study of yourself, and of the ground you stand on, what your combined inward and outward Capability specially is.'[14]

In *Middlemarch* vocation is defined by Ladislaw (though he calls it genius): 'a power to make or do, not anything in general, but something in particular' (ch. 10). It is exemplified not by Lydgate (who is too complex a character to be emblematic) but by Caleb Garth, who speaks in muted Carlylean and 'deeply religious' tones of the importance of work and of business (which are his words for vocation): 'You must be sure of two things: you must love your work, and not be always looking over the edge of it, wanting your play to begin. And the other is, you must not be ashamed of your work' (ch. 56). Like Lydgate's vocation, Caleb's had 'laid hold of his imagination in boyhood' with the force of a religious calling. Business has made a wholesome 'philosophy for him without the aid of philosophers, a religion without the aid of theology' (ch. 24), and given him 'the chance of getting a bit of the country into good fettle ... that those who are living and those who come after will be the better for. I'd sooner have it than a fortune ... It's a great gift of God' (ch. 40). But Caleb Garth is an idealised character – a pastoral type, as we have already seen in a different connection. He lives in a simpler world than that of the novel's other characters, a world where business never meant money transactions or handling capital, but 'the skilful application of labour' (ch. 56). The choice of career is a much more difficult matter for several characters in the novel who have no God or inherited social position to bestow the gift of vocation.

Ladislaw and Fred Vincy are two of these characters: another is Farebrother, though he is seen from a different point of view because he is older and his vocational choice is behind him, not in front of him. Early on, Farebrother observes to Lydgate that 'you are in the right profession, the work you feel yourself most fit for. Some people miss that, and repent too late ... I am not a model clergyman – only a decent makeshift' (ch. 17). And one feels sure he is speaking from experience when he tells the Garths that 'I would do anything I could to hinder a man from the fatal step of choosing the wrong profession' (ch. 40). As we shall see in a later chapter, there is around Farebrother's character a certain aura of self-suppression and incompleteness; it is hard not to associate this with his dubious vocational choice. For Fred Vincy, the choice of clergyman would not be dubious; it would clearly be wrong. Having been 'born the son of a Middlemarch manufacturer', Fred is 'inevitable heir to nothing in particular' (ch. 12) and has difficulty in imagining 'what secular avocation on earth was there for a young man (whose friends could not get him an "appointment") which was at once gentlemanly, lucrative, and to be followed without special knowledge' (ch. 56). The only answer seems to be to go into the church; but, as Mary Garth caustically points out, this would make him ridiculous: 'His being a clergyman would be only for gentility's sake, and I think there is nothing more contemptible than such imbecile gentility' (ch. 52). The man chosen by the daughter of Caleb Garth must be made of sterner stuff, for Mary, too, has a Victorian ideal of vocation that involves useful activity. 'How can you bear', she tells Fred, 'to be so contemptible, when others are working and striving, and there are so many things to be done – how can you bear to be fit for nothing in the world that is useful?' (ch. 25).

The choice of career is as pressing a concern for Ladislaw as it is for Fred. None of the traditional professions 'civil or sacred' (ch. 9) – that is, law, medicine or the church – initially appeals to Ladislaw, who prefers to explore artistic avenues for the expression of his particular 'genius'. But this pursuit only makes him into a dilettante and it eventually becomes clear to him that his vocation does not lie in creative directions. When he returns to England and becomes a newspaper editor, the reader begins to see the truth of Dorothea's shrewd prediction: 'people may really have in them some vocation which is not quite plain to themselves ... They may seem idle and weak because they are growing' (ch. 9). What is growing in Will is an 'ardent' interest in the political situation, to which his 'sense of duty' is finally beginning to respond. This sense 'must often wait for some work which shall take the place of dilettanteism and make us feel that the quality of our action is not a matter of indifference' (ch. 46). It is in the offstage world of public affairs in London – the city that was the final destination of the protagonist of *Sartor Resartus* – that Ladislaw finds his vocation.

The silent partner in Ladislaw's post-Middlemarch public life is Dorothea Brooke. The question of whether this young woman of heroic potential finds appropriate vocational fulfilment in this role has long been mooted by readers of *Middlemarch*, many of whom have agreed with the 'many who knew her [who] thought it a pity that so substantive and rare a creature should have been absorbed into the life of another, and be known only in a certain circle as a wife and mother' (finale). I propose to defer consideration of this contentious issue to a later chapter; what should be considered here is the social context in which Dorothea attempts to realise her maximum of capability.

There are two passages early in *Middlemarch* which heavily underline the ill-effects of provincial society on the aspiring 19-year-old Dorothea. The first speaks of her 'altogether ardent, theoretic, and intellectually consequent' nature 'struggling in the bands of a narrow teaching, hemmed in by a social life which seemed nothing but a labyrinth of petty courses, a walled-in maze of small paths that led no wither' (ch. 3). The second concerns Dorothea's reluctance to admit 'any error in herself. She was disposed rather to accuse the intolerable narrowness and the purblind conscience of the society around her' (ch. 4). It is important not to make too much of these rhetorical passages, for the most salient aspect of both is that they represent Dorothea's own views of her situation in provincial society, and not necessarily the narrator's. On the other hand, the views expressed in the prelude and the finale to the novel are clearly the narrator's. They raise a crucial question: the extent to which *Middlemarch* is a contribution to what Victorians called the Woman Question – more precisely, the extent to which the novel suggests that Dorothea's unheroic lot is the result of the position of women in nineteenth-century society. Although it does so vaguely, the prelude speaks of 'the social lot of women', 'the common yearning of womanhood', and the 'inconvenient indefiniteness' which 'some' consider characteristic of woman's nature. And we have already seen that the original version of the penultimate paragraph of the finale enumerated specific aspects of society's treatment of women that were said to be negative determinants in Dorothea's life.

This question has been debated ever since *Middlemarch* was published. R. H. Hutton, for example, complained in his review that the prelude and the finale mistakenly attempted 'to represent the book as an elaborate contribution to the "Woman's" question; [for] the creative power of the author is yoked to no specific doctrine'.[15] Even in the light of recent feminist commentary on *Middlemarch*,[16] it is hard not to feel that Hutton had a point – as Eliot herself presumably realised when she changed the controversial passage in the finale. On the other hand, it is unquestionably the case that the dictation of custom and male assumptions concerning women's inferiority are fundamentally important aspects of the stories of the novel's female characters; and what the narrator of *Felix Holt* says of Esther Lyon, that novel's central character, is equally true of the females in *Middlemarch*: 'After all she was a woman, and could not make her own lot ... her lot is made for her by the love she accepts' (ch. 43). The key to resolving this question is to make a distinction between social criticism and social notation. On the thematic level the prelude does seem to overemphasise the importance of the Woman Question. But on the level of social-historical observation of the real, minute processes that cumulatively shape a person's lot there is abundant evidence of society's unenlightened assumptions and attitudes concerning the nature of women.

Consider first the views expressed by characters in the novel. For Sir James Chettam, 'a man's mind ... has always the advantage of being masculine ... and even his ignorance is of a sounder quality' (ch. 2); he further asserts that it is a woman's duty 'to be cautious and listen to those who know the world better than she does' (ch. 72). Mr Brooke believes that 'there is a lightness about the feminine mind' that made it suitable for 'music, the fine arts, that kind of thing' (ch. 7); but as for the love of knowledge, it 'doesn't often run in the female line; or it runs underground like the rivers in Greece you know – it comes out in the sons' (ch. 5). Lydgate considers women appropriate companions for hours of light relaxation, not for serious pursuits. Caleb Garth accurately reflects the social and legal realities of the period when he tells Mary that 'a woman, let her be as good as she may, has got to put up with the life her husband makes for her' (ch. 25). Borthrop Trumbull observes that 'a man whose life is of any value should think of his wife as a nurse' (ch. 32). Casaubon expresses a common nineteenth-century view when he speaks of the 'characteristic excellence' and 'great charm' of woman's nature being 'its capability of an ardent self-sacrificing affection' (ch. 5).ˑ With this assumption, it would never occur to him to 'think as much about his own qualifications for making a charming girl happy as he thinks of hers for making himself happy' (ch. 29). And even more telling are the views of two of the most attractive and intelligent women in the novel: Mrs Garth, who believes that her sex 'was framed to be entirely subordinate' (ch. 24); and Dorothea Brooke herself, who even when a little girl had as her great desire 'to help some one who did great works, so that his burthen might be lighter' (ch. 37) rather than to do great works herself. And while she 'used to despise women a little for not shaping their lives more, and doing better things' (ch. 54), Dorothea becomes more tolerant after her marriage gives her fuller experience of a woman's lot.

It is also important to notice that the unusually gifted Dorothea is not the only character in *Middlemarch* shown to be affected by cultural assumptions concerning female inferiority. There is Letty Garth, the young sibling of Mary, for example, 'whose life was much checkered by resistance to her depreciation as a girl' (ch. 57), the depreciator being her brother Ben, whose insistence that 'it was clear girls were good for less than boys' (finale) makes him a prepubescent epitome of the Middlemarch male in his attitude to the female. Another example is Rosamond Vincy, who is in her own way as hemmed in by petty circumstances as Dorothea – the difference being that what the latter attempts to overcome the former incarnates. Rosamond is admitted to be 'the flower of Mrs Lemon's school, the chief school in the county, where the teaching included all that was demanded in the accomplished female – even to extras, such as the getting in and out of a carriage' (ch. 11). As a result of this conventional education, Rosamond 'never showed any

unbecoming knowledge, and was always that combination of correct
sentiments, music, dancing, drawing, elegant loveliness, which made the
irresistible woman for the doomed man of that date' (ch. 27). This glossy
finish has made Rosamond superficially attractive but inwardly vacuous:
she aspires only to the middle-class heaven of rank, and after her marriage
discovers that flirtations are necessary to satisfy her vanity and to fill her
days. But even then she finds herself 'oppressed by [an] ennui' (ch. 59)
that – so limited are her inner resources for all her superficial attainments
– she can only think to assuage by 'the agreeable titillation of vanity and
sense of romantic drama' that comes with intensified flirtation (ch. 75).

A similarly inadequate education – the codification of society's attitude
to women – afflicts Dorothea in a different but equally serious way. The
narrator observes in chapter 3 that, had she been a less exceptional person
with 'some endowment of stupidity and conceit',

> she might have thought that a Christian young lady of fortune should
> find her ideal of life in village charities, patronage of the humbler
> clergy, the perusal of 'Female Scripture Characters', unfolding the
> private experience of Sara under the Old Dispensation, and Dorcas
> under the New, and the care of her soul over her embroidery in her own
> boudoir – with a background of prospective marriage to a man who, if
> less strict than herself, as being involved in affairs religiously
> inexplicable, might be prayed for and seasonably exhorted.

But Dorothea is not such a limited and stupid person, though she is an
inadequately educated one. That 'toy-box history of the world adapted to
young ladies, which had made the chief part of her education' (ch. 10),
provides as scant nourishment for her intellect or altruistic yearnings as
her deficient aesthetic training does for her feelings. Indeed, the social
reason Dorothea is drawn to Casaubon is that he is the only man in her
acquaintance who eschews the 'small-talk of heavy men' (ch. 3) and who
seems to offer her understanding, sympathetic guidance and intellectual
stimulation. Similarly, one reason she is later drawn to Ladislaw is simply
that – unlike the other men in her society – he listens to her, seems to
understand her and thereby offers some alleviation of 'the stifling
oppression of that gentlewoman's world ... that had been her brief
history since she had left off learning morning lessons and practising silly
rhythms on the hated piano' (ch. 28).

But of course there is a great deal more to Dorothea's relations with
Casaubon and Ladislaw than what can be gathered under the heading of
the Woman Question, just as there is a great deal more involved in the

story of Lydgate's professional failure than determination by public opinion. In *Middlemarch* George Eliot is not solely concerned to study the influence of society on the individual. She is not only a social historian, but also a moralist, a psychologist and an aesthetic teacher. To get below the social surface of her characters and to enlarge on the ethical and philosophical implications of her history she needed to develop a fictional persona who would be a surrogate of herself within the text. It is to this pervasive and fundamentally important presence in *Middlemarch* that we must now turn our attention.

CHAPTER 4
The Narrator

Middlemarch employs one of the principal conventions of nineteenth-century fiction, that of the omniscient narrator. Eliot uses the convention in all of her novels, and it is hard not to think that the god's-eye view was for her the natural and proper way to tell a story. The naturalness is of course illusory, as J. Hillis Miller's helpful description of this sophisticated and complex device makes clear:

> The term 'omniscient narrator' has tended to obscure clear understanding of the narrating voice in Victorian fiction. The theological overtones of the word 'omniscient' suggest that such a narrator is like a God, standing outside the time and space of the action, looking down on the characters with the detachment of a sovereign spectator who sees all, knows all, judges all, from a distance. The narrators of Victorian novels rarely have this sort of omniscience. This perfect knowledge is rather that of pervasive presence than that of transcendent vision. When Dickens, George Eliot, and Trollope move to the other side of the mirror and enter into the role of the personage who tells the story they do not take up a position outside the world of the novel, as a watchtower of vision down on it. They move within the community. They identify themselves with a human awareness which is everywhere at all times within the world of the novel. This awareness surrounds and permeates each individual human mind and therefore is able to know it perfectly from the inside, to live its life ... There is relatively little of what has come to be called the 'antinovel' in Victorian fiction. There are few places where the narrator explicitly confesses that the novel is a novel, though many aspects of the narrative language may implicitly recognize this. For the most part, the narrators of Victorian novels talk as if they were confronting directly or in historical retrospect a world independent of their knowledge of it, but a world over which they happen to have extraordinary powers. The novelist

himself knows that the world is an invented one, that it exists only in the words he makes up and puts down on the page. The narrator whose role he plays exists as much on the other side of the mirror as any of the characters. He takes the story as authentic history. He is like an immanent God who has perfect knowledge not of his own creation, but of the creation of another God, an externally existing world which he has somehow been able to penetrate, flowing into it like an ubiquitous sea or like a pervasive perfume which can pierce the most hidden recesses, entering freely everywhere.[1]

Narrators can be omniscient in three ways: temporally, spatially and psychologically.[2] In *Middlemarch* the last two modes are the most important, but the first is also employed. One aspect of the narrator's temporal omniscience is his knowledge of the past and his ability to place the characters in historical perspective. Dorothea Brooke is contrasted with St Theresa of Avila, for example, and the reader is informed that in Mr Brooke 'the hereditary strain of Puritan energy was clearly in abeyance' (ch. 1). The narrator also has the power, though it is equally seldom exercised, to know the personal pasts of his characters: of Lydgate, for example, whose 'moment of vocation' in childhood is recounted, as is the peculiar episode of his infatuation with the French actress Laure and its abrupt termination when she reveals that she had meant to stab her unwanted actor husband during a performance. The reader is also given an authoritative recapitulation of Bulstrode's early days as a member of the Calvinist dissenting church at Highbury, his business association with Mr Dunkirk, and the cruel deception practised on his widow.

Just as he has the power to know the past of his characters, the narrator also knows their future – what lies in store for them beyond the 1829–32 present time of the narrative. Until the finale, however, this power is almost never used. One of the rare exceptions is in chapter 20 when we are told that 'in certain states of dull forlornness' Dorothea all her life continued to see in her mind's eye the oppressive vastness of St Peter's, which like the rest of Rome has had a destabilising effect on her. Another facet of this kind of omniscience is seen in the narrator's comments on the present-time action of the novel from the point of view and the knowledge available in the late 1860s. As Steven Marcus has noted of Eliot's novels: 'both writer and audience share a modern sensibility and consciousness, and ... are engaged in common in reflecting upon the immediately pre-modern'.[3] In chapter 19, for example, the narrator comments on the paucity of information about Christian art then available to travellers on the Continent, and in chapter 3 he notes that Dorothea is wearing a straw bonnet 'which our contemporaries might look at with conjectural curiosity as at an obsolete form of basket'. Most often, this perspective is used to make modestly telling ironic points of a *plus ça change* variety: 'in those days the world in general was more ignorant of good and evil by forty years than it is at present' (ch. 19); 'in those days human intercourse was not determined solely by respect' (ch. 40); and in chapter 1 mention of the value of Mr Brooke's estate draws forth the ponderously sarcastic reflection that the well-to-do society of that earlier day was innocent 'of that gorgeous plutocracy which has [since then] so nobly exalted the necessities of genteel life'.

None of these examples, however, is particularly salient or important, and on the whole it is fair to say that the narrator's explicit then-now contrasts do not figure significantly in *Middlemarch*. The principal exception to this generalisation is the way in which Dorothea Brooke is associated with the future: 'But perhaps no persons then living', the narrator observes early in the novel, '– and certainly none in the neighbourhood of Tipton – would have had a sympathetic understanding for the dreams of a girl whose notions about marriage took their colour entirely from an exalted enthusiasm about the ends of life, an enthusiasm which was lit chiefly by its own fire' (ch. 3). Dorothea's distinction gives her a privileged position in the reader's eye and further suggests that there is a special bond between them – as there clearly is between the narrator and Dorothea. By the last paragraph of *Middlemarch* the reader has a deeper understanding of the nature of this bond and of its place in the novel's humanistic economy of salvation. For Dorothea's 'unhistoric acts' have been 'incalculably diffusive', and one indication of their contribution to 'the growing good of the world' is that contemporaries of the narrator in the 1870s can now recognise the special distinction of Dorothea's nature that her contemporaries were unable to appreciate forty years earlier.

The powers of spatial omniscience, which enable the narrator to know what is going on in different places at the same time, are fully exploited in *Middlemarch*. Their frequent exercise is essential to the conduct of the narrative, which moves back and forth among several groups of characters, shifting from business office to parlour, public house to boudoir, from the library at Lowick to the drawing-room in Lydgate's too expensive house, from the lawn near the great conservatory at Freshitt Hall to the Garths' pleasant garden; and so on. The same powers are also essential to the novel's social-historical panorama and the principal way through which Eliot is able to indulge 'the habit of my imagination to strive after as full a vision of the medium in which a character moves as of the character itself' – a habit in the exercise of which Eliot went on to admit of a 'tendency to excess'.[4] (It was her name for what Henry James politely called her 'redundancy of touch'.) Through these powers the reader is taken into the scruffy room at the Red Lion in Houndsley where Fred Vincy dines with Mr Horrock and Mr Bambridge, into Mrs Dollop's public house in Slaughter Lane, and under the archway of the Green Dragon where, on seeing Bulstrode ride by, Mr Bambridge is reminded of a story he picked up about him in another town. It enables the reader to learn what Mrs Bulstrode and Mrs Plymdale talk about during a morning visit; how Farebrother's mother, aunt and sister receive his guests; how Featherstone's blood-relations get on together in the kitchen and parlour at Stone Court; how Borthrop Trumbull conducts an auction; and so on. Finally, spatial omniscience is also thematically important. Its comprehensive overview shows the interplay of private life and public life and makes visible 'the play of minute causes' (ch. 6) that precipitates events and helps to determine the futures of the characters. In chapter 11 it is not so much a weakly personified Destiny as it is the narrator himself who holds the script: 'But any one watching keenly the stealthy convergence of human lots, sees a slow preparation of effects from one life on another, which tells like a calculated irony on the indifference or the frozen stare with which we look at our unintroduced neighbour. Destiny stands by sarcastic with our *dramatis personae* folded in her hand.'

The third kind of omniscience is psychological: the power to penetrate the consciousness of the characters and provide authoritative accounts and analyses of their motives and emotions. For all the central characters in *Middlemarch*, outside views are complemented by extended inside views. The narrator's usual practice is first to show a character from the outside and then to move within. Casaubon, for example, is first seen from the point of view of Dorothea and the country gentry, but it is not long before the narrator is suggesting that he may not be 'fairly represented in the minds of those ... personages who have hitherto delivered their judgments concerning him', and inviting the reader to 'turn from outside estimates of [Casaubon] to wonder, with keener interest, what is the report of his own consciousness about his doings or capacity' (ch. 10). Nor is it long after the reader has been introduced to Lydgate that the narrator announces that he now has 'to make the new settler ... better know to anyone interested in him than he could possibly be even to those who had seen the most of him since his arrival in Middlemarch' (ch. 15).

George Eliot is a master of psychological omniscience, and for many readers it is the exercise of this many-splendoured power that more than any other single factor makes *Middlemarch* a great novel. It is certainly the case that the combination and alternation of outside and inside views, public life and private life, the landscape of opinion and the *paysage intérieur*, the social web and the 'subtle muscular movements' of consciousness (ch. 68), provide the organising principle of many of the novel's chapters and give to the narrative as a whole its basic rhythm – the 'systole and diastole' that Lydgate insists are essential to all inquiry, in which a person's mind 'must be continually expanding and shrinking between the whole human horizon and the horizon of an object-glass' (ch. 63). Lydgate makes this observation just before a New Year's party at the Vincys'; the scene affords a perfect illustration of the systole and diastole of the narrator's fictional inquiry. In the middle of his account of what guests are saying to and about each other, he suddenly switches to a close-up view of the face of Lydgate's wife, which is then followed by a brief but equally penetrating psychological notation:

> Rosamond was perfectly graceful and calm, and only a subtle observation such as the Vicar had not been roused to bestow on her would have perceived the total absence of that interest in her husband's presence which a loving wife is sure to betray, even if etiquette keeps her aloof from him. When Lydgate was taking part in the conversation, she never looked towards him any more than if she had been a sculptured Psyche modelled to look another way: and when, after being called out for an hour or two, he re-entered the room, she seemed unconscious of the fact, which eighteen months before would have had the effect of a numeral before cyphers. In reality, however, she was intensely aware of Lydgate's voice and movements; and her pretty good-tempered air of unconsciousness was a studied negation by which she satisfied her inward opposition to him without compromise of propriety.

The range and depth of the narrator's powers of psychological omniscience will be abundantly instanced in the following chapter's discussion of the character and characterisation of the novel's principal players. For the present, two general points may be made. The first is that one can have too much of a good thing, and just as there is a tendency to excess in the narrator's use of spatial omniscience, so, too, there is a certain redundancy of touch in the exercise of his powers of psychological omniscience. One example involves Joshua Rigg, Featherstone's illegitimate son who unexpectedly sells Stone Court soon after he has inherited the estate and subsequently leaves Middlemarch for good. Rigg is a strictly peripheral character and his selling of the property could have been satisfactorily reported in a sentence by any of a number of characters. Instead we are given this:

> as Warren Hastings looked at gold and thought of buying Daylesford, so Joshua Rigg looked at Stone Court and thought of buying gold. He had a very distinct and intense vision of his chief good, the vigorous greed which he had inherited having taken a special form by dint of circumstance: and his chief good was to be a money-changer. From his earliest employment as an errand-boy in a seaport, he had looked through the windows of the money-changers as other boys look through the windows of the pastry-cooks; the fascination had wrought itself gradually into a deep special passion; he meant, when he had property, to do many things, one of them being to marry a genteel young person; but these were all accidents and joys that imagination could dispense with. The one joy after which his soul thirsted was to have a money-changer's shop on a much-frequented quay, to have locks all around him of which he held the keys, and to look sublimely cool as he handled the breeding coins of all nations, while helpless Cupidity looked at him enviously from the other side of an iron lattice. The strength of that passion had been a power enabling him to master all the knowledge necessary to gratify it. And when others were thinking that he had settled at Stone Court for life, Joshua himself was thinking that the moment now was not far off when he should settle on the North Quay with the best appointments in safes and locks.

The analysis is not implausible, but to what end is it made? The reader has seen far too little of Rigg to be interested in what makes him tick or to be able to assess the accuracy of the analysis. Nor can this little portrait of obsession be usefully related to other material in the novel. No wonder the narrator himself finally breaks off, exclaiming 'Enough. We are concerned with looking at Joshua Rigg's sale of his land from Mr Bulstrode's point of view' (ch. 53).

This passage is also a negative example of another general point. Psychological omniscience is most tellingly and helpfully used in the presentation of characters who unfold during the course of the novel rather than static characters. With Caleb Garth, Mary Garth and Mr Brooke, for example, the narrator's use of psychological omniscience is wisely limited to an introductory character sketch, after which the character's speech and actions are in the main left unglossed. Among characters who do unfold – the expression is the narrator's – psychological omniscience is most tellingly used in the presentation of those among them who are morally flawed. The climactic engagement scene between Dorothea and Ladislaw in chapter 83 has its felicities, as we shall see, but quality of psychological notation is not among them. From this point of view the episode cannot hold a candle to the one-page scene at the end of chapter 31 in which Lydgate and Rosamond become engaged, a virtuoso display of psychological omniscience on the narrator's part in which there is only one line of dialogue. The explanation of the difference between these two engagement scenes is that Dorothea and Ladislaw are too unflawed, the quality and breadth of their emotion too pure and too encompassing, to allow for psychological complexity. Conversely, psychological omniscience has its limitations as an instrument of characterisation when the subject is too flawed or too morally corrupt. Inside views of Bulstrode can do little more than detail his metronomic debates with his conscience and his programmatic rationalisations of his selfish actions. To reveal Bulstrode's depths, George Eliot had to employ what for her were most unusual means, as we shall later see.

The narrator of *Middlemarch* is not only omniscient. Like Thackeray's and Trollope's third-person narrators he is also intrusive. In *Middlemarch*, as we have seen, Eliot is primarily concerned to offer a vivid representation of her realistic subject. But this by no means precludes the addition of intrusive narratorial comment, including judgements on characters, remarks on how the story is being told, direct addresses to the reader, and generalisations and miscellaneous observations on a variety of subjects. This conspicuous feature of the omniscient narration of nineteenth-century novels became quite unfashionable during the heyday of modernist aesthetic criteria deriving from the dicta and the practice of Flaubert and Henry James. The former had insisted that 'great Art is scientific and impersonal' and that the author/narrator 'must be in his work as God is in creation, invisible yet all powerful; we must sense him everywhere but never see him.'[5] For James, 'the only reason for the existence of a novel' was that it attempted 'to represent life'. When the attempt was relinquished, as when Trollope allowed his narrators asides and digressions that broke the representational illusion, the result was 'a terrible crime', a betrayal of the novelist's 'sacred office'.[6] In time James even came to cast a cold eye on impersonal omniscient narration ('the mere muffled majesty of irresponsible "authorship"'), preferring an 'indirect and oblique' third-person point of view limited to what was experienced, thought and observed by a single character or a very small number of characters.[7]

These criteria were a principal reason for the neglect of *Middlemarch* during the 1920s and 1930s, and even today the narrator's intrusions can be a considerable obstacle to the reader's engagement with the text. The intrusions may be divided into three groups: the direct comments on characters; the generalisations, sententiae and dicta; and the direct addresses to 'you', the reader. In the first two groups there are unquestionable examples of what might be called narratorial spots of commonness. The comments on his characters sometimes seem occasioned by the narrator's intermittent inability to leave well enough alone. Signposting unnecessarily supplements showing, and the reader's involvement with the character is interrupted. For example, just before Mr Brooke makes an ass of himself addressing the electors of Middlemarch from the balcony of the White Hart in chapter 51, the narrator prolixly interpolates: 'Pray pity him; so many English gentlemen make themselves miserable by speechifying on entirely private grounds: whereas Mr Brooke wished to serve his country by standing for Parliament – which indeed may also be done on private grounds, but being once undertaken does absolutely demand some speechifying.' Perhaps the narrator thought he was being witty? In another example, the problem is his indulgent affection for a character, which spills gauchely on to the page: 'pardon these details for once', he says parenthetically, 'you would have learned to love them if you had known Caleb Garth' (ch. 23). But no reader of *Middlemarch* can know Caleb Garth in the flesh and the only way he can come to approximate the narrator's love is through suggestive details – not through interpolated testimonials.

There are also some infelicitous asides concerning Casaubon; but it is Rosamond Vincy who brings out the worst in the narrator. At the beginning of chapter 75, for example, the subject is the vanity of Rosamond, who is said to be 'one of those women who live much in the idea that each man they meet would have preferred them if the preference had not been hopeless'. She is shown titillating both her 'vanity and sense of romantic drama' by day-dreaming about her relationship with Will Ladislaw: 'He would have made, she thought, a much more suitable husband for her than she had found in Lydgate.' At this point the narrator should have stopped; but he cannot forbear to provide in the following sentence a censorious and totally unnecessary gloss for Rosamond's self-indulgent musings: 'No notion could have been falser than this, for Rosamond's discontent in her marriage was due to the conditions of marriage itself.' In another passage, the narrator's animus is so pronounced as to make one doubt his reliability, which is based on the reader's sense of the absolute compatibility of the teller and the tale. The passage is in chapter 31. The narrator has been describing Rosamond's increasing unhappiness because Lydgate, to whom she considers herself virtually engaged, has ceased to visit her: 'Poor Rosamond lost her appetite and felt as forlorn as Ariadne – as a charming stage Ariadne left behind with all her boxes full of costumes and no hope of a coach.' As R. H. Hutton observed: 'that is palpably an unkind author's criticism not founded on truth. Rosamond is thin, and selfish, and self-occupied, but she is not stagey. Her grief, such as it was, though of a feeble and thready kind, was perfectly genuine. The prick of the needle was due to literary malice.'[8]

One must be careful, however, not to make too much of these intrusive infelicities, for their effect is not seriously damaging to the verisimilitude of the characters in the novel. Surely no serious reader was ever in danger of regarding the superbly drawn Rosamond as a 'charming stage Ariadne'. Indeed, even F. R. Leavis failed entirely to notice that there was 'animus in the presentment'.[9] Moreover, in the case of the most notorious example of the narrator's intrusive remarks it is even possible to be downright positive. It occurs at the beginning of chapter 29: 'One morning, some weeks after her arrival at Lowick, Dorothea – but why always Dorothea? Was her point of view the only possible one with regard to this marriage? I protest ...' This outburst is certainly abrupt, and it has been thought ill-considered and gauche; but its intention (and, for readers like myself, its effect) is just the opposite of making Dorothea and her husband appear puppets. It rather signals the narrator's commitment to a comprehensive and impartial depiction of the inner life of both characters, neither of whom is allowed to remain a one-dimensional figure with whom the reader can remain uninvolved. The intrusion further suggests that the narrator is aware of the special bond between himself and Dorothea and determined to minimise its effect on the narrative. His doing so involves the overcoming of a form of self-absorption (for Dorothea is unquestionably the character with whom the narrator most closely identifies) and the recognition of 'an equivalent centre of self' (ch. 21) in others. Since these are the very things that Dorothea must herself learn to overcome and recognise during the course of the novel, the narrator's determination to see a complex emotional situation not only from Dorothea's point of view becomes a prolepsis of Dorothea's impressive mental act during her night of suffering in chapter 80: 'She began now to live through that yesterday morning deliberately again, forcing herself to dwell on every detail and its possible meaning. Was she alone in that scene? Was it her event only?'

The second group of narratorial intrusions in *Middlemarch* consists of the discursive generalisations and aphorisms with which the text is peppered. Here, too, there are infelicities and embarrassments. It is not hard to compile a list of sayings that are either stilted, simplistic, bloated, run-of-the-mill, gratuitous, or clumsily ironic. To cite only a few examples:

Mortals are easily tempted to pinch the life out of their neighbour's buzzing glory, and think that such killing is no murder. (ch. 21)

We mortals, men and women, devour many a disappointment between breakfast and dinner-time; keep back the tears and look a little pale about the lips, and in answer to inquiries say, 'Oh, nothing!' Pride helps us; and pride is not a bad thing when it only urges us to hide our own hurts – not to hurt others. (ch. 6)

When the animals entered the Ark in pairs, one may imagine that allied species made much private remark on each other, and were tempted to think that so many forms feeding on the same store of fodder were eminently superfluous, as tending to diminish the rations. (I fear the part played by the vultures on that occasion would be too painful for art to represent, those birds being disadvantageously naked about the gullet, and apparently without rites and ceremonies.) (ch. 35)

to most mortals there is a stupidity which is unendurable and a stupidity which is altogether acceptable – else, indeed, what would become of the social bonds. (ch. 58)

It was presumably to clinkers like these that Walter Allen was referring when he made some harshly critical comments about George Eliot's 'intrusive, indeed obtrusive' narratorial comment. Fielding persuades the reader 'of the truth of his interpretation of what he is narrating by his appeal both to sweet reasonableness and to worldly experience'. Eliot, in contrast, 'lectures us and sometimes even hectors us. She lacks tact, as she lacks wit, except a ponderous irony. She gives the impression, in fact, of not quite knowing whom she is addressing. Her style is not subtle or easy enough; she is too self-conscious.'[10] Put differently, what Allen is saying is that the key to success in the deployment of intrusive comment is the creation of a distinctive persona and voice. The narrator himself seems aware of this when in his brief digression on Fielding's digressions he speaks of Fielding's bringing 'his arm-chair to the proscenium [to] chat

with us in all the lusty ease of his fine English' (ch. 15). Lusty ease is not a
quality of the voice of the narrator of *Middlemarch*, and neither on the
whole is wit. George Eliot is no Thackeray. The voice of *Middlemarch* is
more serious and sombre than that of Fielding's or Thackeray's narrators.
It is the voice of a person whose eye, like the mature eye of George Eliot's
favourite poet, has long kept watch on man's mortality. The voice belongs
to a persona that was first described by the Victorian critic Edward
Dowden, who distinguished between George Eliot 'the actual historical
person' and the 'second self' who narrates her novels. The latter was 'a
great nature, which has suffered and has now attained, which was
perplexed and has now grasped the clue – standing before us not without
tokens on lip and brow of the strife and the suffering, but resolute, and
henceforth possessed of something which makes self-mastery possible'.
To none of his characters is he 'cold or indifferent'; he is 'present in the
midst of them, indicating, interpreting'. The reader learns of 'those
abstractions from the common fund of truth which the author has found
most needful to her own deepest life. We feel ... in the presence of a soul
and a soul which has had a history.'[11] Dowden's impressionistic
description is heavy and portentous and as such nicely suggests the
sententious and moralising qualities in the narrator's voice that tend to
come out when he clears his throat to generalise or that, when he attempts
wit, often result only in an elephantine lightness.

It would be unfair and distinctly misleading, however, to end
discussion at this point. The first thing to be said in the narrator's defence
is that his sayings tend to bring out the worst qualities in his style and
voice and as such are unrepresentative. For example, if the italicised bit of
generalisation in the following sentence from the beginning of chapter 45
were removed, the notation would be much sharper (though, to be fair, it
would make one notice that it would be better if *tone* replaced *shade*):
'What the opposition in Middlemarch said about the New Hospital and
its administration had certainly a great deal of echo in it, *for heaven has
taken care that everybody shall not be an originator*; but there were
differences that represented every social shade ...' Or consider the
shrewd observation made about Farebrother in chapter 17: 'The Vicar's
frankness seemed not of the repulsive sort that comes from an uneasy
consciousness seeking to forestall the judgment of others, but simply the
relief of a desire to do with as little pretence as possible.' This is crisp and
telling because it is specific. Were the same notation inflated into an
aphorism, it is hard to imagine it not becoming soggy. As a final example,
consider the fine simile in chapter 61 concerning Bulstrode's tormented
consciousness: 'he felt the scenes of his earlier life coming between him

and everything else, as obstinately as when we look through the window from a lighted room, the objects we turn our backs on are still before us, instead of the grass and the trees'. The tendency of the narrator towards generalisation is present in the references to 'we' and 'us', but not strongly enough to cause the notation to swell into an aphorism that would surely have weakened the striking comparison of Bulstrode's oppressive anxieties to a common optical occurrence.

The other point to be made is that by no means all of the discursive generalisations in the novel fall into the same categories as the examples quoted above. Those are more than compensated for by the many sayings in the text that are apt, striking, penetrating, moving, and/or profound, some of which can even – so Isobel Armstrong has urged in a spirited defence – withstand comparison with those of Samuel Johnson.[12] Let us begin with the generalisation in chapter 36 that is prompted by an account of Mr Vincy's less than firm resolution: 'a disagreeable resolve formed in the chill hours of the morning had as many conditions against it as the early frost, and rarely persisted under the warming influences of the day'. Out of context the reflection would be trite, if nicely turned; in context it works well because it is suited to its subject, Mr Vincy's character being hardly out of the ordinary. And the aphorism might even be thought to be making a knowing wink back at him in its closing reference to 'the warming influences of the day', which can refer not only to the sun but also to the strong drink of which Mr Vincy is fond. Another minor felicity is the following: 'the early months of a marriage often are times of critical tumult – whether that of the shrimp-pool or of deeper waters – which afterwards subsides into a cheerful peace' (ch. 20). What gives this saying its froth is of course *shrimp-pool*; if *shallows* were substituted, it would subside into platitude.

Now let us look at some of what I take to be the best of the discursive generalisations in *Middlemarch*:

There are characters which are continually creating collisions and nodes for themselves in dramas which nobody is prepared to act with them. (ch. 19)

the egoism which enters into our theories does not affect their sincerity; rather, the more our egoism is satisfied, the more robust is our belief. (ch. 53)

We are on a perilous margin when we begin to look passively at our future selves, and see our own figures led with dull consent into insipid misdoing and shabby achievement. (ch. 79)

If we know how to be candid, we shall confess [that self-discontent makes] more than half our bitterness under grievances, wife or husband included. (ch. 58)

If we had a keen vision and feeling of all ordinary human life, it would be like hearing the grass grow and the squirrel's heart beat, and we should die of that roar which lies on the other side of silence. (ch. 20)

He was simply a man whose desires had been stronger than his theoretic beliefs, and who had gradually explained the gratification of his desires into satisfactory agreement with those beliefs. If this be hypocrisy, it is a process which shows itself occasionally in us all, to whatever confession we belong, and whether we believe in the future perfection of our race or in the nearest date fixed for the end of the world; whether we regard the earth as a putrefying nidus for a saved remnant, including ourselves, or have a passionate belief in the solidarity of mankind. (ch. 61)

The first two examples might be said to offer only worldly wisdom; but such wisdom is hardly common coin and both sayings are sharply focused and trenchant. The third example bites deeper, as does the more straightforwardly articulated fourth example, the last phrase of which, seemingly an afterthought, in fact drives home the painful home-epic truth. The fifth example is not so much a distillation of mature experience as the residue of the intense perceptual experiences of youth – more Wordsworthian than Johnsonian. It recalls some similarly ravishing reflections in Eliot's early novels and is evidence that the narrator of *Middlemarch* has a memory that is still half passionate and not merely contemplative. Much would have been lost if the narrator had attempted to point a moral to adorn his piercing notation. Alas, this is just what he does. The sentence about 'the other side of silence' is followed by a gratuitous bellow: 'As it is, the quickest of us walk about well wadded with stupidity.' The final example is especially interesting because in it the narrator's moral scrutiny is indirectly brought to bear on himself. We have seen that he is not a catastrophist concerned with the end of the world; but he does have a uniformitarian belief in the gradual improvement of the race and certainly has 'a passionate belief in the solidarity of mankind'.

In her article on the sayings in *Middlemarch*, Isobel Armstrong argued that they serve to increase the reader's participation in the novel: 'Eliot's procedure depends upon the constant corroboration and assent of the reader to her sayings, [which become] the growing-point of imaginative involvement in the novel.'[13] This aspect of the sayings relates them to the third and last cluster of intrusive comments: the direct addresses to 'you', the reader, and the similar references to 'our' and 'we'. Examples abound: 'this trait is not quite alien to us, and ... claims some of our pity' (ch. 10); 'we all of us ... get our thoughts entangled in metaphors, and act fatally on the strength of them' (ch. 10); 'Mr Casaubon ... was spiritually a-hungered like the rest of us' (ch. 29); 'irritated feeling with him, as with all of us, seeks rather for justification than for self-knowledge' (ch. 34); 'is it not rather what we expect in men, that they should have numerous strands of experience lying side by side and never compare them with each other?' (ch. 58); 'that things are not so ill with you and me as they might have been, is half owing to the number who lived faithfully a hidden life, and rest in unvisited tombs' (finale). The relationship of narrator to reader, of 'I' to 'you', is not simply a rhetorical one, nor is it essentially preceptorial – though there are good many things the narrator wants us to know. The relationship is rather based on a similar range of experience, shared beliefs and a shared fund of human wisdom.

This relationship provides the explanation of a seeming discrepancy in the novel that has been separately noted by two philosophical critics, Peter Jones in his *Philosophy and the Novel* and K. M. Newton in his *George Eliot, Romantic Humanist: A Study of the Philosophical Structure of her Novels*. To cite the former: 'the omniscient author appears immune from precisely those obstacles to knowledge encountered by her characters, and to which we are all alleged to be subject in everyday life'.[14] The wrong way for a non-philosophical critic to explain this apparent discontinuity would be to say that epistemological relativism is a characteristic of the world of the novel, but the convention of a god's-eye narrator is for good reason used to present this world and one must simply accept this convention of omniscience, just as one must accept the convention of divine intervention in the *Iliad*. The right way to explain the matter would begin by noting that just as on the historical level *Middlemarch* is told from the viewpoint of looking back after forty years on an earlier state of social development, so on the personal level the novel is narrated from the point of view of middle-age looking back on youth. *Middlemarch* is primarily about 'young lives' (finale), about 'the season of hope' during which youth is apt 'to think its emotions, partings, and resolves are the last of their kind. Each crisis seems final, simply because it is new' (ch. 55). The omniscience of the narrator is not so much god-like as generational. There are no *ex cathedra* pronouncements; there is, rather, a constant appeal to a shared fund of human experience and a

consensus of human wisdom that is the closest possible approximation to
the now superseded divine wisdom. Virginia Woolf's famous comment
was perfectly correct: *Middlemarch* is a novel for grown-up people, for
members or would-be members of what the narrator of *The Mill on the
Floss* called 'the natural priesthood' of the middle-aged, their knowledge
different in degree but not in kind from the fallible, struggling young men
and women whose stories are told in the novel. There is no discrepancy
between the limited knowledge of the characters and the omniscient
knowledge of the narrator. There is, rather, a gradualist distinction – in
Middlemarch as in *In Memoriam* – between knowledge and wisdom, a
wisdom that is not transcendent but 'the empiricism of the inner life',
which is 'grounded in sorrow' and has as its precondition what Tennyson
calls love and Eliot calls fellow-feeling.[15]

CHAPTER 5

Character and Characterisation

for character too is a process and an unfolding.
Middlemarch, ch. 15

In recent years it has become increasingly difficult for literary critics to talk about fictional characters as if they were 'real' persons having a psychological existence independent of the novel that contains them, rather than (as one deconstructive critic puts it) 'powerful phantasms of personalities' generated by the text. Critics are now clearly aware of the dangers involved in such discourse: for example, the risk of co-option – of the critic unwittingly speaking 'as though he were one of the invented characters in the novel, the narrator'.[1] The danger is particularly acute in discussing a novel like *Middlemarch* in which, as we have seen, the narrator is concerned to create a community of interest and a consensus of judgement between himself and his readers. The risks can, however, be considerably reduced if character is considered in tandem with characterisation – with the ways in which, and the adequacy with which, the fictional personage is presented. Dangers will doubtless remain, but the attempt nevertheless has to be made, for any adequate consideration of *Middlemarch* must include discussion of the characters in which one's disbelief in their reality is suspended. Not to make this act of fictional faith would impoverish any account of Eliot's novel, one of the most impressive and deeply satisfying aspects of which is the depiction of character. It is here that George Eliot's philosophical, social-historical and moral concerns are fused with her abundant natural gifts as a novelist – for dialogue and characterisation by speech, for social and psychological notation, for the interplay of inside and outside views and the enriching mixture of showing and telling.

Of course, not all of the characters who figure in *Middlemarch* in more than a passing way are fully characterised. Such figures are minor not only because they are cast in supporting roles but also because they do not unfold during the novel and are mainly presented from the outside. Victorian reviewers, for whom character was pretty much everything, delighted in these fictional personages for their own sakes, and it would be well if contemporary commentators could recover some of this capacity for enjoyment, for too often the novel's minor characters are noticed only to the extent that they have a perceived thematic or structural role to play or are able to become grist for some interpretative mill. Tact and discretion are needed to avoid making either too much or too little of them. Some of these characters are more interesting and more satisfactorily rendered than others. Sir James Chettam, for example, has a place in the novel's social panorama and a small role in Dorothea's story, but in his own right he is a weak characterisation, 'a blooming Englishman of the red-whiskered type' (ch. 2) and little else. A pleasant disposition and loyal-hearted nature seem the sum of his personal qualities, while the wish that 'people would behave like gentlemen' is his 'comprehensive programme for social well-being' (ch. 38). Even the impercipient Mr Brooke can adequately sum him up: 'Chettam is a good fellow, a good sound-hearted fellow, you know; but he doesn't go much into ideas' (ch. 4). The one time in the novel when he does become of more interest is when the narrator, whose favourite subject is egotism, pauses for a paragraph to analyse his 'amiable vanity'. Celia Brooke, whom Chettam marries, is an equally thin characterisation. Some inside information about her is provided in two places early on, but after that Celia becomes tedious almost as soon as she begins to speak. As her sister playfully but tellingly observes, she is 'fit hereafter to be an eternal cherub and [is] hardly more in need of salvation than a squirrel' (ch. 4).

Borthrop Trumbull is much better done. He is frankly and unapologetically a humour character and bit of local colour, with no significant function to perform. He is nicely deployed: his four appearances are at widely spaced intervals and in each case touch on a different one of the novel's major story-lines. In Trumbull's first appearance in Featherstone's kitchen in chapter 32 the narrator alerts the reader to his 'sincere sense of his own merit' and to the fact that 'his admiration was far from being confined to himself, but was accustomed professionally as well as privately to delight in estimating things at a high rate. He was an amateur of superior phrases ... If anyone had observed that Mr Borthrop Trumbull, being an auctioneer, was bound to know the nature of everything, he would have smiled and trimmed himself silently with the sense that he came pretty near that.' Amusing illustrations of these qualities are then provided, as Trumbull reads aloud from a Scott novel, the title of which he mispronounces, offers an assessment of its author and of the ham that he swallows 'with alarming haste', and in taking his leave volunteers some insights into why he has never married: 'Some men must marry to elevate themselves a little, but when I am in need of that, I hope someone will tell me so – I hope some individual will apprise me of the fact.' In his next appearance, in chapter 45, Trumbull is treated for pneumonia by Lydgate, whom he assures: 'you are not speaking to one who is altogether ignorant of the *vis medicatrix*'. But his big scene is the Larcher auction over which he presides in chapter 60. It reaches its high point when Trumbull waxes particularly eloquent over 'a painting of the Italian school – by the celebrated *Guydo*, the greatest painter in the world, the chief of the Old Masters, as they are called'.

Two other humour characters excellently hit off are Mrs Cadwallader, the Mrs Poyser of *Middlemarch*, and Mr Brooke. The former is almost wholly characterised through her distinctive voice – rightly so since she is the finest wit in the novel, compelling attention through the biting candour of her worldly wisdom and the sparkle of her pitiless banter as she scatters her bad words for everyone. She is appropriately introduced in the sixth chapter not by a character sketch but through a page of dialogue with Mrs Fitchett, the lodge-keeper at Tipton, during which she successfully barters a pair of tumble pigeons for a brace of fowl – a brief scene that economically illustrates Mrs Cadwallader's impecuniousness, shrewdness, free-speaking, and knowledge of country manners. Mr Brooke, the most prominent humour character in *Middlemarch*, is also given a wholly distinctive voice, but in addition the narrator supplies an initial character sketch to establish his well-meaning but ineffectual nature, his 'too rambling habit of mind ... acquiescent temper, miscellaneous opinions, and uncertain vote' (ch. 1). And from time to time throughout the novel he will provide bits of information about what is going on inside his head. Henry James described Mr Brooke as being drawn 'with the touch of a Dickens chastened and intellectualized'.[2] This seems just right: Mr Brooke never quite becomes the comic caricature he sometimes seems close to becoming and would have become in Dickens's hands. His voice is immediately recognisable, from his first appearance in chapter 2, through his address to the Middlemarch electors from the balcony of the White Hart, to the close of the novel when with characteristic indirection he leads up to the subject of Dorothea's impending remarriage by first speaking of poaching and then summing up his genial sense of human affairs: 'There's something singular in things; they come round, you know' (ch. 84). In the finale, Mr Brooke's prolixity is neatly made the agent of the genial sense or comic vision with which the story of the country gentry families comes round. Just as his loquacity in letter-writing had been responsible for the invitation that brought Ladislaw to Lowick and planted the seeds of Chettam–Brooke disruption, so a similarly overfluent missive leads to the invitation to Dorothea and her new husband to visit Tipton and hence to their reconciliation with the Chettams. In a novel as philosophically and morally serious as *Middlemarch*, there is perhaps too much over-simplification in this comic resolution. One might similarly reflect that on the whole the narrator's presentation of the gentry is rather too uncritical, even indulgent. Mr Cadwallader is an unsatisfactory clergyman even by the undemanding standards of traditional Anglicanism; his wife's endless sarcasms are at everyone's expense but her own; and it would be difficult to gainsay A. O. J. Cockshut's description of Mr Brooke's moral character as laziness masquerading as moderation and strong practical sense.[3] What these reflections point towards is a certain generic discontinuity in *Middlemarch*: in the presentation of the country gentry conventions of comedy are used that are not employed in the presentation of other groups from lower down the social scale. The implications of this discontinuity raise questions concerning the unity and cohesiveness of Eliot's novel that will be considered in a later chapter.

There is also a degree of oversimplification in the characterisation of Caleb Garth, whom James also described as being drawn with the touch of a chastened and intellectualised Dickens, though in this case he must have been referring not to Dickens's comic characters but to his idealised ones. There is no hint of base metals in the sterling figure of Caleb Garth, the personification of probity and fellow-feeling, who is as colourfully emblematic of the positive value of work as the labourers in Ford Madox Brown's exemplary Victorian painting. Caleb Garth's daughter Mary has inherited much of her father's wholesomeness and is given something of his emblematic quality. But she is a less simplified and therefore more interesting character because of her acuteness of perception and trenchancy of judgement – 'she gauges everybody', as Farebrother remarks in chapter 17. When coupled with her plainness and narrowed prospects, these qualities give her the potential for resentment. Unfortunately, this interest is not allowed to develop; the narrator chooses to keep Mary's story and her character strictly subservient both to that of Fred Vincy and to those of Dorothea and Rosamond, the two central female characters. To ensure that her role remains minor and interest in her limited, Mary is made middle-aged before her time. When the novel opens this young lady has already learned to make 'no unreasonable claims' on life (ch. 33) and is already in possession of the admirable mature qualities needed to overcome her potential for resentment. And her love for Fred is said to have something 'maternal' in it (ch. 25). Her character is fully unfolded; since it is also unflawed there is no need for Mary to be the subject of extended inside views as Dorothea and Rosamond are. A one-paragraph sketch on her first appearance in chapter 12 is sufficient, though it is supplemented by an additional paragraph twenty-one chapters later.

Farebrother is also middle-aged; but not prematurely. He does not unfold either, and his sole function in the novel might be said to be instrumental; to be a wise counsellor to Lydgate and Fred Vincy, to help resolve Fred and Mary's story, and to provide variations on the themes of vocation and the humanistic economy of salvation. But Farebrother, 'the keen-faced handsome little Vicar in his well-brushed threadbare clothes' (ch. 40), is an extremely interesting characterisation in his own right. I do not refer to the fineness of the notation – his way of speaking, his manner, his percipience, tact, and delicacy of feeling. Of greater interest is the way in which, despite his sterling qualities, the reader is made to feel that there is something incomplete or missing, not quite right or possibly deficient, in Farebrother's character. There are one or two places in the novel where he is seen in a negative light. In chapter 72, for example, where Dorothea for the first time feels 'rather discontented' with him because of his reluctance to come to Lydgate's aid – a reluctance that one feels is owing to his seeing Lydgate through the prism of his own flawed character. But of itself this would not adequately explain how a sense of Farebrother's incompleteness is communicated to the reader. It is difficult to explain how unless one is prepared to risk what used to be called the fallacy of imitative form and say that this feeling is owing to a corresponding indefiniteness and incompleteness in Farebrother's characterisation.

The narrator, one notes upon reflection, seems peculiarly reluctant to provide authoritative comment on Farebrother in the form of either a character sketch or an extended inside view. There is an analysis and assessment of the vicar's character in chapters 17 and 18, but this is done from the point of view not of the narrator but of Lydgate, who is young and new to Middlemarch and who has yet to learn what a difference 'want of money' and the hampering, thread-like pressure of small social conditions can make to a man's conduct. Lydgate's final judgement at this point of the novel is that there is 'some pitiable infirmity of will' in Farebrother. But Lydgate had recently voted for Bulstrode's candidate rather than for his friend Farebrother to be chaplain of the new hospital, and one cannot be at all sure that there is not a degree of rationalisation, even of displacement, in his judgement. And after this episode there are no further attempts by anyone to explore the vicar's character. Perhaps the narrator was reluctant to do so because he might have found that Farebrother's deficiency and incompleteness were due to an insufficient degree of egotism, a quality which elsewhere in *Middlemarch* is shown to contaminate by its presence, not by its absence. Whatever the reason,

Farebrother has the distinction of remaining the one imperfectly comprehended character in a novel otherwise bathed in omniscience.

The last minor character I want to examine is Mr Bulstrode's wife Harriet. There is no better example in *Middlemarch* of the narrator's economy of means in both portrayal of character and management of the narrative. Until very late in the novel Harriet Bulstrode receives little attention. It is clear that she is an affectionate and loving wife who reveres her husband, even believing him to be 'one of those men whose memoirs should be written when they died' (ch. 36). It is equally clear that she is fully at home in the town she has lived in all her life. This point is made in the few sentences of generalisation about her in chapter 61, where one is also told that her 'imitative piety and native worldliness were equally sincere'. This narratorial judgement tempers what one has learned about Mrs Bulstrode from Lydgate's passing reflection earlier in the novel about the mixed delights of visiting the Bulstrodes: 'Mrs Bulstrode's *naïve* way of conciliating piety and worldliness, the nothingness of this life and the desirability of cut glass, the consciousness at once of filthy rags and the best damask, was not a sufficient relief from the weight of her husband's invariable seriousness' (ch. 27). And one again notes her love of finery four chapters later when she visits Rosamond to discuss her niece's non-engagement to Lydgate. Even while she is speaking of this serious matter, Mrs Bulstrode cannot keep her eyes from rolling around the 'ample quilled circuit' of Rosamond's charming bonnet.

It might initially seem that none of this crisp but meagre notation prepares one adequately for chapter 74, the only time in the novel in which Mrs Bulstrode is the centre of attention. In the chapter she is shown learning of her husband's public disgrace, going to give him comfort, resigning herself with difficulty to a diminished sorrowful life, and making herself one with her suffering and broken spouse. The unexpectedness of her noble action might be thought to suggest that she is being pressed into the service of the novel's thematic and organisational needs. It is part of the narrator's habitual practice not to present any character in a wholly negative light and Mrs Bulstrode's act does stimulate some sympathy for her appalling husband. Her act also makes for several threads of associative connection between the Bulstrode story and the novel's other central characters. It recalls Dorothea's selfless devotion to her husband Casaubon earlier in the novel and contrasts with Rosamond's chilling response to the plight of her husband Lydgate, who is also involved in the town's suspicions concerning the death of Raffles. And her putting aside her usual fine clothes and jewellery in favour of plain garments more appropriate to her 'new life' will be repeated by Dorothea after her night of sorrow in chapter 80 – both women seeming to know of 'the tradition that fresh garments belonged to all initiation' (ch. 80).

But chapter 74 is more than simply functional. It is important in its own right because one has learned just enough of Harriet Bulstrode to feel what a desolating blow to her her husband's disgrace is. It perforce destroys the admiration she had felt for him; it will separate her from the town where she has lived all her life and hoped to end her days; and, as she instinctively senses and expresses by her change of clothes, it means the end of her ingenuous pleasure in the things of this world. It is because the reader has a felt sense of her desolation as she sobs out farewell to all the gladness and pride of her life that he can find believable and moving the corresponding intensity of the 'leap of her heart' towards her husband and the 'great wave' of new compassion and tenderness that courses through her. It is the most simply affecting instance in all of *Middlemarch* of the operation of the humanistic economy of salvation and the transforming potential of intense fellow-feeling.

The seven major characters in *Middlemarch* are all subjects of extended inside views and penetrating analyses of character and motivation, which complement what one learns of them through their speech and actions, and their interaction with other characters. The reader's knowledge of each is further assisted by implicit or explicit comparison with the others. All the central characters exist within the same ideological and thematic frameworks examined in earlier chapters. For example, the moral character of each can be focused and assessed by gauging the degree of egotism or self-absorption as opposed to the degree of fellow-feeling and altruistic concern, and by applying George Eliot's favourite litmus-paper tests of a good character: the ability to see connections between and relate different strands of experience; and the quality and breadth of emotion.

The seven characters are Ladislaw and Fred Vincy, Casaubon and Bulstrode, Lydgate and Rosamond, and Dorothea. The last is the dominant presence in *Middlemarch* and will be discussed in a separate chapter not only because her importance to the novel warrants it, but also because the character–characterisation lens is not the appropriate one for bringing her most clearly into focus. The first pair are weakly characterised and do not have the depth and richness of the other two pairs, the latter of which – Lydgate and Rosamond – are the novel's greatest characterisations. The weakness of the characterisations of Ladislaw and Fred Vincy is related to their lack of vocation during almost all of the time period covered by the novel. To flesh out her characters, George Eliot's narrator needs a good deal of circumstantial notation which is much better supplied by characters who are in a state of being rather than a state of becoming. (The exception is Dorothea – another reason for treating her separately.) When the character of her fictional creations is not in a state of being, is 'abundant in uncertain promises' (ch. 47) – the phrase is used of Ladislaw and fits Fred Vincy equally well – uncertainty and vagueness are likely to be found in their characterisations as well.

When the narrator speaks of character as an 'unfolding', he may be said to be making an implicit distinction between those whose characters are in the process of formation (growing) and those whose characters are already essentially complete but will be more fully revealed by changes in the environment (unfolding). The characters of Casaubon, Bulstrode, Lydgate and Rosamond are all in a state of being rather than of becoming and do not really grow or change much during the course of the novel. But the character of each is more and more fully revealed as his or her circumstances change. The point is worth emphasising, for a number of commentators have taken Farebrother to be the author's mouthpiece when, smiling gently at Dorothea's ardent assertion of Lydgate's innocence in the matter of Raffles's death, he tells her: 'character is not cut in marble – it is not something solid and unalterable. It is something living and changing, and may become diseased as our bodies do' (ch. 72). Since Farebrother is wrong about Lydgate, and would be equally incorrect if, *mutatis mutandis*, he were to apply his generalisation to himself, it would seem distinctly dubious to assume that he is here speaking for George Eliot. It is true that Lydgate does change somewhat during the course of the novel. As we shall see, he learns to compare different strands of his experience and to bring to bear on his personal life some of his scientific rigour. He also learns to recognise Dorothea's exceptional qualities. But these are comparatively minor matters. The essence of Lydgate's story and the precondition both of the depth of his characterisation and of the reader's involvement in his lot is not that his character changes but that it is laid bare. As the novelist Brian Moore has shrewdly observed: 'failure is a more interesting condition than success. Success changes people ... whereas failure leaves you with a more intense distillation of that self you are.'[4]

There has long been a consensus that Ladislaw is the most inadequately drawn of the novel's principal characters. 'The author,' observed Henry James, 'who is evidently very fond of him, has found for him here and there some charming and eloquent touches; but in spite of these he remains vague and impalpable to the end.'[5] This insubstantiality is accentuated by the fact that Ladislaw is idealised or romanticised (either positively or negatively) or his character in some other way exaggerated by everyone in the novel who comments on him. Lydgate describes his appearance as 'a sort of Daphnis in coat and waistcoat' (ch. 50). Mr Brooke is undecided whether he is 'a kind of Shelley' (ch. 37) or 'a sort of Burke with a leaven of Shelley' (ch. 51). To his detractors Ladislaw is even more exotic. Mr Hawley describes him as being of 'any cursed alien blood, Jew, Corsican, or Gypsy' (ch. 71); Mrs Cadwallader's memorable epithets include 'a sort of Byronic hero – an amorous conspirator' (ch. 38) and (best of all) 'an Italian with white mice' (ch. 50); and Mr Keck, editor of *The Trumpet*, calls him a Polish spy and an energumen (ch. 46).

What is most damaging to Ladislaw's presentation is that the narrator idealises him. In one place his smile is described as being 'pleasant to see as the breaking of sunshine on the water' (ch. 47) and in another as 'a gush of inward light illuminating the transparent skin as well as the eyes, and playing about every curve and line as if some Ariel were touching them with a new charm' (ch. 21). Elsewhere the narrator notes that his hair and eyes also seem to be 'sending out light' (ch. 28) and that when his hat is off and his head thrown backward, showing his delicate throat as he sang, he looked 'like an incarnation of the spring' (ch. 47). Will's internal qualities are equally filigreed and equally ethereal: his delicate generosity is said to be only one 'among the more exquisite touches in nature's modelling of him' (ch. 79); his emotions are of such 'very impressible stuff [that] the bow of a violin drawn near him cleverly, would at one stroke change the aspect of the world for him' (ch. 39). And, worst of all, his feelings at a certain moment are described as 'perfect, for we mortals have our divine moments, when love is satisfied in the completeness of the beloved object' (ch. 37).

Ladislaw's self-image early in the novel is similarly romanticised and, though his creative posturings are presently dropped, 'the impression ... that he is a *dilettante*', as Henry James observed, 'is never properly removed',[6] not even by his growing concern with vocation and the public good. And certainly not by the notations that point up his fey side: leading 'a troop of droll children ... out on gypsy excursions to Halsell Wood at nutting-time' or improvising a 'Punch-and-Judy drama' for them while they feast on gingerbread around a bonfire; stretching himself at full length on the rug while conversing in the houses that receive him; and treating quaint little Miss Noble with extravagant courtesy (ch. 46). A more complex and interesting side of Ladislaw is suggested when he becomes Rosamond's confidant, but because of thematic necessity this relationship is never developed beyond the needs of the converging story-lines. Since 'our good depends on the quality and breadth of our emotion', Will's emotions must be unflawed in order to make appropriate the great good of his final union with the equally idealised Dorothea. It is this necessity that accounts for Will being virtually untouched by the moral stupidity into which the narrator assures us we are all born. He is too much the exemplar of quality and breadth of emotion to be an interesting characterisation in his own right. The outward and visible sign of his emotional quality is the purity and intensity of his feeling for Dorothea, and this is the only aspect of him in which the narrator is deeply interested. For all its social-historical interest, almost all of Ladislaw's vocational development takes place offstage. His central scenes are the seven private 'interviews' (as Eliot called them in the 'Quarry for *Middlemarch*') with Dorothea, which mark the stages of their relationship from first acquaintance to their final coming together, never more to part. But in these scenes, which will be closely examined in the next chapter, the splendid Dorothea is the dominant character and rightly receives the lion's share of the reader's attention and interest.

Fred Vincy is a more rounded and a more realistically presented character than Ladislaw; but this does not make him more interesting. Two genetic reasons for the weakness of this character have been suggested earlier: the change of direction in the 'Middlemarch' manuscript after it was joined to 'Miss Brooke'; and the fact that in *Middlemarch* Eliot no longer seemed deeply interested in the Wordsworthian piety that is the root of Fred and Mary's relationship. But the visible reason for Fred's insufficiency as a central character in *Middlemarch* is that all his qualities – including his weaknesses, aspirations and potential strengths – are so routine and unexceptional that it is hard for the reader to become interested in him. The young man's egotism is of a wholly run-of-the-mill sort, as is his particular spot of commonness: the implicit conviction 'that he at least ... had a right to be free from anything disagreeable. That he should ever fall into a thoroughly unpleasant position – wear trousers shrunk with washing, eat cold mutton, have to walk for want of a horse, or to "duck under" in any sort of way – was an absurdity irreconcilable with those cheerful intuitions implanted in him by nature' (ch. 23). Equally commonplace is his callow self-pity, his trusting in his luck and his feeling that only the love of a good woman can save him. Godfrey Cass in *Silas Marner* is a good example of how much richer a characterisation George Eliot can make out of these same character traits when they are pitched in a more intense key and belong to a character in a state of being rather than of becoming. Fred Vincy is most like a young man in a Trollope novel. The comparison was first suggested in general terms by R. H. Hutton, who nicely defined the essential difference between Eliot's powers of characterisation and those of her contemporary:

> Mr Trollope scours a still greater surface of modern life with at least equal fidelity; but then how much less is the depth of drawing behind his figures! One would know all his characters if one met them in actual life, and know a great deal more of them than we do of ninety-nine out of every hundred of our actual acquaintances, but then he seldom or never picks out a character that it is not perfectly easy to draw in the light fresco of our modern-society school. He gives you where it is necessary the emotions proper to the situations, but rarely or never the emotions which lie concealed behind the situations and which give a kind of irony to them. His characters are carved out of the materials of ordinary society; George Eliot's include many which make ordinary society seem a sort of satire on the life behind it.[7]

That is to say, it is not that there is very much wrong with the character/characterisation of Fred Vincy; it is rather that, for a principal figure in *Middlemarch*, there is not nearly enough that is right with it.

With the next pair of characters to be considered, George Eliot is strikingly successful in giving 'the emotions which lie concealed behind the situations'. But in each case she uses a different method to achieve this. For all practical purposes Casaubon and Bulstrode do not figure in the novel at the same time. Only after the former's death halfway through does the latter begin to emerge as a central figure. The reason is obvious: the characters are too alike in their atrophied capacity for fellow-feeling, their costive nature, and their intense fear of disclosure of information about their deepest selves. And, as we saw in the previous chapter, both are so repugnant that the narrator resorts to intrusions in order to compel a little sympathy for them. The shrivelled selves of Casaubon and Bulstrode pose another problem for the narrator: how to avoid having a desiccated characterisation because of the character's desiccation. This is avoided by treating each character intensively over a relatively short span of time during which each is made to undergo a situation of unprecedented stress that becomes the climactic, indeed the climacteric, experience in each life, and which is only resolved by death for one and total humiliation for the other.

An abundance of telling external notation is used to suggest Casaubon's inner nature: his smile 'like pale wintry sunshine' (ch. 3); his house, with the suggestive connotations of its name – Lowick – and its 'air of autumnal decline' (ch. 9); his habitual refusal to offer an opinion of his own; his dislike of physical contact; his way of saying 'yes' with 'that peculiar pitch of voice which makes the word half a negative' (ch. 20); and so on. But the principal entrance to the icy core of Casaubon's inner being is through the extended inside views of his character and thoughts that the narrator offers at several points. They are, however, inside views that are subtly different in effect from those accorded the other central characters. While on the one hand the narrator makes intrusive comments in order to stir up sympathy for Casaubon's blighted character, on the other hand he creates the opposite effect through keeping a certain distance from him even while offering inside views. This is done by avoiding the use of *style indirect libre* (or free indirect style), the narratorial device which reports a character's thoughts and words in a mixture of *oratio recta* (direct speech) and *oratio obliqua* (indirect speech) and tends to collapse the distance between narrator and character. Roy Pascal explains:

> Free indirect speech occurs frequently [in *Middlemarch*] in longer passages and short snatches, within the framework of the narratorial material. It is used for any character, though of course more frequently for the main character ... Dorothea, since it necessarily implies a special concern for and intimacy with the character. The frequency of its incidence must affect the reader's response, since it tends to establish bonds not only of familiarity but also sympathy. It is significant that it is hardly used at all for Mr Casaubon, whom we get to know almost entirely through narratorial description and comment [i.e. through extended inside views], through his occasional contributions to conversation, and through the medium of the other characters. The effect is a feeling that his inner life is secretive and alien, and perhaps hollow and unworthy of the reader's respect. Will Ladislaw, by contrast, is through the use of free indirect style recommended to our sympathetic attention from his first appearance, long before we have any grounds for believing he has an important part to play in the story.[8]

The reader is first introduced to Casaubon's point of view in the tenth chapter, when it is learned that as the date of his marriage approached Casaubon 'did not find his spirits rising'. The condition is puzzling since 'there was nothing external by which he could account for a certain blankness of sensibility which came over him just when his expectant gladness should have been most lively'. One's awareness of 'hidden conflicts' (ch. 20) in Casaubon increases during the scenes in Rome when several intemperate words suggest 'a sort of jealousy which needs very little fire; it is hardly a passion, but a blight bred in the cloudy, damp despondency of uneasy egoism' (ch. 21). This is not 'the common jealousy of a winter-worn husband: it [is] something deeper, bred by his lifelong claims and discontents' (ch. 37). What Casaubon is jealous of is Dorothea's opinion of him, which he is convinced is put in jeopardy by her conversations with Ladislaw. The most sustained inside view of Casaubon comes in chapter 29 when it is revealed through the narrator's masterful analysis that the source of his malaise is a deficiency in the quality and breadth of his emotion, which manifests itself most pitiably in his shrinking from pity. Casaubon's 'small hungry shivering self' is 'sensitive without being enthusiastic' and too languid 'to thrill out of self-consciousness into passionate delight'. His greatest fear is that his shrunken inner self should be known for what it is: 'that proud narrow sensitiveness which has not mass enough to spare for transformation into sympathy, and quivers thread-like in small currents of self-preoccupation or at best of an egoistic scrupulosity'. Marriage, 'the new bliss [that] was not blissful to him', is consequently fated to become what religion and erudition and even authorship itself have already become for him – not a living activity but a simulacrum, an 'outward requirement [that he] was bent on fulfilling unimpeachably'.

But Casaubon has married Dorothea Brooke, his spiritual and psychological opposite, in whom runs 'a current into which all thought and feeling were apt sooner or later to flow – the reaching forward of the whole consciousness towards the fullest truth, the least partial good' (ch. 20). As this warm current continues to flow around his frigid reserve, Casaubon's 'proud suspicious reticence' (ch. 29) and 'hidden alienation' (ch. 50) make his wife's shows of compassion 'necessarily intolerable'. He lives in a state of 'perpetual suspicious conjecture' that Dorothea's opinions of him are 'not to his advantage' and as time passes becomes more and more certain 'that she judged him, and that her wifely devotedness was like a penitential expiation of unbelieving thoughts' (ch. 42). Only once before his death is Dorothea able to pierce her husband's morbid self-consciousness. The moment comes unexpectedly at the end of chapter 42: as he wearily climbs the staircase from his desk to his bed Casaubon is surprised to see Dorothea waiting up for him:

"Dorothea!" he said, with a gentle surprise in his tone. 'Were you waiting for me?'

'Yes, I did not like to disturb you.'

'Come, my dear, come. You are young, and need not to extend your life by watching.'

When the kind quiet melancholy of that speech fell on Dorothea's ears, she felt something like the thankfulness that might well up in us if we had narrowly escaped hurting a lamed creature. She put her hand into her husband's, and they went along the broad corridor together.

It is an exceptionally delicate moment that is all the more affecting because the narrator is wise enough not to try to explain Casaubon's unprecedented openness to compassion and even to a human's touch. It is this moment, rather than any of the narrator's intrusive asides, that most stirs the reader's sympathy for Casaubon.

While Henry James considered Casaubon 'an excellent invention', he was unhappy with Bulstrode, in whose story he found 'a slightly artificial cast, a melodramatic tinge, unfriendly to the richly natural coloring of the whole'. Bulstrode was 'too diffusely treated; he never grasps the reader's attention'.[9] A melodramatic tinge there undeniably is; but, as we shall see, it is precisely because of the unusual coloration that the reader's attention is forcefully grasped. The brief character sketch of Bulstrode given early in the novel does include some inside information: 'It was a principle with Mr Bulstrode to gain as much power as possible, that he might use it for the glory of God. He went through a great deal of spiritual conflict and inward argument in order to adjust his motives, and make clear to himself what God's glory required' (ch. 16). This information, however, does not take one below the surface of Bulstrode's inner self and in fact might even be considered a summary account of how he regards his transactions with his conscience. It is not until much later in the novel that a deeper and more accurate picture of his inner nature begins to unfold.

Bulstrode's thought processes must seem to most readers of *Middlemarch* what they seemed to Lydgate, who found his opinions contemptible, his metaphors broken, his logic bad, and his motives 'an absurd mixture of contradictory impressions' (ch. 67). This is presumably the reason that Eliot found it necessary to have her narrator insist that, although the specifics of the way Bulstrode's mind works may be attributable to distortions 'peculiar to Evangelical belief' (more particularly to the Calvinistic strain of it), in its generic aspect his psychology illustrates the universal tendency of general doctrine to corrupt morality if unchecked by fellow-feeling (ch. 61). On the one hand, Bulstrode is 'doctrinally convinced that there [is] a total absence of merit in himself' (ch. 57), that he is a sinful vessel to be consecrated by whatever use it pleases God to make of it. He further believes that human events, if properly interpreted, can give indications of the use to which Providence wishes its instrument to be put. On the other hand, Bulstrode's nature is characterised by 'selfish passions' (ch. 70), a 'tenacious nerve of ambitious self-preserving will, which had continually leaped out like a flame' (ch. 71), and 'an immense need of being something important and predominating' (ch. 61). At the crucial turning-points in his life general doctrine and individual egotism have collaborated in a series of self-serving rationalisations in which the glory of God, God's sake, God's service, and the cause of true religion have been made to justify the immoral and inhuman acts that have served to make Bulstrode wealthy and powerful and thereby given him the wherewithal to fulfil his desire of 'being an eminent Christian' (ch. 53).

At the beginning of chapter 53, Bulstrode is at the height of his worldly success and self-satisfaction. Of course he is doctrinally convinced of his worthlessness; 'but that doctrinal conviction may be held without pain when the sense of demerit does not take a distinct shape in memory'. And Bulstrode's memories are of far-off evenings when 'he was a very young man and used to go out preaching beyond Highbury'. He has as yet no cause to remember quite different aspects of his Highbury life – his dubious business partnership with Mr Dunkirk and his gaining the Dunkirk fortune for himself by withholding from his widow information concerning the existence and whereabouts of her lost daughter – an act characteristically rationalised by aligning his motives with a grotesque distortion of what 'God's glory required'. It is just at this high point of felicity that Raffles comes back into Bulstrode's life. This 'loud red figure' (ch. 53), 'very florid and hairy', with 'the air of a swaggerer' and 'the stale odour of travellers' rooms in the commercial hotels of the period' (ch. 41), notes sarcastically that his return is 'what you might call a providential thing' and 'perhaps ... a blessing to both of us'. But it is a very different providence from the one Bulstrode has long been invoking.

The authorial providence that brings Raffles back involves a note stuck in a brandy-flask and an excessive amount of coincidence. These contrivances have usually been regarded as comprising a serious artistic defect in *Middlemarch*, damaging to its seriousness, its realism and its claim to show the gradual action of ordinary rather than exceptional causes. The note stuck in the brandy-flask certainly seems Dickensian in the pejorative sense of being an unrealistic, implausible manipulation of plot for melodramatic purposes. But, when placed in context, it can be seen as part of a more thoughtful and serious use of Dickensian motifs. If the end of chapter 41 – where the paper gets stuck in the flask – is looked at closely, more evidence of Eliot's indebtedness to her older contemporary can be seen.

Raffles's presence in the 'moist rural quiet' is there said to be as incongruous 'as if he had been a baboon escaped from a menagerie'. And his social manner is described as follows: 'Mr Raffles on most occasions kept up the sense of having been educated at an academy, and being able, if he chose, to pass well everywhere; indeed, there was not one of his fellow-men whom he did not feel himself in a position to ridicule and torment.' If the startling and artificial figure of speech in the first passage suggests the Dickensian motif of evil invading a country sanctuary (like Fagin at the window of the house where Oliver Twist has found succour), the second passage even more strongly recalls the specific figure of Rigaud, the swaggering evil force in *Little Dorrit* who also ludicrously thinks of himself as a gentleman. What these similarities suggest is that the return of Raffles is not simply Dickensian in the superficial melodramatic sense; it is, rather, part of an appropriation of what David Carroll calls an 'essential method of Dickens's later novels [in which] two characters intimately tied together by exploitation seek their independence through further exploitation'.[10] To put it more simply, Raffles the tormentor is Bulstrode's *Doppelgänger*. Once this is realised the whole brilliant sequence involving Bulstrode and Raffles comes into focus. The loud red figure of Raffles has risen before Bulstrode 'as if by some hideous magic' (ch. 53), and seems the residue of 'a loathsome dream' – like 'a dangerous reptile' leaving 'slimy traces' on all 'the pleasant surroundings of his life' (ch. 68). This figure, 'worse than a nightmare' and seemingly sent by 'the spirit of evil', is Bulstrode's hidden self, his 'incorporate past' (ch. 53) and the personification of the morally polluted underside of his present life.

The introduction of a full-fledged psychological double into a realistic study of provincial life is by far the riskiest chance taken by George Eliot in *Middlemarch*. It is unquestionably unfriendly to the richly natural colouring of the whole. But on its own terms the symbiotic relationship is handled with impressive boldness and assurance. And it does enable the author both to have her cake and to eat it. While one of Eliot's cardinal tenets is that all her characters must be presented in a sympathetic light, another is her belief in the operation of an implacable nemesis which punishes serious moral transgressions (it is the offshoot of Eliot's Victorian sense of the 'peremptory and absolute' nature of duty).[11] In *Adam Bede*, her first novel, the former tenet had been grossly breached because the nemesis that pitilessly pursued and punished Hetty Sorrel was obviously endorsed – if it was not fuelled – by the narrator.[12] But in *Middlemarch* the function of nemesis is assigned to Raffles, a character within the novel, leaving the narrator free to be the compassionate moralist who insists that Bulstrode's rationalisations were 'a process which shows itself occasionally in us all' (ch. 61).

When Raffles first reappears in Middlemarch, Bulstrode gives him money so that he will go away and promises regular sums if he will stay away. But of course Raffles returns, for 'his eagerness to torment was almost as strong in him as any other greed'. His manner upsets Harriet Bulstrode and makes her husband realise that 'the loss of high consideration from his wife,' as from everyone else who did not clearly hate him out of enmity to the truth, would be as the beginning of death to him'. He also realises 'with cold certainty at his heart' that Raffles will continue his torments 'unless providence sent death to hinder him'. To propitiate this 'threatening Providence', Bulstrode attempts to make belated financial restitution to Ladislaw for what he had done to his mother, but an expected 'scene of self-abasement' (ch. 61) becomes more painful when Ladislaw scornfully refuses his money.

As time passes, Bulstrode's imagination continually intensifies 'the anguish of an imminent [public] disgrace' (ch. 68). Release from his torment seems a possibility when Raffles returns to Middlemarch with delirium tremens, which Bulstrode interprets as 'a sort of earnest that Providence intended his rescue from worse consequences'. If so, then 'the will of God might be the death of that hated man' (ch. 69). This train of thought continues until Bulstrode is virtually plotting Raffles's murder. When it is clear that 'the enemy of his peace' is in fact about to expire because of his contrivings, Bulstrode feels 'more at rest than he had done for many months. His conscience is soothed by the enfolding wing of secrecy, which seemed just then like an angel sent down for his relief' (ch. 70). But his providence has not delivered him; not even the death of his dark double, 'the haunting ghost of his earlier life' (ch. 71), can stop Bulstrode's descent into the black tunnel of total humiliation. The only light at its end is not that of providence, nor is it some prepubescent embodiment of the good, which is with what Dickens counters the evil force of Rigaud in *Little Dorrit*. It is, rather, the warmly human figure of Harriet Bulstrode, who when she takes her broken husband into her arms makes him once again friendly to the richly natural colouring of the novel.

Tertius Lydgate and Rosamond Vincy are the two most subtly and vividly realised characters in *Middlemarch* and the scenes between them the novel's most brilliant, nuanced and intelligent passages. As we have already seen, Lydgate is an exceptional person of rare potential: his professional goals of scientific discovery and improvement in public health give him the dual distinction of devotion to 'intellectual conquest and the social good' (ch. 15). We have also seen that the emotional intensity of his nature is forcefully conveyed through Eliot's substituting an account of her own creative passion for his similar intellectual passion. But when the novel's most important standard of judgement – the quality and breadth of emotion on which one's good depends – is applied to Lydgate his character is found to be seriously flawed. The standard is rigorously – perhaps one should even say ruthlessly – applied. Lydgate's professional life ends in failure and his private life in unhappiness not because of some vicious mole of nature in him but simply because of a deficiency or impercipience that the narrator claims is commonly found in men. The flaw is observable even on Lydgate's first appearance in the novel. His reaction to Dorothea Brooke, whom he meets at her uncle's dinner party in chapter 10, is that 'she is a good creature ... but a little too earnest. It is troublesome to talk to such women ... She did not look at things from the proper feminine angle. The society of such women was about as relaxing as going from your work to teach the second form, instead of reclining in a paradise with sweet laughs for bird-notes, and blue eyes for a heaven' (ch. 11).

When this flaw is placed under the microscope in chapter 15, during the narrator's first extended inside view of Lydgate, it is identified as 'spots of commonness'. They are found in 'the complexion of his prejudices, which, in spite of noble intention and sympathy, were half of them such as are found in ordinary men of the world: that distinction of mind which belonged to his intellectual ardour, did not penetrate his feeling and judgment about furniture, or women', or the desirability of his good birth being known. Put simply, there is a discontinuity between the fineness of mind and intensity of emotion that distinguish Lydgate's professional work and the comparative coarseness, even vulgarity, of his views on other subjects. In a subsequent analysis of Lydgate's social views in chapter 36, the narrator returns to the subject:

But it had never occurred to him that he should live in any other than what he would have called an ordinary way, with green glasses for hock, and excellent waiting at table. In warming himself at French social theories he had brought away no smell of scorching. We may handle even extreme opinions with impunity while our furniture, our dinner-giving, and preference for armorial bearings in our own case, link us indissolubly with the established order. And Lydgate's tendency was not towards extreme opinions: he would have liked no barefooted doctrines, being particular about his boots: he was no radical in relation to anything but medical reform and the prosecution of discovery. In the rest of practical life he walked by hereditary habit; half from that personal pride and unreflecting egoism which I have already called commonness, and half from that *naïveté* which belonged to preoccupation with favourite ideas.

Lydgate's 'unreflecting egoism' makes him particularly susceptible to the considerable charms of Rosamond Vincy. Their first meeting is at Stone Court where Rosamond has come with her brother in the hope of becoming acquainted with the handsome and well-connected young doctor. When she rises to leave, Lydgate follows her with his eyes: 'Every nerve and muscle in Rosamond was adjusted to the consciousness that she was being looked at. She was by nature an actress of parts that entered into her *physique*: she even acted her own character, and so well, that she did not know it to be precisely her own'. As Lydgate hands Rosamond her riding whip, their eyes meet in that unmistakable way that signifies mutual attraction. He turns a little paler than usual; she blushes deeply and feels 'a certain astonishment' even though what has happened 'was just what [she] had contemplated beforehand' (ch. 12).

The notation in this brief meeting is superb: Rosamond's consuming egotism is shown to be both calculating and yet, like Lydgate's (though in a more complicated way), unreflecting – for the character that she is acting is not someone else's but her own. Since almost all of what we later learn of Rosamond is seminally present in this scene, it is not surprising to learn that 'of all the characters she had attempted [George Eliot] found Rosamond's the most difficult to sustain'.[13] The difficulty, however, is not apparent in the text. Despite a few heavy-handed and dispensable narratorial intrusions, Rosamond's character unfolds magnificently as the novel goes on. There are, for example, the precise notations of her accomplished role-playing and 'quick imitative perception' (ch. 36). She 'could say the right thing; for she was clever with that sort of cleverness which catches every tone except the humorous. Happily she never attempted to joke, and this perhaps was the most decisive mark of her cleverness.' When Lydgate asks what she saw while in London, she answers that she has seen very little: 'A more naïve girl would have said, "Oh, everything!" But Rosamond knew better' (ch. 16). And when Lydgate is unexpectedly called in from the street to attend her ill brother, she leaves the room as he enters, 'waiting just long enough to show a pretty anxiety conflicting with her sense of what was becoming' (ch. 26). She is on stage even when alone: 'now more than ever she was active in sketching her landscapes and market-carts and portraits of friends, in practising her music, and in being from morning till night her own standard of a perfect lady, having always an audience in her own consciousness' (ch. 17). The musical performance is particularly good, for with 'her executant's instinct' Rosamond has perfectly copied her teacher's manner of playing, and gives forth 'his large rendering of noble music with the precision of an echo. It was almost startling, heard for the first time. A hidden soul seemed to be flowing forth from Rosamond's fingers' (ch. 16).

With the help of the narrator's omniscient perspective, the reader can see Rosamond's performance at the piano for what it is. Lydgate's reaction is different: he was 'taken possession of, and began to believe in her as something exceptional' rather than something essentially hollow. His illusion intensifies as their relationship develops, his spots of commonness making him confident that Rosamond would be the perfect wife, having 'that feminine radiance, and distinctive womanhood which must be classed with flowers and music'. As the narrator notes, Lydgate has never applied to 'the complexities of love and marriage [the] testing vision of details and relations' that he brings to his scientific work (ch. 16). His involvement soon reaches the stage of 'that peculiar intimacy which consists in shyness':

> They were obliged to look at each other in speaking, and somehow the looking could not be carried through as the matter of course which it really was. Lydgate began to feel this sort of consciousness unpleasant, and one day looked down, or anywhere, like an ill-worked puppet. But this turned out badly: the next day, Rosamond looked down, and the consequence was that when their eyes met again, both were more conscious than before. (ch. 27)

This leads on to an 'intimacy of mutual embarrassment' which forces the frank recognition of 'mutual fascination'. The result is the lively intercourse of flirtation. But this in turn leads to a complication caused by the different value that the egotism of each places on flirtation. For Lydgate, who does not want to marry, 'the play at being a little in love was agreeable, and did not interfere with graver pursuits': 'the primitive tissue was still his fair unknown'. But Rosamond, who does want to marry, does not distinguish 'flirtation from love, either in herself or in another' (ch. 27). When he realises the perceived seriousness of his flirtation, Lydgate decides to stop seeing Rosamond; but they nevertheless become engaged during their next meeting eleven days later. The psychological nuance in this brief scene is important. Lydgate has decided to call at the Vincys rather than leave a message for Mr Vincy because of his unreflecting egotism: he imagines how gratifying to himself it will be to have a few playful words with Rosamond on the subject of his resolve to put flirtation behind him. But Rosamond has been deeply hurt by Lydgate's avoidance of her and when he rises to leave she cannot quite sustain the role of 'self-contented grace'. Her manner betrays a 'certain helpless quivering' and as her tears rise she momentarily becomes 'as natural as she had ever been when she was five years old'. Lydgate had merely flirted with the artificial role-playing Rosamond; but he now falls in love with the 'natural' Rosamond, being completely mastered by 'the onrush of tenderness at the sudden belief that this sweet young creature depended on him for her joy' (ch. 31). It is paradoxically at the very moment when Lydgate's spots of commonness have been overwhelmed by the outflow of powerful feeling that his sad fate is sealed, for never again in his presence will Rosamond fail to act out the artificial character that she does not realise is precisely her own.

The period of their engagement is a time of egotistic satisfaction to both parties as they together spin the 'gossamer web' of 'young love-making ... the things whence its subtle interlacings are swung are scarcely perceptible: momentary touches of the finger-tips, meetings of rays from blue and dark orbs, unfinished phrases, lightest changes of cheek, faintest tremors'. Rosamond's state is that of 'the water-lily's expanding wonderment at its own fuller life', while Lydgate is assured that he has found the woman who can 'create order in the home and accounts' and yet keep the ability to 'transform life into romance at any moment', and who is 'instructed to the true womanly limit and not a hair's-breadth beyond – docile, therefore, and ready to carry out behests that come from beyond the limit'. In short, he foresees 'the innate submissiveness of the goose as beautifully corresponding to the strength of the gander' (ch. 36). But what he does not see is Rosamond as she really is. When she says that her need of wedding clothes may mean that the date of their wedding cannot be moved forward as much as he would like, Lydgate thinks that she is either 'tormenting him prettily' (ch. 36) or really does shrink from speedy marriage. But Rosamond has spoken the complete truth: it is only her trousseau that is on her mind. She does employ dissimulation, however, in connection with her keen desire to visit Lydgate's relations at Quallingham during their wedding tour. She would like, she says, to see where her husband-to-be grew up, and to imagine him there when he was a boy. But what she really wants is the chance to display herself in a more exalted social circle than any she has yet known.

The early days of their marriage are as idyllic as Lydgate and Rosamond have imagined them. But the husband's mounting debts soon make him begin to feel 'the biting presence of a petty degrading care, such as casts the blight of irony over all higher effort'. Around the same time he begins to realise that his wife's nature is far from being innately submissive. It is in chapter 58 that 'the terrible tenacity of this mild creature' and their 'total missing of each other's mental track' fully come home to him. Because she is gratified to be seen in public with a baronet's son, Rosamond goes out riding with the visiting cousin of Lydgate despite his insistence that she give up the exercise during her pregnancy. Rosamond does not waste her energy 'in impetuous resistance', for 'what she liked to do was to her the right thing, and all her cleverness was directed to getting the means of doing it'. A miscarriage is the result. It rouses Lydgate, who has hitherto walked by habit, not by self-criticism, to 'discern consequences which he had never been in the habit of tracing' as he begins to apply to his private life 'some of the rigour (by no means all) that he would have applied in pursuing experiment'. He also begins for the first time to compare the different 'strands of experience' in his life. He wonders if his wife has the capacity to murder, as did Laure, the French actress; and, as the reader has been doing for some time, he contrasts Dorothea's treatment of her husband with Rosamond's treatment of him. In the chapter's final pages husband and wife sit down together to talk. As she comes towards him 'in her drapery of transparent, faintly-tinted muslin, her slim yet round figure never looked more graceful'. Lydgate is also moved by the 'untarnished beauty' of her face, which stirs the memory of the early moments of his love, and brings a 'roused tenderness'. But the subject of their talk must be the urgent need to economise and the husband's need of wifely assistance in the hour of financial crisis. 'What can *I* do, Tertius?' is Rosamond's answer: the words fall 'like a mortal chill' on Lydgate's reawakened tenderness and make him look forward with dread to their future discussions about money. For her part, Rosamond sits perfectly still: 'the thought in her mind was that if she had known how Lydgate would behave, she would never have married him'. And she is 'quite sure that no one could justly find fault with her'.

Lydgate's 'creeping self-despair which comes in the train of petty anxieties' intensifies as a result of subsequent scenes with Rosamond in chapters 64 and 65. His 'bitter and moody state' is by now continually widening his wife's alienation from him. When he does make efforts to repair the relationship Rosamond welcomes 'the signs that her husband loved her and was under control. But this was something quite different from loving *him*.' The distinction is not lost on Lydgate, who comes to perceive that, if his marriage is not to be 'a yoked loneliness', he must find the will 'to go on loving without too much care about being loved' (ch.

66). In short, Rosamond has mastered her husband. She is able to do this because she draws a terrible strength from having no real character of her own, 'her nature [being] inflexible in proportion to its negations'. Lydgate, however, has nothing comparable within him from which to draw strength and to protect him from Rosamond's 'torpedo contact'. The metaphor is scientific, not ballistic – a torpedo fish has electric apparatus for numbing or killing its prey – and nicely suggests the quiet but deadly effect on Lydgate of his wife's 'negative character'. As his financial situation deteriorates, Lydgate becomes more and more desperate. The man who had once found a 'pitiable infirmity of will' in the whist-playing Farebrother now himself gambles to raise money. The ambitious professional man who had chosen to practise in the provinces rather than in London in order to stay clear of time-wasting entanglements is now 'ready to curse the day on which he had come to Middlemarch' (ch. 73). When it becomes clear that he will have to leave, his bleak future is already in his mind's eye: 'I must do as other men do, and think what will please the world and bring in money; look for a little opening in the London crowd, and push myself; set up in a watering-place, or go to some southern town where there are plenty of idle English, and get myself puffed, – that is the sort of shell I must creep into and try to keep my soul alive in' (ch. 76). This 'narrowed Lot' Lydgate accepts with 'sad resignation. He had chosen this fragile creature, and had taken the burthen of her life upon his arms. He must walk as he could, carrying that burthen pitifully' (ch. 81). That is the last one hears of Lydgate except for the brief report in the finale that he died early, always considered himself a failure, and once found a striking metaphor for the black hole of Rosamond's negative character that had absorbed his energies and ideals: 'He once called her his basil plant; and when she asked for an explanation, said that basil was a plant which had flourished wonderfully on a murdered man's brains.'

CHAPTER 6
Dorothea

In these delicate vessels is borne onward through the ages the treasure of human affections.

Daniel Deronda, ch. 11

From one point of view, that of the prelude to *Middlemarch*, Dorothea Brooke is an exceptional figure of heroic capabilities and radiant goodness, a latter-day Saint Theresa, a quester after 'some illimitable satisfaction, some object which would never justify weariness, which would reconcile self-despair with the rapturous consciousness of life beyond self'. In her exalted spiritual nature, Dorothea may be associated with the rare breed of Protestant heroines in post-Reformation English literature, who include the · Lady in Milton's *Comus*, Richardson's Clarissa, Browning's Pompilia, James's Isabel Archer and Shaw's Saint Joan. From another point of view, however, that of the historian of the English novel, Dorothea may be seen as a less exceptional character belonging to a less exalted lineage – that of the heroines of many eighteenth- and nineteenth-century novels by women writers, including Jane Austen's Emma Woodhouse and Fanny Price, and Charlotte Brontë's Jane Eyre and Lucy Snowe. Margaret Doody has described the paradigm:

> It is the story of a woman gifted with some talents and a deep capacity both for affection and responsibility who is to some important degree at odds with the world in which she finds herself. Unlike Clarissa, she is not called upon to make archetypal choices, and may be moving towards some kind of happiness or at least partial fulfillment; she desires to understand the world and to contribute something to it, but her abilities are often frustrated by poverty of education and incomplete experience. Her life is manifestly an affair of irritation and anxiety, though the reader is taught to measure society against her good will. She desires to move outward into society, but it will not respond to her. She is frequently an orphan or half-orphan, and parents or parent substitutes are inadequate or unsympathetic, overconventional or hostile. The heroine is often presented with the foil of a female character of her own age who is smaller-minded and, through greed or

timidity, more willing to act a conventional female role. The heroine herself tries to be both just and generous, but her intentions are often balked by her own ignorance or defects, and by the nature of her world. She desires above all the love of a man who is her equal, but such love is very hard to come by.[1]

For a proper understanding of Dorothea's development during the course of *Middlemarch*, it is important to recognise that her story fits the second schema at least as well as it does the first.

These different schemata also have a bearing on the question of whether Dorothea is an idealised character or a realistically drawn one. This question has occasioned a good deal of critical debate and it would be well at the outset of our discussion to see if it can be satisfactorily answered. Those who wish to deny that Dorothea's character is idealised usually talk about the irony in her presentation and point to those places in the text where a deflating or wry tone is found, and where there is evidence of a distance between what Dorothea thinks about herself or what another character thinks about her, and what the narrator says or implies.

Certainly there are a number of places in which Dorothea's innocence, youthful intensities, lack of experience and self-knowledge, shortsightedness and even wilfulness are directly or indirectly pointed up, and where there is a discrepancy between what she says and what she feels. There are a number of instances in the opening chapter of *Middlemarch*; for example: 'Riding was an indulgence which she allowed herself in spite of conscientious qualms; she felt that she enjoyed it in a pagan sensuous way, and always looked forward to renouncing it.' Similar notations occur periodically as the novel progresses. In chapter 34, Dorothea watches Featherstone's funeral from an upper window at Lowick 'with the interest of a monk on his holiday tour'; when Will Ladislaw recounts his family history three chapters later, she listens keenly, looking with serious intentness before her, 'like a child seeing a drama for the first time'; in chapter 44 she is said to look 'at the affairs of Middlemarch by the light of the great persecutions'; and in chapter 39, when she ardently describes her religion to Ladislaw, he may exclaim 'God bless you for telling me', but the narrator is sufficiently uninvolved in their conversation to be able to note that they 'were looking at each other like two fond children who were talking confidentially of birds'. It is also the case that these notations are supplemented by the observations of Dorothea's sister Celia and Mrs Cadwallader. The former notes that 'Dorothea is not always consistent' (ch. 1); that 'she likes giving up' (ch. 2); that 'it is impossible to satisfy you; yet you never see what is quite plain' (ch. 4); and that 'you are wanting to find out if there is anything uncomfortable for you to do ...' (ch. 50). The worldly wisdom of the rector's wife is equally blunt. In chapter 6 she observes that 'there is a great deal of nonsense in her – a flighty sort of methodistical stuff', and that 'Miss Brooke [is] a girl who would have been requiring you to see the stars by daylight'. And after Casaubon's death she notes Dorothea's tendency to be 'playing the tragedy queen and taking things sublimely' (ch. 54).

On the other hand, the narrator far more frequently speaks of Dorothea in tones reminiscent of those of the prelude: there are numerous references to her 'ardent' nature and repeated reminders of the purity and elevation of her inner being, which is characterised by 'the reaching forward of the whole consciousness towards the fullest truth, the least partial good' (ch. 20). And the witness of Celia and Mrs Cadwallader would carry more weight if the former were less scatter-brained and the latter less predictably sarcastic. Even then, however, they would be far outweighed by the remarks of a number of characters in the novel who see Dorothea as an exalted, unique being. Even if Ladislaw's many comments are not cited (on the grounds that he is hardly impartial), there is abundant testimony in *Middlemarch* to Dorothea's exceptional nature: Sir James Chettam believes that 'it is a pity she was not a queen' (ch. 54) and that a second marriage would be 'a sort of desecration' for her (ch. 55); and Tantripp, Dorothea's maid, at one point feels 'an irrepressible movement of love towards the beautiful, gentle creature' whom she serves (ch. 48). Rosamond at first assumes that animosity is the reason Dorothea returns to see her in chapter 81. But by the time the visit is over Rosamond has come to feel that she 'must be better than any one'. Lydgate, as we have seen, was initially unimpressed by Dorothea; but by the climax of the novel he, too, has come to idealise her: 'This young creature has a heart large enough for the Virgin Mary' (ch. 76). And Caleb Garth's rapturous description of Dorothea's voice – 'it reminds me of bits in the "Messiah"' – '"and straightway there appeared a multitude of the heavenly host, praising God and saying"' (ch. 56) – is only one of a number of testimonials to the splendour of the most intangible of Dorothea's physical characteristics. For the Shelleyesque Ladislaw, it is 'like the voice of a soul that had once lived in an Aeolian harp' (ch. 9); for Lydgate it is the voice 'of deep-souled womanhood' (ch. 58); and for the narrator 'her speech [is] like a fine piece of recitative' (ch. 5), and 'as clear and unhesitating as that of a young chorister chanting a *credo*' (ch. 39).

The two different lenses – the idealised and the ironic – through which Dorothea is alternately seen are both present in the climactic scene between her and Lydgate in chapter 76. The narrator first speaks of Dorothea's 'noble nature, generous in its wishes, ardent in its charity'. But he also speaks of Dorothea's description of what she will do for Lydgate as a 'childlike picture'. And when the narrator speaks of Dorothea's 'ready understanding of high experience' a parenthetical qualification immediately follows: 'Of lower experience such as plays a great part in the world, poor Mrs Casaubon had a very blurred shortsighted knowledge, little helped by her imagination.' On the evidence of this scene, it would not be difficult to argue that the presentation of Dorothea is either inconsistent or ambivalent. The truth of the matter is less complex; it is summarised in the narrator's generalisation about Dorothea in the following chapter, which may be regarded as a synthesis of the irony and the idealising that both figure in her presentation. In 'Dorothea's nature', the reader is told, her 'passionate faults lay along the easily counted open channels of her ardent character; and while she was full of pity for the visible mistakes of others, she had not yet any material within her experience for subtle constructions and suspicions of hidden wrong. But that simplicity of hers, holding up an ideal for others in her believing conception of them, was one of the great powers of her womanhood' (ch. 77). That is to say, Dorothea's faults are superficial, the result of her outward-flowing, ardent, but not yet fully matured goodness. If she is 'childlike', it is for the reason given early in the novel: her nature is 'entirely without hidden calculation either for immediate effects or for remoter ends' (ch.5). As for the parenthetical reference to Mrs Casaubon's 'very blurred shortsighted knowledge' of 'lower experience', the comment is too clumsy (especially in the substitution of the formal 'Mrs Casaubon' for Dorothea's Christian name, which is used by the narrator elsewhere in the chapter), too gratuitous, and too inappositely intrusive to carry much weight.

Like it or not, then, Dorothea is in the main an idealised character. She does exist on a different spiritual plane from the other characters in the novel (with the partial exception of Ladislaw). But, having said this, one must go on to note with surprise that in a novel by a master psychologist and explorer of the depths of the human personality no attempt at all is made to explain how Dorothea Brooke, the novel's central character, came to have her ardent nature – her insatiable thirst and quenchless burning. In chapter 21 the narrator insists that 'we are all of us born in moral stupidity, taking the world as an udder to feed our supreme selves: Dorothea had early begun to emerge from that stupidity'. But the reader has to take the narrator's word on this important matter, for despite the length and comprehensiveness of *Middlemarch* one learns virtually nothing about Dorothea's life before she was 19 (her age when the novel opens). All one can glean from over 600 pages is that 'when she was a child she believed in the gratitude of wasps and the honourable susceptibility of sparrows' (ch. 22); that even when she was a little girl she thought she would like to devote her life to helping someone who did great works (ch. 37); that her parents had died around the time of her puberty (ch. 1); that · since childhood she had been concerned about her religious beliefs (ch. 39) and had at some point prayed frequently and as 'fervidly as if she thought herself living in the time of the Apostles' (ch. 1). All of these scattered details tally with the idealised picture of Dorothea in the present time of the novel and not one of them suggests the least tincture of moral stupidity in her. For just as in Catholic theology the Virgin Mary (to whom Dorothea is more than once compared) is said to have been untouched by the stain of original sin, so Dorothea Brooke in *Middlemarch* seems untouched by the otherwise universal ('all of us') primal taint of moral stupidity.

Of the psychological roots of this immaculately conceived character the reader learns nothing. In the case of Lydgate, the novel's other central character, the reader was given early on an extended flashback which convincingly described his moment of vocation, and a detailed analysis of the genesis of his determining characteristic, the spots of commonness. And in the case of the visionary Daniel Deronda, the title character of George Eliot's next novel, there is an elaborate attempt to account for his exalted spiritual nature. Deronda, like Dorothea, has 'the imaginative need of some far-reaching relation to make the horizon of his immediate, daily acts' and longs 'for some ideal task' (ch. 63). But, as is not the case with Dorothea, the roots of Deronda's yearnings are convincingly explored. The 'main lines' of his character (ch. 16) are shown to be determined by the early pain of 'his first sorrow' (ch. 35). It occurred around the time of his puberty, when he began to suspect that he was illegitimate and that a secret surrounded his birth. This impression gives him 'something like a new sense in relation to all the elements of his life', intensifies his 'inward experience', makes his imagination 'tender', and gives him 'an acute sympathy' (ch. 16).

Perhaps something analogous happened to Dorothea Brooke about the age of her puberty and her parents' death to account for her distinctive, visionary nature. The speculation is of course wholly idle, for in *Middlemarch* George Eliot is uninterested in Dorothea's ideal or spiritual nature *per se*, and it cannot be said that its depiction is an impressive achievement. What Eliot is interested in doing is stylising and simplifying Dorothea's character in order to be able to illustrate with exemplary clarity two of the principal themes of *Middlemarch*: the relation of the gifted individual to modern society; and the workings of the humanistic economy of salvation. But there is in Dorothea's story another key thematic thread which is distinct from, though closely related to, the social theme and the secular religious theme, and in which her ideal qualities play little part. It concerns what the prelude rather obscurely calls 'the common yearning of womanhood'. Its subject is the development of a young woman as she journeys towards a degree of self-knowledge and a recognition of her true emotional needs. In the depiction of this development there is a richness, a complexity and a power that justifies Dorothea's position as not only the thematic centre of *Middlemarch*, but also its premier character. It is this development that will now be examined as we chart the stages by which the 'girl whose notions about marriage took their colour entirely from an exalted enthusiasm about the ends of life, and did not include even the honours and sweet joys of the blooming matron' (ch. 3), dwindles into a wife and mother.

The general shape of Dorothea's passage will not be surprising to students of nineteenth-century literature. It is a re-enactment of the movement – from youth to maturity, from subjectivity to objectivity, from egotism ('a tumultuous preoccupation with her personal lot', ch. 20) to the realisation of an 'equivalent centre of self' in others, from isolation to community – that is commonly found in the central works of the Victorian period. Teufelsdröckh, for example, the central figure in Carlyle's *Sartor Resartus*, moved from egotism and visionary bafflement through indifference and a '*Divine Depth of Sorrow*' to a renewal founded on renunciation (with which alone 'Life, properly speaking, can be said to begin') and the abandonment of the quest for happiness in order to do the duty that lay nearest.[2] The same kind of passage was vigorously schematised in Matthew Arnold's 1849 poem 'Resignation', which contrasts romantic questers enthralled with 'self-ordained' labours, who flee 'the common life of men', to other natures who through experience have come to replace passionate intensity with a 'sad lucidity of soul', to unite themselves with 'the general life', and to 'bear rather than rejoice'. There is a difference, however, between these versions of the Victorian rite of passage into adult life and the progression of Dorothea Brooke in *Middlemarch*. The difference lies in Eliot's greater emphasis on the importance of emotional fulfilment. Unlike those of Carlyle's Teufelsdröckh or the speaker of Arnold's poem, Dorothea's development involves a recognition of her sensual nature. This subject is important but its presentation oblique, and before proceeding it will be well to consider carefully the place of sexuality in Dorothea's development.

Indirection and inference are George Eliot's characteristic methods of presenting sexual subject-matter. Steven Marcus, for example, has admitted that it took him a long time to grasp what Eliot's first work of fiction, 'The Sad Fortunes of the Rev. Amos Barton', 'was so mutedly trying to say'. Only when he realised that Milly Barton, the mother of six, died as a result of yet another miscarriage did Marcus become aware of 'the presence of some extraordinary sexual rapport' between her and her husband which, he reasonably claimed, was the basis of their 'passionately happy marriage' and to what the terminally overworked Milly was referring in her dying words to her husband: 'You – have – made me – very – happy.'[3] And, in a *tour d'horizon* of all the fiction, Juliet McMaster has shown that 'Eliot made it her business to be full and explicit about sensuous experience' and that, although 'the restrictions of her day precluded the direct and literal description of sexual relations, George Eliot is nonetheless able to convey all she needs by shifting to the figurative level'.[4]

At the beginning of *Middlemarch*, Dorothea's ideas about marriage seem unconnected with passion or sexuality. It is, she says, 'a state of higher duties. I never thought of it as mere personal ease' (ch. 4). As the narrator observes:

> Dorothea, with all her eagerness to know the truths of life, retained very childlike ideas about marriage. She felt sure that she would have accepted the judicious Hooker, if she had been born in time to save him from that wretched mistake he made in matrimony; or John Milton when his blindness had come on; or any of the other great men whose odd habits it would have been glorious piety to endure; but an amiable handsome baronet, who said 'Exactly' to her remarks even when she expressed uncertainty, – how could he affect her as a lover? The really delightful marriage must be that where your husband was a sort of father, and could teach you even Hebrew, if you wished it. (ch. 1)

These notions are a droll index of the intensity of Dorothea's religious disposition and a reflection of her ardent yearning for some ideal 'life beyond self' to which she can devote her energies. But other things that one learns about her in the opening chapters suggest that there is a strong sensuous streak in Dorothea's nature that goes against the grain of her desire to explore the high places of the *via negativa*. The often-remarked-on scene with the jewels at the end of chapter 1 is a case in point. Dorothea first declares a complete lack of interest in the gems that Celia is eager to divide between them. But a 'new current of feeling, as sudden as the gleam' from the fine emerald and diamond ring that has caught her eye, leads her to exclaim how very beautiful the gems are and to reflect that 'it is strange how deeply the colours seem to penetrate one, like scent. I suppose that is the reason why gems are used as emblems in the Revelation of St John. They look like fragments of heaven.' She then puts the ring and a matching bracelet on her beautiful finger and wrist. 'And all the while', the narrator shrewdly notes, 'her thought was trying to justify her delight in the colours by merging them in her mystic religious joy.' The point is no less telling for being patent: there is a sensuous emotional side as well as an ascetic side to Dorothea's nature, but she instinctively tries to suppress the former because she wishes to have her consciousness wholly filled with the 'visionary future' (ch. 3) rather than the physical present.

There is a similar contrast – a boldly emblematic one – in chapter 19 when Dorothea, dressed not unlike a nun in 'Quakerish grey drapery' with her long cloak fastened at the neck, is seen in the Vatican standing near where the statue of 'the reclining Ariadne, then called the Cleopatra, lies in the marble voluptuousness of her beauty, the drapery folding around her with a petal-like ease and tenderness'. It is, as Ladislaw's German friend Naumann observes, 'a fine bit of antithesis'. He goes on to make the same conceptual transference that George Eliot wants the reader to make: the voluptuous Ariadne stands for the physical and sensuous nature of the 'breathing blooming' Dorothea, whose form, 'not shamed' by that of Ariadne, lies concealed beneath her grey drapery: 'antique form animated by Christian sentiment', as Naumann puts it, 'sensuous force controlled by spiritual passion'.

In chapter 20 the same point that was made dramatically with the jewels and symbolically with the statue is made through detailed psychological notation. In an analysis of the growing strain in Dorothea's relations with her new husband, the narrator notes that Casaubon's dislike of any physical contact or intimacy frustrates Dorothea's natural tendency to express her 'girlish and womanly feeling' through 'those childlike caresses which are the bent of every sweet woman'. Dorothea's frustration is compounded by her sense of humiliation at finding 'herself a mere victim of feeling, as if she could know nothing except through that medium: all her strength was scattered in fits of agitation, of struggle, of despondency, and yet again in visions of more complete renunciation, transforming all hard conditions into duty'. The *mere* in the phrase 'a mere victim of feeling' is an instance of *style indirect libre*: it registers Dorothea's undervaluation of feeling at this point in her development,

not that of her creator, who believes that there is little of human value that
is not grounded in the truth of feeling. The rest of the quotation shows
Dorothea practising the same suppression of feeling as in the scene with
the jewels: she struggles to reach the visionary path of renunciation and
duty, and to leave behind the low and vexatious road of feeling.

Casaubon's dislike of physical contact, including even the hand of his
beautiful young bride, comes as no surprise to the reader of *Middlemarch*,
who by chapter 20 has developed a perfectly understandable interest in
learning as much as he can about the physical relations between the newly-
weds. In his letter proposing marriage, Casaubon had spoken of 'an
affection hitherto unwasted' (ch. 5) and later, in commenting on another
instance of his recoil from the touch of the affectionate Dorothea, the
narrator notes that 'There was something horrible to Dorothea in the
sensation which this unresponsive hardness inflicted on her. That is a
strong word, but not too strong: it is in these acts called trivialities that the
seeds of joy are for ever wasted' (ch. 42). The striking imagery of
unwasted affection and wasted seed is suggestive, even if we do not
choose to be as blunt as Richard Ellmann: 'Mr Casaubon chooses self-
isolation like choosing self-abuse. The image of Onan is invoked to
symbolize his spirit, which in turn is reflected in his physical denial.'[5]
Other details concerning Casaubon's emotional life have similarly
unwholesome connotations and similarly suggest an unconsummated
union. At the beginning of chapter 7, for example, the narrator observes
that while in offering marriage to Dorothea he had 'determined to
abandon himself to the stream of feeling' he was surprised to discover
'what an exceedingly shallow rill it was'. This leads him to speculate that
'the poets had much exaggerated the force of masculine passion', though
it also crosses his mind that 'there was some deficiency in Dorothea to
account for the moderation of his abandonment'. From his marriage he
both expects to 'receive family pleasures' and to 'leave behind him that
copy of himself which seemed so urgently required of a man – to the
sonneteers of the sixteenth century' (ch. 29). But for Casaubon any
procreative urgency seems merely cerebral or bookish, and as the day of
his marriage approaches he does not 'find his spirits rising' (ch. 10) and
is in other ways presumably untumescent.

It is details such as these that should be kept in mind in approaching
one of the two most spectacular passages in *Middlemarch* (the other is the
description of Lydgate's scientific passion in chapter 16): the account of
Dorothea's 'oppressed heart' and consciousness as she cries bitterly to
herself in Rome at the opening of chapter 20, the 'dream-like strangeness
of her bridal life' having been intensified by the 'stupendous

fragmentariness' of the ancient city and its 'oppressive masquerade of ages, in which her own life too seemed to have become a masque with enigmatical costumes':

> To those who have looked at Rome with the quickening power of a knowledge which breathes a growing soul into all historic shapes, and traces out the suppressed transitions which unite all contrasts, Rome may still be the spiritual centre and interpreter of the world. But let them conceive one more historical contrast: the gigantic broken revelations of that Imperial and Papal city thrust abruptly on the notions of a girl who had been brought up in English and Swiss Puritanism, fed on meagre Protestant histories and on art chiefly of the hand-screen sort; a girl whose ardent nature turned all her small allowance of knowledge into principles, fusing her actions into their mould, and whose quick emotions gave the most abstract things the quality of a pleasure or a pain; a girl who had lately become a wife, and from the enthusiastic acceptance of untried duty found herself plunged in tumultuous preoccupation with her personal lot. The weight of unintelligible Rome might lie easily on bright nymphs to whom it formed a background for the brilliant picnic of Anglo-foreign society; but Dorothea had no such defense against deep impressions. Ruins and basilicas, palaces and colossi, set in the midst of a sordid present, where all that was living and warm-blooded seemed sunk in the deep degeneracy of a superstition divorced from reverence; the dimmer yet eager Titanic life gazing and struggling on walls and ceilings; the long vistas of white forms whose marble eyes seemed to hold the monotonous light of an alien world: all this vast wreck of ambitious ideals, sensuous and spiritual, mixed confusedly with the signs of breathing forgetfulness and degradation, at first jarred her as with an electric shock, and then urged themselves on her with that ache belonging to a glut of confused ideas which check the flow of emotion. Forms both pale and glowing took possession of her young sense, and fixed themselves in her memory even when she was not thinking of them, preparing strange associations which remained through her after-years. Our moods are apt to bring with them images which succeed each other like the magic-lantern pictures of a doze; and in certain states of dull forlornness Dorothea all her life continued to see the vastness of St Peter's, the huge bronze canopy, the excited intention in the attitudes and garments of the prophets and evangelists in the mosaics above, and the red drapery which was being hung for Christmas spreading itself everywhere like a disease of the retina.

The paragraph begins dispassionately with the erudite and well-travelled narrator setting out a striking 'historical contrast'. But the passage soon begins to re-enact, not simply to describe, the impact of Rome on Dorothea's consciousness. And just as she has no 'defense against deep impressions', so the narrator becomes increasingly unable to control the powerful impressions and jarring images that the passage has begun to generate. In the reference to 'weight of unintelligible Rome' there is a strong echo of 'the heavy and the weary weight/Of all this unintelligible world' of Wordsworth's 'Tintern Abbey', which is lightened only by transporting moods equal in intensity but antithetical in nature to the mood that has gripped Dorothea. There is the oppressive and minatory juxtaposition of artefacts from the alien past and the warm-blooded, degenerate present (an almost lurid transmogrification of the Ariadne–Dorothea contrast in the previous chapter); there is the startling image of an electric shock which, when it is used elsewhere in the novel in connection with Dorothea, refers to the intensity of her emotional reaction to Ladislaw or of his to her; there is the abrupt flash-forward to the states of 'dull forlornness' in Dorothea's later life as the passage reaches its climax; and finally there is the red drapery being hung for Christmas in St Peter's spreading itself everywhere 'like a disease of the retina' – at which point the passage has become wholly expressive of Dorothea's disturbed consciousness and not at all representational. White is the liturgical colour for Christmas; as in a painting by Munch, the red is supplied, so to speak, by a disease of the inner eye.[6]

That Eliot was not fully in control of this torrential passage is suggested by the narrator's weak recoil from its implications at the beginning of the following paragraph, which offers as explanation a reductive generalisation concerning Dorothea's 'not ... very exceptional' inner state: 'many souls in their young nudity are tumbled out among incongruities and left to "find their feet" among them, while their elders go about their business'.[7] But, if culture shock seems an inadequate explanation of Dorothea's hypersensitive revulsion, what is the reason for it? The key to the answer lies in the collocation of the 'stupendous fragmentariness' of Rome and the 'dream-like strangeness of [Dorothea's] bridal life'. Her vision of Rome, we may say, is a 'masque with enigmatical costumes' which expresses obliquely what even so strait-laced a critic as Gordon Haight calls the 'violent and painful' nature of Dorothea's 'initiation into matrimony'.[8]

In the light of the evidence we have reviewed, then, it is difficult not to conclude that Dorothea and Casaubon's marriage was either frustratingly unconsummated or unsatisfactorily consummated, that Casaubon was in any case sexually inadequate and emotionally petrified, that there was consequently sexual friction between cold husband and affectionate wife, and that the acute degree of Dorothea's destabilisation indicates that sexual currents run deep in her.[9] Thus, although the narrator avers in chapter 28 that 'No one would ever know what [Dorothea] thought of a wedding journey to Rome', the reader in fact knows a fair amount about what has transpired. And even before Casaubon's death midway through the novel the reader might well be asking himself the same question that Lydgate wonders about only much later in the novel: 'Casaubon must have raised some heroic hallucination in her. I wonder if she could have any other sort of passion for a man?' (ch. 76).

The man in question is of course Ladislaw, and ever since *Middlemarch* was first published commentators have found the depiction of Dorothea's relationship with him unsatisfactory. Among the most interesting and impressive analyses is that of Barbara Hardy, who argues that '*Middlemarch* is only restrictedly truthful in its treatment of sexuality'. The 'important thing' is not 'the absence of sexual realism achieved through a detailed clinical report, but the absence or presence of that psychological realism which makes the characters appear as sexual beings'. George Eliot is reticent but not silent about the sexual side of the Dorothea–Casaubon relationship, but 'she leaves things out in her treatment of Dorothea and Will'. The omission is 'an unrealistic element in an unusually realistic novel'. The 'unhappy consequences of restricted treatment of sex' in their relationship is 'the psychological and structural flaw in *Middlemarch*'. Sensibility replaces sexuality in the Dorothea–Ladislaw relationship, and 'when they are together, physically or in the thoughts of each other ... the romantic glow seems false and the childlike innocence implausible and inappropriate'.[10] It is difficult to quarrel directly with this shrewd analysis. The principal problem, as I see it, is that like most of the other characters in *Middlemarch* Ladislaw idealises Dorothea and seems happiest when warming himself in the radiant glow of her childlike ardour. Dorothea's inner life is, however, a good deal richer and more complex than Ladislaw realises. It can best be brought into focus if Dorothea's development during the novel is examined with minimal reference to Ladislaw's idealised perceptions of her. If this is done, an instinctively affectionate nature and a powerful desire, in neither of which there is any reason to think that sexuality does not have a part, can be seen to characterise Dorothea's long-germinating love for Ladislaw.

There are two strands in Dorothea's development during the course of

Middlemarch. One involves the passage from subjectivity to objectivity through sorrow, sad experience and the recognition of an equivalent centre of self in others. The second is composed of the stages by which she comes to recognise the primacy of the feelings and the importance of emotional fulfilment. Let us begin with Dorothea's reaction in chapter 5 to Casaubon's letter proposing marriage. She trembles and sobs, casts herself, 'with a childlike sense of reclining', on what she takes to be 'the lap of a divine consciousness which sustained her own'; her 'whole soul was possessed by the fact that a fuller life was opening before her'. The reader trembles as well, but for a different reason. Casaubon's letter, which Dorothea reads in the subjective light of 'the radiance of her transfigured girlhood', is in fact a chilling missive, in the circumlocutions and stiff formality of which there is no hint of ardour, strong emotion or noble purpose. It is important, however, not to make too much of the ironic discrepancy; to do so could lead to a simplistic relegation of Dorothea's intense emotions to the category of the preposterously immature. If the object towards which she channels her spiritual energies is wholly unworthy of her, her choice is not bizarre or inexplicable. It is ultimately one of the results of the disappearance of God during the nineteenth century. As the narrator explains in chapter 10: 'something she yearned for by which her life might be filled with action at once rational and ardent; and since the time was gone by for guiding visions and spiritual directors, since prayer heightened yearning but not instruction, what lamp was there but knowledge? Surely learned men kept the only oil; and who more learned than Mr Casaubon.' It is a penetrating and prescient analysis which must strike a responsive chord in university teachers of literature who annually observe young persons – usually female – bringing to the acquisition of knowledge and the study of literature expectations that neither can properly satisfy. But if knowledge is not the lamp, what illumination is there for an intense young woman seeking fulfilment and a 'life beyond self'?

As we have already seen, the word 'childlike' is again used about Dorothea in the passage where she is 'humiliated to find herself a mere victim of feeling' (ch. 20). The subject of feeling comes up again two chapters later during her second private interview with Will Ladislaw. For Will the ideal human condition is not that of self-suppression, of the 'martyrdom' that he accuses Dorothea of practising, but that of the poet, in whose soul 'knowledge passes instantaneously into feeling, and feeling flashes back as a new organ of knowledge'. Dorothea rightly points out that this is an incomplete description of the poet, for it leaves out the writing of poems. It is also a most dubious description, for it seems to assign feeling only a secondary or reactive, not a primary and initiating, role. This part of the description is none the less endorsed by Dorothea, who says she understands 'what you mean about knowledge passing into feeling, for that seems to be just what I experience'. What Dorothea is saying might seem close to George Eliot's remark in a late notebook that 'Feeling is a sort of knowledge'.[11] Close – but not identical; at this point in Dorothea's development, it is important to note that in what she thinks about feeling (which is not necessarily the same as what she actually feels) there is an overemphasis on the head (knowledge) and an insufficient emphasis on the heart (emotions).

In the same interview, Ladislaw uses the imagery of sacrifice and imprisonment to describe the nature of Dorothea's life with Casaubon: 'I suspect you have some false belief in the virtues of misery, and want to make your own life a martyrdom ... you will go and be shut up in that stone prison at Lowick: you will be buried alive.' The same imagery is deployed by the narrator in his first description of Dorothea after her return to Lowick at the beginning of chapter 28. It is, as Frank Kermode has said, a 'wonderful moment'. [12] From her window Dorothea sees the 'uniform whiteness' of the snow-covered 'distant flat' and the equally monotonous and monochromic 'low-hanging uniformity of cloud'. The furnishings of her room seem comparably dismal, even ghostly. But Dorothea herself is vividly alive, even dazzling: 'She was glowing from her morning toilette as only healthful youth can glow: there was a gem-like brightness on her coiled hair and in her hazel eyes; there was warm red life in her lips; her throat had a breathing whiteness above the differing white of the fur.' The startling contrast, which recalls the early scene with the jewels and the juxtaposition of Dorothea and the statue of Ariadne, is powerfully suggestive: while Dorothea's life at Lowick and her devotion to her husband bespeak self-sacrifice, renunciation and the acceptance of duty, her wonderful body bespeaks throbbing life, and has a sensual, not a supernal, glow which is totally out of place in her present surroundings.

It is of essential importance to charting Dorothea's development to note that this scene is set in her blue-green boudoir at Lowick, the room in which most of the key episodes in her inner life are to take place. The room is first described in chapter 9: its furniture of faded blue; the group of family miniatures on the wall; the tapestry showing a peculiar 'blue-green world with a pale stag in it'. Most important, there is in this upper room a bow window that looks down on the avenue of limes on the south-west front of the house, 'with a sunk fence between park and pleasure-ground, so that ... the glance swept uninterruptedly along a slope of greensward till the limes ended in a level of corn and pastures, which after seemed to melt into a lake under the setting sun'.

As the glowing Dorothea in her 'blooming full-pulsed youth' stands in this room in chapter 28, she feels a sense of 'moral imprisonment which made itself one with the chill, colourless, narrowed landscape, with the shrunken furniture, the never-read books, and the ghostly stag in a pale fantastic world that seemed to be vanishing from the daylight' and that recalls nothing so much as one of the enigmatical costumes of Dorothea's weird reverie in Rome. In this 'disenchanted' chamber, 'deadened as an unlit transparency', in which 'all existence seemed to beat with a lower pulse than her own' and 'every object was withering and shrinking away from her', there is one object that, when her glance falls on it, finally cancels Dorothea's 'nightmare' and provides the chapter's second wonderful moment. The object is a miniature of Casaubon's aunt Julia, who was Will Ladislaw's grandmother. As Dorothea gazes at the picture its colours deepen, the lips and chin of the dead woman seem to get larger, and the hair and eyes seem to be sending out light. It is as if Dorothea has transferred to the miniature something of her own vibrant blooming life, just as she had earlier transferred to the Vatican draperies something of her inner turmoil. She has also communicated to the miniature her own unconscious desire for Will Ladislaw, for under the power of her observation the face of the long dead Julia is transformed into the smiling face of the young man who in turn makes Dorothea smile. Perhaps we should call the transformation effected by Dorothea a creative, even a poetic act. ('We are all of us imaginative in some form or other', as the narrator remarks in another connection in chapter 34, 'for images are the brood of desire.') If so, we must also say that it has nothing to do with knowledge passing into feeling; it is, rather, the power of intense feeling and emotional need creating not an idea or an ideal, but a representation of the object of its desire.

In chapter 37 there is another scene between Dorothea and Will and another scene in which she meditates alone in the blue-green boudoir. The former instances the 'sense of young companionship' that is an aspect of Dorothea's delight in seeing Will. It is said to be 'like a lunette opened in the wall of her prison, giving her a glimpse of the sunny air'. During their meeting Ladislaw is pleased to perceive 'what Dorothea was hardly conscious of – that she was travelling into the remoteness of pure pity and loyalty towards her husband'. After their conversation, during which she has learned Ladislaw's family history, there are 'fresh images' that gather round the miniature of aunt Julia as Dorothea sits alone in her boudoir. She has by now – it is late in the summer following her January return to the snow-covered estate – grown fond of the 'pallid quaintness' of the room that is now filled with memories of her inner struggles to find the spiritual resolve to discharge the duties of her marriage. She is particularly helped by looking along the avenue of limes 'toward the arch of western light'. This sunset vision, with its transcendent connotations, is said to have gained a communicating power with her. But what most helps to 'concentrate her feelings' is that 'delicate miniature of aunt Julia, so like a living face that she knew'. It is in gazing at this picture that Dorothea has a 'vision' that is 'like a sudden letting in of daylight' – that is, a vision that is the opposite of the sunset vision of higher duties. The second vision tells her that she must persuade her husband to share their wealth with the impecunious Ladislaw. But the only result of her intercession is a deepened estrangement between husband and wife. The narrator calls Dorothea's purpose innocent and pure, but the reader may be forgiven for doubting whether her naïveté and altruism were wholly responsible for her so completely misjudging her husband's reaction, and for wondering if the imperfect sublimation of her powerful emotional attraction to Ladislaw has not been a contributing factor. The conscious expression of this emotion takes the form of an act of seeming disinterest. But for the careful reader the source and motive of Dorothea's act may seem as different from her other unselfish acts as her daylight vision is from her sunset vision.

The next time that Dorothea meditates in the blue-green boudoir occurs in chapter 42, just after she has been struck by a sense of something horrible in her husband's 'unresponsive hardness'. She is too absorbed with her own emotions to notice that the bow window opens on to a glorious afternoon, or to be bothered by the dazzling sun rays: 'if there were discomfort in that, how could she tell that it were not part of her inward misery?' Dorothea's anger and resentment are intense: 'in such a crisis', the narrator remarks, 'some people begin to hate'. But the result of Dorothea's 'meditative struggle' shows that the ideal or spiritual side of her nature is still dominant: 'resolved submission' finally does come to supersede resentment and potential hatred as 'the noble habit of the soul reasserts itself'. This psychological process seems credible, even though it is insufficiently dramatised to be fully convincing. But it does not cover the full range of Dorothea's inner life – as the next chapter makes clear. As Dorothea drives away from Lydgate's home, where she has been startled to find Ladislaw alone with Rosamond, the only matter 'explicitly in her mind' is the errand concerning her unwell husband. But it is not what is in her mind, but what is in her feelings, that brings tears and 'a vague discomfort', and makes her 'confusedly unhappy': it is that the clear 'image' she has had of her desire now seems 'mysteriously spoiled'.

It is the following spring when Dorothea is next found in her boudoir, now become a compartment of the 'virtual tomb' in which she lives (ch. 48). She is reading inspirational literature to fuel her resolved submission to her shrunken life; but 'the sustaining thoughts which had become habits' are cold comfort. They seem 'to have in them the weariness of long future days in which she would still live with them for her sole companions'. It is 'another and a fuller sort of companionship' that she is 'hungering for', as well as for 'objects who could be dear to her, and to whom she could be dear'. It comes as no surprise that the only 'object' of her desire specifically named is Will Ladislaw. Two chapters later Casaubon has died and Dorothea learns for the first time of the codicil to his will. She is deeply affected by what she learns and feels a 'vague alarmed consciousness that her life was taking on a new form, that she is undergoing a metamorphosis'. At the same time – it is a striking notation – she feels 'a sudden strange yearning of heart towards Will Ladislaw'. The reason given is that before learning of the codicil 'it had never ... entered her mind that he could, under any circumstances, be her lover'. The narrator's explanation is correct, but incomplete; while it may not have entered Dorothea's conscious mind that Ladislaw could be her lover, he had sometime before been entered on her emotions as the object of her desire.

In chapter 54, after a three-month stay with her sister at Freshitt, Dorothea resolves to satisfy her 'great yearning' and 'deep longing' to return to live at Lowick. The reason she gives Celia is the wish to know the Farebrothers better, and to talk with Mr Farebrother about what needs to be done in Middlemarch. But the real reason is her longing to see Will Ladislaw: 'her soul thirsted to see him'. Before her husband's death Dorothea had noticed Ladislaw in the church at Lowick one Sunday. So intense is her desire for his presence that as she is about to enter the church for the first time after her return she has a hallucination, believing that he is sitting in the pew where he had sat before. In the same chapter Dorothea is once again found alone in her boudoir. The time is late morning; a map of her property and other documents are spread before her. But she is looking out along the avenue of limes to the distant fields. The familiar scene seems changeless to her and 'to represent the prospect of her life, full of motiveless ease – motiveless, if her own energy could not seek out reasons for ardent action'. The reason for her lack of energy is suggested in the next sentence, which notes the contrast between her 'heavy solemnity of clothing' – the widow's cap and black crape dress that Tantripp later calls her mistress's 'hijeous weepers' (ch. 80) – and her young face 'with its recovered bloom'. This is a deliberate repetition and conflation of the earlier pictorial contrasts between grey-clad Dorothea and voluptuous Ariadne in chapter 19 and frozen landscape and blooming youth in chapter 28. It suggests that Dorothea's sensuous emotional nature is still suppressed, and that she is still without a channel through which her longings can flow towards their desired object. Dorothea's reverie is interrupted by her maid's announcement that Ladislaw is below and would like to see her. As they greet each other, a 'deep blush which was rare in her' comes upon Dorothea 'with painful suddenness'. Will has come to announce that he is leaving Middlemarch, and before their brief interview is terminated by the arrival of Sir James Chettam she has time to ask him if he would like to take with him the miniature of his grandmother that hangs in the blue-green boudoir. Since he declines, the miniature is in its accustomed place when in the next chapter Dorothea takes it down from the wall, places it in her palm, makes a bed for it there, and leans her cheek against it. The narrator's comment is that 'she did not know then that it was Love who had come to her briefly, as in a dream before awaking'.

There is another telling repetition in chapter 62. As Dorothea is driving in her carriage, tears again begin to roll down her cheeks just as they had done in chapter 43. The reason is the same, Mrs Cadwallader having just informed her that 'Mr Orlando Ladislaw is making a sad dark-blue scandal by warbling continually with your Mr Lydgate's wife'. This comes just before the crucial sixth meeting alone between Dorothea and Will, at the climax of which Dorothea realises in 'one flash' that Ladislaw loves her and not someone else. Her first emotions are joy and a tremendous sense of release: 'it was as if some hard icy pressure had melted, and her consciousness had room to expand: her past was come back to her with larger interpretation'. But part of Dorothea's joy is disinterested, for she now knows that Ladislaw is not demeaning himself through a sordid entanglement with another man's wife. And her joy is not lessened but 'perhaps' made 'more complete' by what she feels certain is their 'irrevocable parting'. That is to say, even at this late point Dorothea's deepest emotions are sufficiently suppressed to keep her from fully realising that she loves and desires Ladislaw. Indeed, she is later said to entertain 'no visions of their ever coming into nearer union, and yet she had taken no posture of renunciation. She had accepted her whole relation to Will very simply as part of her marriage sorrows' (ch. 77). Such passive resignation is not the whole story of Dorothea's inner life, however, as she herself finally comes to realise when she again visits Lydgate's house and again discovers Ladislaw alone with Rosamond, this time in what appears a distinctly compromising situation.

Thus is precipitated Dorothea's night of sorrow in chapter 80. When she is once again alone, presumably in her blue-green boudoir, she is shaken by 'waves of suffering'. (In *Middlemarch* passion and sexual attraction come as electric shocks, while suffering and sorrowful compassion come in waves, as they did to Harriet Bulstrode in chapter 74.) She feels 'the clutch of inescapable anguish', presses her hands hard on the top of her head, and moans out: 'Oh, I did love him.' It is only now, 'with a full consciousness which had never awakened before', that 'she discover[s] her passion to herself'. Since Dorothea is now aware of her passion for Ladislaw she must assume a 'posture of renunciation'. This she successfully does and after a night of anguish, during which she looks 'into the eyes of sorrow' and is sustained by her store of 'vivid sympathetic experience' of the troubles of others, which returns to her now 'as a power'. By this time there is daylight in her room and Dorothea goes to the window:

> She opened her curtains, and looked out towards the bit of road that lay in view, with fields beyond, outside the entrance-gates. On the road there was a man with a bundle on his back and a woman carrying her baby; in the field she could see figures moving – perhaps the shepherd with his dog. Far off in the bending sky was the pearly light; and she felt the largeness of the world and the manifold wakings of men to labour and endurance. She was a part of that involuntary, palpitating life, and could neither look out on it from her luxurious shelter as a mere spectator, nor hide her eyes in selfish complaining.

This scene is of course emblematic. It is in fact a set piece that has close affinities with other key moments in nineteenth-century literature which describe or signify the transition from subjectivity to objectivity, from self-consciousness to the awareness of a life beyond self, of what Wordsworth in book 13 of *The Prelude* called the 'temperate show/Of objects that endure'. To cite only two examples: there is the climactic moment at the end of Tennyson's 'Holy Grail' idyll in which the unsought vision of an agricultural labourer, 'Who may not wander from the allotted field/Before his work be done', is presented as the positive alternative to the destructive spiritual quests of Arthur's knights; and there is the closing section of Tolstoy's *Anna Karenina,* in which a casual remark by a peasant changes the course of Levin's life and brings to at least a temporary end his fruitless speculations concerning the meaning of life.

For some readers of *Middlemarch*, what Dorothea sees when she opens the curtains is more stagey than emblematic and too contrived to be effective. It is certainly the case that Dorothea's epiphany (as it has been called) lacks the poetic intensity of the end of 'The Holy Grail' and the dramatic immediacy of the close of *Anna Karenina*. But those who find the moment forced have perhaps failed to notice how carefully George Eliot has prepared for it through the detailed notations in earlier chapters of what at different times and in different moods Dorothea has seen from the same window. What she sees in chapter 80 is significantly different, for her vision is no longer coloured by her mental state, as it was in the sunset vision of chapter 37, which was suffused with her spiritual yearnings, or in her view of the 'changeless prospect' in chapter 54, when Dorothea had projected into the landscape the sense of her own stagnant life. The landscape in chapter 80 rather contains human figures representative of the general life of ordinary humanity that instil in Dorothea a felt awareness of a meaning and purpose in ordinary human existence, and of a 'life beyond self' achieved through labour and endurance rather than through what have been called 'heroic exertions of the ego'.[13]

Dorothea's vision in chapter 80 is the climax of one strand in her development. The climax of the other – her learning the importance of feeling and emotional fulfilment – comes three chapters later in her final meeting with Ladislaw. The scene is not nearly as powerful and satisfying as many readers (including myself) would have liked it to be. This is because George Eliot has scripted the scene to point up the childlike qualities of Dorothea and Will. As the chapter opens, for example, the former has discovered that she has 'O dear! Nothing' to do in the village and turns to 'her particular little heap of books on political economy and kindred matters', on which she is entirely unable to concentrate. Then Ladislaw is announced by quaint little old Miss Noble, who fingers the tortoise-shell lozenge-box he had given her, thus assuring that his Peter Pan qualities will be foremost in the reader's mind. In addition, the script fails to include any detailed notation of Dorothea's thoughts and feelings. Her passion is suggested only indirectly through the too theatrical device of the vivid flashes of lightning. One reason for playing down this scene must have been to avoid suggesting that there was any active desire in Dorothea's coming together with Will, for any such suggestion would have run counter to the implications of her selfless vision in chapter 80. Thus, Eliot has the two stand 'with their hands clasped, like two children, looking out on the storm', and when they kiss 'tremblingly' has the narrator report that 'it was never known which lips were the first to move

towards the other lips'. Another reason is to underline the home-epic
simplicity of Dorothea and Will's union. The childlike qualities are not
pointed up for ironic purposes, as they were early in the novel, but rather
to help emphasise that the young woman of heroic spiritual ambition has
dwindled into someone more like her sister Celia than like St Theresa of
Avila.

At the end of the scene, Dorothea declares her willingness to embrace
what she thinks of as poverty, announcing in 'a sobbing childlike way,
"We could live quite well on my own fortune – it is too much – seven
hundred a year – I want so little – no new clothes – and I will learn what
everything costs"'. It is all quite charming and in its way affecting, but
one does regret that the scene is pitched in so minor a key, for it tends to
obscure the importance to Dorothea's story of her physical union with the
man she loves and desires. It was perhaps for this reason that in the finale
George Eliot was at pains to emphasise the fundamental importance of
Dorothea's emotional fulfilment. Dorothea and Will, the narrator says,
'were bound to each other by a love stronger than any impulses which
could have marred it. No life would have been possible to Dorothea
which was not filled with emotion, and now she had a life filled also with
... beneficent activity.' The beneficent activity is the afterglow of
Dorothea's vision in chapter 80 and the realisation of her distinctively
Victorian belief that 'if we had lost our own chief good, other people's
good would remain' (ch. 83). But Dorothea's 'chief good' is emotional
fulfilment, which she reaches through union with the object of her desire,
not through its renunciation. That is the deepest reason why 'the many
who knew her [who] thought it a pity that so substantive and rare a
creature should have been absorbed into the life of another' were never
able to state exactly 'what else that was in her power she ought rather to
have done'.

CHAPTER 7

The Parts and the Whole

Middlemarch *is a treasure-house of details, but it is an indifferent* *whole.*

Henry James

In March 1873, Henry James wrote a long letter to his American friend Grace Norton. At one point he brought up the subject of George Eliot's recently published novel. No, James had not written the review of *Middlemarch* in the *Nation*. His had been displaced at the eleventh hour by one 'which is doubtless better as going more into details'; but he hoped his review would appear elsewhere. The letter then continued:

> I wondered whether you were hearing anything about George Eliot. Her book, with all its faults, is, it seems to me, a truly immense performance. My brother William lately wrote me that he was 'aghast at its intellectual power'. This is strong – and what one says of Shakespeare. But certainly a marvellous *mind* throbs in every page of *Middlemarch*. It raises the standard of what is to be expected of women – (by your leave!) We know all about the female heart; but apparently there is a female brain, too ... I have read very little else this winter and written little, though something ... criticism of all kinds seems to me overdone, and I seriously believe that if nothing could be 'reviewed' for fifty years, civilization would take a great stride. To produce some little exemplary works of art is my narrow and lowly dream. They are to have less 'brain' than *Middlemarch*; but (I boldly proclaim it) they are to have more *form*.[1]

James's review did appear in a different periodical and, as we have seen, it contained high (but not unqualified) praise for *Middlemarch*. James's admiration remained high. According to Leon Edel, his biographer, the greatest tribute that James paid Eliot's novel was the writing of his own novel *The Portrait of a Lady* (1881), the single subject of which is a young American woman possessed of 'a certain nobleness of imagination' and of a 'finer mind' and 'larger perception' than 'most of the persons among whom her lot was cast' – in other words, a New World Dorothea Brooke.[2] In a certain sense, says Edel, the story of Isabel Archer affronting her

destiny can be called a 'George Eliot novel' written in the way James
believed she should have written.[3]

Another of James's 'little exemplary works of art' was *The Tragic Muse*
(1890). In the preface he added when the novel was republished in the
New York Edition of his works, James recalled its genesis and reviewed
the artistic decisions he had had to make. These reflections throw much
light on his notions of fictional form and his attitude to sprawling novels
like *Middlemarch*. James remembered debating with himself whether to
attempt to bring together into one work two separate stories or 'cases' –
one political, the other theatrical – that he had had in the back of his mind
for some time. He feared that 'the joining together of these interests,
originally seen as separate, might, all disgracefully, betray the seam, show
for mechanical and superficial. A story was a story, a picture a picture,
and I had a mortal horror of two stories, two pictures in one.' It was true
that he had on occasion seen two or more pictures in one, in 'certain
sublime Tintorettos at Venice', for example, one of which 'showed
without loss of authority half a dozen actions separately taking place'. But
this had clearly required 'a mighty pictorial fusion, so that the virtue of
composition had somehow thereby come all mysteriously into its own'.
Of course there would be no difficulty in bringing his two cases together
'if composition could be kept out of the question'. But this James could
not bring himself to do, for 'a picture without composition slights its most
precious chance for beauty'. In the absence of composition

> there may ... be life, incontestably, as [Thackeray's] 'The Newcomes'
> has life, as [Dumas's] 'Les Trois Mousquetaires', as Tolstoi's 'Peace
> and War', have it; but what do such large loose baggy monsters, with
> their queer elements of the accidental and the arbitrary, artistically
> *mean*? We have heard it maintained, we well remember, that such
> things are 'superior to art'; but we understand least of all what *that* may
> mean, and we look in vain for the artist, the divine explanatory genius,
> who will come to our aid and tell us. There is life and life, and as waste is
> only life sacrificed and thereby prevented from 'counting', I delight in
> a deep-breathing economy and an organic form. My business was
> accordingly to 'go in' for complete pictorial fusion, some such common
> interest between my two first notions as would, in spite of their birth
> under quite different stars, do them no violence at all.[4]

With these preoccupations, it is no wonder that James found
Middlemarch 'an indifferent whole'. Was he entirely fair to George Eliot's
'truly immense performance'? *Middlemarch* unquestionably has 'brain'
and has 'life', and just as certainly does not have 'a deep-breathing

economy' or a 'complete pictorial fusion' of its elements. But it does not necessarily follow that it lacks a distinctive form, that the whole is not greater than the sum of its parts, or that it should be added to the list of 'large loose baggy monsters' whose artistic meaning was obscure. After all, for a Victorian novelist, George Eliot was unusually concerned with the question of artistic form and with the design and wholeness of her compositions. There is, for example, her intriguing little essay of 1868, 'Notes on Form in Art'. In it Eliot is explicitly concerned with poetry, not with prose fiction. But poetry is considered 'in its wider sense as including all literary production' in which 'the choice & sequence of images & ideas – that is, of relations & groups of relations – are more or less not only determined by emotion but intended to express it'. This being so, it is not unreasonable to regard the essay as relevant to Eliot's theory of the novel and as containing 'important modifications of her earlier conceptions of realism in fiction'.[5]

For our present purpose the essay is particularly interesting because it addresses itself to the question of the fusion of two or more different stories, subjects or cases. 'Fundamentally, form is unlikeness'; it is that quality which makes something distinct from everything else. One could even say that 'every difference is form'. But with this 'fundamental discrimination is born in necessary antithesis the sense of wholeness or unbroken connexion'. Just as knowledge grows 'by its alternating processes of distinction & combination' (like the systole and diastole of Lydgate's scientific inquiry), so form grows through simultaneous additions of 'unlikenesses' and recognitions at a higher level of likenesses until one arrives at the conception of a whole 'composed of parts more & more multiplied & highly differenced, yet more & more absolutely bound together by various conditions of common likeness or mutual dependence'. Form was basically 'the limit of that difference by which we discriminate one object from another'; the 'highest Form' was found in that object (biological or artistic) in which 'the most varied group of relations [is] bound together in a wholeness'. 'Consensus' was the word used to describe the mutually dependent relationships among the parts of which the whole was composed. In Eliot's scientific terminology, the word expressed 'that fact in a complex organism by which no part can suffer increase or diminution without a participation of all other parts in the effect produced & a consequent modification of the organism as a whole'. In this view, 'forms of art can be called higher or lower only on the same principle as that on which we apply these words to organisms; viz. in proportion to the complexity of the parts bound up into one indissoluble whole'.[6]

Whether or not Eliot was thinking of her 'private projects about an English novel' when she wrote her 'Notes on Form in Art' in 1868, the essay does provide a terminology and a context that could be usefully employed by someone wishing to sort out the question of whether *Middlemarch* was or was not an indifferent whole. Since the essay was not published until 1963, Henry James did not have an opportunity to think about the novel in terms of it. It is unlikely that he would have altered his views, however, for in James's thinking about artistic form the analogy of visual art is dominant and it is not hard to imagine him saying disapprovingly of Eliot's essay and its dominant scientific model just what he said of *Middlemarch* in his review: that it is 'too often an echo of Messrs Darwin and Huxley'. Certainly one would never suppose from the 'Notes' alone that its author was a major creative artist, any more than after reading his *Poetics* one would suppose that Aristotle was. What is conspicuously absent in the 'Notes' is what is so excitingly present in James's writings on aesthetics: their intimate relation to his creative processes.

James could also not have read the several letters in which George Eliot expresses not a theoretical interest in artistic form but a practical concern with the shape and the wholeness of *Middlemarch*. In July 1871, for example, while still at work on the novel, she wrote to her publisher: 'I hope there is nothing that will be seen to be irrelevant to my design, which is to show the gradual action of ordinary causes rather than exceptional, and to show them in some directions which have not been from time immemorial the beaten track – the Cremorne walks and shows of fiction. But the best intentions are good for nothing until execution has justified them.' Over a year later, with her great labour finally completed, she observed:

> One healthy condition at least for me is that I have finished my book and am thoroughly at peace about it – not because I am convinced of its perfection, but because I have lived to give out what it was in me to give and have not been hindered by illness or death from making my work a whole, such as it is. When a subject has begun to grow in me I suffer terribly until it has wrought itself out – become a complete organism; and then it seems to take wing and go away from me.

In February 1873, at the end of a letter commenting on reviews of the novel, Eliot spoke of 'her ideal – to make matter and form an inseparable truthfulness'. And later the same year she reflected that

If it were true [that her novels fragmented easily], I should be quite stultified as an artist. Unless my readers are more moved towards the ends I seek by my works as wholes than by an assemblage of extracts, my writings are a mistake. I have always exercised a severe watch against anything that could be called preaching, and if I have ever allowed myself in dissertation or in dialogue [anything] which is not part of the *structure* of my books, I have there sinned against my own laws.[7]

While the degree of Eliot's concern with the design, wholeness and organic completeness of her novel was unusual in a Victorian novelist, it is commonly found in modern commentators on *Middlemarch*, for many of whom it seems axiomatic that unity is a prerequisite for artistic success and a *sine qua non* for a great work of literary art. As John Bayley has observed: 'The usual critical instinct is to show that the work under discussion is as coherent, as aware, as totally organised, as the critic desires his own representation of it to be.'[8] A flagrant example is found in W. J. Harvey's introduction to his widely used Penguin English Library edition of *Middlemarch*. Behind the patter of the following passage one can just see the critic rolling up his shirtsleeves and settling down to the skilled, no-nonsense performance of his ritual office, the demonstration of unity:

> with George Eliot, thanks largely to her philosophic power, all is disciplined to the demands of the whole. Certainly we enjoy the liveliness of individual characters - Casaubon, Mr Brooke, Mrs Cadwallader, Featherstone are all vivid creations - but they are only strands in a total pattern. Henry James was certainly right when he called *Middlemarch* a 'treasure-house of detail' [sic]; certainly wrong when he judged it 'an indifferent whole'. The novel's greatness lies in its overall design; in discussing this I shall break it down into what may be called the unities of narration, theme, society, and vision. But these categories, though convenient, must do less than justice to so well integrated a novel; George Eliot's philosophic vision is expressed through the fineness and sureness of her artistic powers.[9]

A transatlantic example of the same itch to establish the unity of *Middlemarch* is found in U. C. Knoepflmacher's *Religious Humanism and the Victorian Novel: George Eliot, Walter Pater and Samuel Butler*. Although his subject did not require any such commentary, Knoepflmacher none the less began his chapter on the novel with the following:

Middlemarch is the most organic of George Eliot's novels. Its Carlylean plot-'filaments' are so skillfully woven together that the critic who wants to unravel them is almost forced to echo Tertius Lydgate's complaint: 'I find myself that it's uncommonly difficult to make the right thing work: there are so many strings pulling at once.' The novel's 'strings' interlace into a three-dimensional web. Its scope, which produces the inevitable comparison with *War and Peace*, is achieved through the controlled motions of an unusually large number of characters, linked either by genealogical ties or by those intricate causal 'relations' George Eliot calls 'the irony of events'. Its depth, however, is produced through the creation of three concentric orbits or spheres of action. In the innermost sphere, four separate, yet complementary, plots are set in motion... In the next sphere the movement of these four plots is connected with the more slack 'provincial life' of the Middlemarch community. In the outermost sphere, the progression of the Middlemarchers is related to the advancement of the English nation as a whole through allusions to the social, religious, and scientific reforms of the period, and associated with the history of Western civilization through references to past events and discoveries, as well as to figures of tradition and myth... In *Middlemarch* the 'pulling strings', which even baffle the morphological expert Lydgate, are woven into a construct of which the final texture is different from and weightier than the mere sum of its parts.[10]

As these examples suggest, there are dangers and embarrassments involved in the critical preoccupation with unity – at least when the subject is *Middlemarch*. One of the principal dangers is the tendency to overemphasise form and design at the expense of content. The danger was warned against long ago by E. M. Forster in his *Aspects of the Novel*. (Forster was speaking specifically of the aesthetic principles and practice of Henry James, but his remarks apply equally well to the practice of the many modern critics who are the heirs of James's aesthetics.) 'A pattern must emerge', noted Forster, and 'anything that emerged from the pattern must be pruned off as wanton distraction. Who so wanton as human beings?' Can a rigid pattern 'be combined with the immense richness of material which life provides'? The answer was no, for 'the novel is not capable of as much artistic development as the drama: its humanity or the grossness of its material (use whichever phrase you like) hinder it. To most readers of fiction the sensation from a pattern is not intense enough to justify the sacrifices that made it.'[11]

Another danger is that a preoccupation with unity can lead to programmatic discourse, to the ignoring of patent discontinuities and of clear qualitative distinctions, and even to what might be called interpretative totalitarianism as the critic attempts to justify the presence of all features in a text and to demonstrate how they are significant and related to some putative totality – be it the organic whole of establishment criticism or the black hole of deconstructive criticism. Two small examples of the sometimes barbarous results of such critical operations are provided by the narrator of *Middlemarch* himself. One of them occurs in chapter 41 when he attempts to finesse a patently inorganic contrivance which is used to link two of the novel's principal plots. That the lost grandson of Mrs Dunkirk, Bulstrode's first wife, should have come to stay in the same Midlands town where Bulstrode himself has settled after leaving London is implausible enough. The coincidence is compounded when it is further revealed that Bulstrode's second wife, the sister of Mr Vincy, has a relation (Mr Featherstone) whose illegitimate son (Joshua Rigg) has had a stepfather (Raffles) who had many years before been a London associate of Bulstrode's and had connived with him to keep Mrs Dunkirk from learning of the existence of her daughter and grandson (Will Ladislaw). No wonder that George Eliot found it necessary to summarise the connections for herself in the 'Quarry for *Middlemarch*'. That she was keenly aware of the negative implications of this mishmash for the organic completeness of her novel is clear: at the beginning of the chapter in which Raffles makes his first appearance Eliot has her narrator make a pre-emptive intrusion:

Who shall tell what may be the effect of writing? If it happens to have been cut in stone, though it lie face downmost for ages on a forsaken beach, or 'rest quietly under the drums and tramplings of many conquests', it may end by letting us into the secret of usurpations and other scandals gossiped about long empires ago: – this world being apparently a huge whispering-gallery. Such conditions are often minutely represented in our petty lifetimes. As the stone which has been kicked by generations of clowns may come by curious little links of effect under the eyes of a scholar, through whose labours it may at last fix the date of invasions and unlock religions, so a bit of ink and paper which has long been an innocent wrapping or stop-gap may at last be laid open under the one pair of eyes which have knowledge enough to turn it into the opening of a catastrophe. To Uriel watching the progress of planetary history from the Sun, the one result would be just as much of a coincidence as the other.

The arch and laboured quality of this 'rather lofty comparison' makes it similar in kind to the unsuccessful intrusive generalisations examined in an earlier chapter. Particularly infelicitous is the tabloid sensationalism of the fourth sentence ('As the stone ...'). But since the particular piece of 'writing' in question turns out to be the note with Bulstrode's name on it that Raffles sticks in his brandy-flask the passage may be more particularly regarded as an example of factitious literary critical discourse in which the attempt is made to supply awkward features of a text with a significance and a 'meaning'. One notes particularly the flashy but non-substantive displays of erudition: the unidentified quotation about drums and tramplings; the references to acoustic effects like those in the dome of St Paul's Cathedral; and the allusion to another literary work – Milton's *Paradise Lost*, in the third book of which the angel Uriel, the 'regent of the sun', is described as having 'the sharpest sighted spirit of all in heaven'. None of this clumsy razzle-dazzle, however, can stop the recognition that the note in the brandy-flask is the node of a complex of coincidence glaringly out of place in a novel devoted to showing 'the gradual action of ordinary causes rather than exceptional'. And the figure of Uriel watching from the sun is additionally disruptive. In order to watch the earth from the sun the angel's sharp sight must have been endowed with telescopic powers. But, as we have seen, it is not telescopic but microscopic observation that makes possible the immanent (not transcendent) omniscience of the narrator's god's-eye view. That is to say, in the attempt to disguise one inorganic feature of *Middlemarch*, the narrator has introduced another.

The other passage in which through her narrator George Eliot supplies a literary critical gloss for an extraneous feature of the text is in chapter 35. It concerns Featherstone's droll blood-relations, his death and the reading of his two wills, to which matters chapters 32, 33 and 35 are devoted. The relatives have a small contribution to make to the social panorama side of *Middlemarch*, and are entertaining in their own right. In case the reader is slow to realise this, the narrator supplies cues, noting how often Mary Garth's lips curled with amusement as she remembered the relatives' 'drollery', and how Fred Vincy gave way to helpless laughter after observing two of them in the kitchen at Stone Court. Duration, however, is the enemy of amusement. Left on stage too long, the relatives become a conspicuous example of what Eliot admitted was her tendency to excess. Here is the passage in which she tries to turn a perceived sow's ear into a silk purse:

And here I am naturally led to reflect on the means of elevating a low subject. Historical parallels are remarkably efficient in this way. The chief objection to them is, that the diligent narrator may lack space, or (what is often the same thing) may not be able to think of them with any degree of particularity, though he may have a philosophical confidence that if known they would be illustrative. It seems an easier and shorter way to dignity, to observe that – since there never was a true story which could not be told in parables where you might put a monkey for a margrave, and vice versa – whatever has been or is to be narrated by me about low people, may be ennobled by being considered a parable; so that if any bad habits and ugly consequences are brought into view, the reader may have the relief of regarding them as not more than figuratively ungenteel, and may feel himself virtually in company with persons of some style. Thus while I tell the truth about loobies, my reader's imagination need not be entirely excluded from an occupation with lords; and the petty sums which any bankrupt of high standing would be sorry to retire upon, may be lifted to the level of high commercial transactions by the inexpensive addition of proportional ciphers.

Again the tone is forced, arch and self-conscious, and again the narrator strains to impute meaning and significance. The attempt this time involves a symbolic interpretation in which through conceptual transference something is made to stand for something else, as in pastoral or romance. But what this passage perhaps most resembles (surprising as it may initially seem) is one of the many digressions in Melville's *Moby-Dick*. Ishmael, its retrospective narrator, is committed to the principle that a certain significance lurks in all things, else all things are of little worth, and is continually attempting, sometimes through trial and error, to discover the meaning of the events and scenes he has observed and to find the right literary schema through which to re-present them to the reader. These attempts are an integral part of the movement of *Moby-Dick*, which was a self-conscious modernist novel long before its time. The case is quite different with *Middlemarch*, however. George Eliot's novel postulates a different relationship between narrator and subject and operates on very different principles, perhaps the most important of which is that the narrator is a historian describing 'real' events which are significant because they are part of the life of a particular time and place, not because they stand for something other than themselves. Again, one finds that, in the attempt to integrate extraneous material into her desired whole, George Eliot has only compounded the problem through her narrator's inept critical legerdemain.[12]

Few of the modern critical attempts to show that *Middlemarch* is a unified whole are as crude as the narrator's discourse in these two passages, but some of them are no more convincing. In thinking about these attempts it is useful to keep in mind Austin M. Wright's description of the 'four common ways' in which critics have attempted to describe the wholeness of a literary text. In the first, the *assertive*, 'unity is described – if at all – by metaphors and analogies, figures emphasizing the integrity of the whole but not usually distinguishing it from other wholes'. In the second, the *aggregative* way, 'unity is described by the enumeration of a series of recurring or limiting features found in the work'. Patterns of images, themes, motifs, point of view, setting, even language can all be regarded as 'unifying principles'; the critic tries to identify as many of these strands as possible in order to 'build a composite picture'. The third way is *reductive*: 'some relatively simple element with an obviously indivisible structure is abstracted from the work and is postulated as its unifying principle, which the critic then shows to be inherent in the work, connecting the element to as many details as possible'. The fourth way is the *hierarchical*: this method uses the second and third ways but 'arranges them in some order'.[13]

An example of the assertive way has already been seen in Knoepflmacher's fusillade of metaphors and analogies, and of the aggregative way in W. H. Harvey's synopsis of what he proposed to demonstrate concerning *Middlemarch*. An example of the reductive way is David Carroll's article, 'Unity through analogy: an interpretation of *Middlemarch*'. For Carroll, Dorothea Brooke's 'quest for a unifying principle' (ultimately found 'in the nature of one's relations with one's fellow human beings') is also the unifying principle of the novel. It is said to reappear in different guises in other places. The 'first analogy' is Casaubon's search for his Key to all Mythologies; a second is said to be provided by 'the workings of the historical imagination'. A third is Lydgate's search for 'unity in plurality in his anatomical investigations'. And, if one looks carefully enough, it is said that one can discover that the 'ramifications' of the novel's central theme are 'extensive', for 'almost every character in the novel has his or her own cosmology which serves as a guide or a warning to the central search'. The 'final analogy' is said to be provincial society 'becoming aware of its organic unity' and seeking a 'unity in plurality'.[14]

The unsatisfactory attempts of Harvey, Knoepflmacher and Carroll (all of whom were/are among the foremost contemporary commentators on Eliot's work) to demonstrate the unity of *Middlemarch* suggest that, for those for whom unity is the measure of greatness, *Middlemarch* presents a difficult problem. To make a cogent case for the unity of the novel a critic of exceptional skills is required. Mark Schorer was such a critic; his two discussions of unifying elements in *Middlemarch*, both examples of the hierarchical method, comprise perhaps the most compelling case yet made for the novel's wholeness. For Schorer, the novel 'creates a powerful effect of unity'; although 'the dramatic structure ... is not very taut, yet one feels, on finishing the book, that this is a superbly constructed work'. There are, says Schorer, four ways in which this effect is achieved. The most obvious is the introduction into nearly every one of its eight books of 'one large social scene, where representatives of the five stories are allowed to come together'. Of more importance is the fact that 'the major characterizations depend on a single value ... the quality and kind of social idealism as opposed to self-absorption; the minor characterizations create the stuff on which this idealism must operate'. The third means towards unity were the developments by which the major characters became enmeshed in social circumstances. This was the 'true plot' of *Middlemarch* and gave the novel its movement.

The fourth and most important means to unity was found in the language and style of the novel, which 'externalizes a mind and shows that mind to be one'. Of particular importance are the novel's images and metaphors. There were the many metaphors of unification and the many metaphors of antithesis ('the first represent yearnings, the second a recognition of fact'). These were connected with metaphors of appearance versus reality, order versus chaos, shape versus shapelessness, inner versus outer, freedom versus restraint. Another large group of figures related to progress: 'everyone and everything in this novel is moving on a "way"'. Another group were composed of 'complementary metaphors of hindrance to progress'. A fourth were metaphors having to do with purpose, shaping, forming, making, framing. Finally there were the metaphors that Schorer in an excellent phrase identified as those of 'muted apocalypse': the images of light, fire and burning, the frequent metaphors in which things are gloriously transformed, transfused or transfigured, and finally the many instances of George Eliot's 'unquestionably favorite word' – vision.[15]

Schorer's witness to the 'powerful effect of unity' in *Middlemarch* is admirable, but he is none the less much too partial and one-sided in his account of what one experiences in reading the novel. There is far too much detail in the text and far too many generic, genetic and qualitative discontinuities or incompatibilities for the novel to be considered in any meaningful way as a unified composition, a superbly constructed work, or a complete organism. The background noise in the novel includes an appreciable amount of what the narrator has to say directly to the reader.

The 'tempting range of relevancies called the universe' is never completely eschewed in the interests of concentration on 'this particular web'. The language of the narrator, moreover, is not only replete with clusters of images and metaphors; it is also full of a variety of impedimenta – learned allusions, scientific terminology, ponderous witticisms, uniquely penetrating observations, and a great deal of miscellaneous sparkle and dross – that so distracts one's attention from the images and metaphors that it takes a critic of great patience and subtlety first to cull them and then to call them tellingly to one's attention. But *Middlemarch* is simply too long and too dense for image patterns to have much cumulative effect on one's experience of the text. And the central metaphors tend to be deployed so frequently and predictably that they lose their suggestiveness and resonance. After the thirtieth or so appearance of 'ardour' or 'ardent', for example, what reader remembers, however subliminally, that there is fire at the root of the words?

Other examples of disunity in the novel include those features of the text that serve one of the novel's diverse purposes but not others. Much of the material that is excellently deployed for the purpose of filling in the picture of provincial life is to a greater or lesser extent inert when it is looked at from the point of view of theme or idea. In other places there is too much of a good thing, too many divergent points of interest. Take, for example, the Laure episode in chapter 15, which calls attention to a key aspect of Lydgate's character by revealing that before he came to Middlemarch his passionate nature had led him to make a serious misjudgement concerning the nature of women and that he had had first-hand experience of the fact that beautiful women who look as if they need the protection and support of a man can in fact be dangerous. Confusion is created because the three-page episode calls too much attention to itself and is too full of suggestive detail with divergent implications. There is the too striking juxtaposition of Lydgate one night leaving the frogs and rabbits used in his 'galvanic experiments' to go to the theatre at the Porte Saint Martin because of the electric effect on him of an actress 'with dark eyes, a Greek profile, and rounded majestic form'. There is the chilling nonchalance of Laure (the actress) who coolly explains that she meant to kill her husband – 'he wearied me; he was too fond' – and who dismisses Lydgate by observing: 'You are a good young man. But I do not like husbands. I will never have another.' For this Laure has received from some feminist critics a quite disproportionate amount of attention and admiration. One is also distracted by the fact that the melodrama during which she kills her husband is part of an episode which is itself stagey – an implausible and sensationalistic vignette out of keeping with its realistic context. (To realise this one has only to imagine Laure as an English actress whom Lydgate tracks down in Birmingham or Liverpool instead of Avignon.) Finally, and most important, there is the confusion created by the episode's effect on the reader's subsequent reaction to Lydgate's disastrous marriage and harsh fate. The Laure episode encourages the reader to feel that what happens to Lydgate is his own fault. Through his experience in France he had been forewarned about women like Laure and when he made the same mistake a second time he could be said to deserve what he got. A judgement along these lines would help a reader accept rather than criticise the iron law that one's good depends on the quality and breadth of one's emotion, which results in treasure for Ladislaw and the black spot for Lydgate. But it would do so at the heavy cost of increasing the distance between the reader and Lydgate, thereby lessening the intensity of one's sympathetic involvement in his unfolding fate and diluting an affective experience that the narrator believes is comparable to that of traditional tragedy.

Most of the principal discontinuities in the text of *Middlemarch* have been identified and discussed under different headings in earlier chapters: Fred Vincy, whose story sometimes gives the reader the sense of having been transported from Loamshire to Trollope's Barsetshire; the 'loud red figure' of Raffles, the *Doppelgänger* of Bulstrode; the ethereal Ladislaw, who never takes on flesh as do the other major characters; the rosy lens through which the gentry is viewed; and so on. Most important, there are the contrasting studies of Dorothea and Lydgate. Certainly their stories connect at many points and certainly there are many telling thematic counterpoints between them. But each figure nevertheless fills his or her own canvas, and if a pictorial analogy is called for it must be that of a diptych (on each panel of which a different representational style is used), not that of the 'mighty pictorial fusion' of a sublime Tintoretto. When Lydgate and Rosamond are conversing in the little house he rented for them to be so happy in, one forgets all about Dorothea; when she is meditating in her blue-green boudoir or looking from its window down the avenue of limes, the reader is concentrating solely on Dorothea and her inner life, and not at all on Lydgate and his. In chapter 30, Dorothea implores Lydgate to advise her concerning her husband's health. For years after he remembers this 'cry from soul to soul, without other consciousness than their moving with kindred natures in the same embroiled medium, the same troublous fitfully-illuminated life'. One would like to say that *Middlemarch* gave one the same consciousness of Dorothea and Lydgate as kindred natures moving in the same embroiled medium. But it does not.

Yet no 'loss of authority' (James's phrase) is involved in the incomplete fusion of the novel's materials. The histories of Dorothea and Lydgate may not be unified in an aesthetically satisfying way, but they none the less convey what James himself called 'that supreme sense of the vastness and variety of human life ... which it belongs only to the greatest novels to produce'. This same sense is further conveyed by the copious circumstantial detail with which Eliot filled her novel. Its purpose, as she explained in a letter, was to provide 'a sufficiently real back-ground' for a 'presentation' that would 'lay hold on the emotions as human experience'.[16] It was the felt representation of human experience, not the production of exemplary fictional artefacts, that was George Eliot's goal as an artist. In *Middlemarch* this goal was only attained at the cost of the novel's remaining what James quite correctly called an indifferent whole. Since this condition is the unavoidable result of the novel's historical, philosophical, psychological and moral richness, who would have it otherwise?

CHAPTER 8
Critical History

Signs are small measurable things, but interpretations are illimitable.
Middlemarch, ch.3

Anthony Trollope's autobiography, published in 1883, three years after George Eliot's death, included a chapter 'On English Novelists of the Present Day'. Trollope did not hesitate to rank Thackeray as the first of his contemporaries. Eliot was placed second and Dickens, 'the most popular novelist of my time', came third. Thackeray's pre-eminent ranking would not have been considered unusual if it had been made a quarter of a century earlier. George Eliot, for example, had said in 1857 that she regarded him, 'as I suppose the majority of people with any intellect do, on the whole the most powerful of living novelists'.[1] But that was at the beginning of her own career as a novelist. By the time Trollope came to do his sorting out he noted that 'at the present moment' it was George Eliot who was 'the first of English novelists'. He nevertheless ranked her second and gave the following reasons:

the nature of her intellect is very far removed indeed from that which is common to the tellers of stories. Her imagination is no doubt strong, but it acts in analysing rather than in creating. Everything that comes before her is pulled to pieces so that the inside of it shall be seen, and be seen if possible by her readers as clearly as by herself. This searching analysis is carried so far that, in studying her latter writings, one feels oneself to be in company with some philosopher rather than with a novelist. I doubt whether any young person can read with pleasure either *Felix Holt*, *Middlemarch*, or *Daniel Deronda*. I know that they are very difficult to many that are not young.

Her personifications of character have been singularly terse and graphic, and from them has come her great hold on the public, – though by no means the greatest effect which she has produced. The lessons which she teaches remain, though it is not for the sake of the lessons that her pages are read. Seth Bede, Adam Bede, Maggie and Tom Tulliver, old Silas Marner, and much above all, Tito, in *Romola*, are characters which, when once known, can never be forgotten. I

cannot say quite so much for any of those in her later works, because in
them the philosopher so greatly overtops the portrait-painter, that, in
the dissection of the mind, the outward signs seem to have been
forgotten ... It is not from decadence that we do not have another Mrs
Poyser, but because the author soars to things which seem to her to be
higher than Mrs Poyser.

It is, I think, the defect of George Eliot that she struggles too hard to
do work that shall be excellent. She lacks ease. Latterly the signs of this
have been conspicuous in her style, which has always been and is
singularly correct, but which has become occasionally obscure from
her too great desire to be pungent. It is impossible not to feel the
struggle, and that feeling begets a flavour of affectation.[2]

Trollope was not alone in recognising that at the time of her death Eliot
was regarded as the first of English novelists, nor in drawing a distinction
between the early and later work and preferring the former. Leslie
Stephen made the same points in the obituary article in the *Cornhill* in
1881. No one, Stephen felt sure, would disagree with his saying 'that the
work of her first period, the *Scenes of Clerical Life*, *Adam Bede*, *Silas
Marner*, and *The Mill on the Floss*, have the unmistakable mark of high
genius'. But when in her later period Eliot returned to the Midland
settings of her earlier work

she did not regain the old magic. *Middlemarch* is undoubtedly a
powerful book, but to many readers it is a rather painful book, and it
can hardly be called a charming book to any one. The light of common
day has most unmistakably superseded the indescribable glow which
illuminated the earlier writings ... nobody can read [*Middlemarch*]
without the sense of having been in contact with a comprehensive and
vigorous intellect, with high feeling and keen powers of observation.
Only one cannot help regretting the loss of that early charm. In reading
Adam Bede, we feel first the magic, and afterwards we recognise the
power which it implies. But in *Middlemarch* we feel the power, but we
ask in vain for the charm. Some such change passes over any great mind
which goes through a genuine process of development. It is not
surprising that the reflective powers should become more predominant
in later years; that reasoning should to some extent take the place of
intuitive perception; and that experience of life should give a sterner
and sadder tone to the implied criticism of human nature. We are
prepared to find less spontaneity, less freshness of interest in the little
incidents of life, and we are not surprised that a mind so reflective and

richly stored should try to get beyond the charmed circle of its early successes, and to give us a picture of wider and less picturesque aspects of human life. But this does not seem to account sufficiently for the presence of something jarring and depressing in the later work.[3]

The same qualitative distinction between Eliot's early and later work was commonly made in the decades following her death. There is a certain irony here, for while the high regard in which Eliot's novels were held during her life had reached its zenith with the publication of *Middlemarch*, the same novel, differently perceived and coupled with *Romola* and *Daniel Deronda*, contributed to the marked downswing in her posthumous reputation. So did the publication in 1885 of the three volumes of John Walter Cross's official biography, *George Eliot's Life as Related in Her Letters and Journals*. Cross was Eliot's second husband and had known her only during the last decade of her life – her sibylline years. Just as a decade later Hallam Tennyson would present a marmoreal image of Victoria's Laureate in his two-volume *Memoir*, so Cross offered a sombre, idealised portrait of a sententious moralist. For Gladstone, it was 'not a Life at all', but 'a Reticence in three volumes'. To William Hale White ('Mark Rutherford'), who had worked with Eliot at Chapman's for two years in the early 1850s and lived in the same house in the Strand, Cross's portrait was a serious distortion of the young woman he had known:

> To put it very briefly, I think he has made her too 'respectable'. She was really one of the most sceptical, unusual creatures I ever knew, and it was this side of her character which to me was the most attractive ... I can see her now, with her hair over her shoulders, the easy chair half sideways to the fire, her feet over the arms, and a proof in her hands, in that dark room at the back of No. 142, and I confess I hardly recognize her in the pages of Mr. Cross's – on many accounts – most interesting volumes. I do hope that in some future edition, or in some future work the salt and spice will be restored to the records of George Eliot's entirely unconventional life. As the matter now stands she has not had full justice done to her, and she has been removed from the class – the great and noble church, if I may so call it – of the Insurgents, to one more genteel, but certainly not so interesting.[4]

The influence of Cross's life, however, should not be overrated. The literary history of the last decades of the nineteenth century is to a considerable degree the story of the negative reaction of a younger

generation to their high Victorian forebears, and even without an official
biography it was inevitable that Eliot's reputation, together with the
esteem in which *Middlemarch* was held by her contemporaries, would
decline as Victoria's long reign entered its closing phase. The
handwriting was on the wall as early as 1873 when the young Samuel
Butler told Miss Savage: 'I am reading *Middlemarch* and have got
through two-thirds. I call it bad and not interesting: there is no sweetness
in the whole book, and, though it is stuffed full of epigrams, one feels that
they are lugged in to show the writer off. The book seems to me to be a
long-winded piece of studied brag, clever enough I daresay, but to me at
any rate singularly unattractive.'[5] During the next three decades literary
men seemed to go out of their way to give assurances that Eliot was not a
novelist worth reading. In one of his earliest surviving letters, for
example, William Butler Yeats explained why he would not even attempt
Middlemarch. Having read four of Eliot's books (*Silas Marner, Romola,
The Spanish Gypsy*, and a volume of selections) he had determined not to
read another. His seven reasons included these: 'She understands only
the conscious nature of man. His intellect, his morals, – she knows
nothing of the dim unconscious nature, the world of instinct'; 'Her
beloved analysis is a scrofula of literature. All the greatest books of the
world are synthetic, homeric'; 'She has morals but no religion. If she had
more religion she would have less morals'; 'She is too reasonable. I hate
reasonable people.'[6] There was very little on which Yeats and George
Bernard Shaw agreed, but a letter written in 1899 shows that (for quite
different reasons) Shaw was equally certain that Eliot had little to offer.
Her gift was to make 'pictures of English life in the Midlands'. This gift
had been 'paralyzed by the fatalism which was the intellectually morally-
snobbishly correct thing among advanced people in her day'. Decades
later, Shaw returned to the subject in a postscript to *Back to Methuselah*:

> George Eliot ... who, incredible as it now seems, was during my
> boyhood ranked in literature as England's greatest mind, was broken
> by the fatalism that ensued when she discarded God. In her most
> famous novel *Middlemarch*, which I read in my teens and almost
> venerated, there is not a ray of hope: the characters have no more
> volition than billiard balls: they are moved only by circumstances and
> heredity. 'As flies to wanton boys are we to the gods: they kill us for
> their sport' was Shakespeare's anticipation of George Eliot.[7]

It was Eliot's moralising rather than her fatalism which set William
Ernest Henley's teeth on edge: 'It was thought that with George Eliot the

Novel-with-a-Purpose had really come to be an adequate instrument for the regeneration of humanity. It was understood that Passion only survived to point a moral or provide the materials of an awful tale, while Duty, Kinship, Faith were so far paramount as to govern Destiny and mould the world.'[8] Yet another cocky animadversion came from George Moore. In the first edition of his breezy autobiographical memoir, *Confessions of a Young Man* (1888), Moore recalled that as a 'really young' man he had 'hungered after great truths: *Middlemarch, Adam Bede, The Rise and Fall of Rationalism, The History of Civilisation*, were momentous events in my life'. He also had flattering things to say about Eliot's novels in comparison with Hardy's. Moore, however, always knew which way the winds of literary fashion were blowing. When he came to write a preface to the revised 1904 edition of his *Confessions* he observed that he would have had 'nothing to regret, nothing to withdraw', were it not 'for a silly phrase about George Eliot, who surely was no more than one of those dull clever people, unlit by any ray of genius'[9].

There was a comparable ebbing of Eliot's reputation among critics. In his *Corrected Impressions* (1895), George Saintsbury identified *The Mill on the Floss* as Eliot's best novel; *Felix Holt* and *Middlemarch* were 'elaborate studies of what seemed to the author to be modern characters and society – studies of immense effort and erudition not unenlightened by humour, but on the whole dead'.[10] And in his *Short History of English Literature*, which first appeared in 1898 and was often reprinted during the next three decades, Saintsbury gave Eliot only two paragraphs. He did, however, observe that her present reputation was too low and thought that it was 'probable that her four first books in fiction, with passages in all her later, will gradually recover for her, and leave her safely established in, a high position among the second class of English novelists, those who have rather observed than created, rather unlocked a hoard of experience than developed a structure of imagination, who have no very good or attractive style, but write clearly and with knowledge'.[11] In his *Makers of English Fiction* (1905), W. J. Dawson endorsed the view that after Eliot's first four works of fiction there was a steep decline: '*Romola* marks her decadence as an artist, and betrays exhaustion. In *Middlemarch* this decadence is still more pronounced, and it is complete in the utterly tedious *Daniel Deronda*. The reason for this decadence is plain ... George Eliot took herself too seriously as a teacher to maintain for any long period the true freshness and spontaneity of the artist.'[12]

It is true that other commentators were more positive and more insightful. In his *Victorian Prose Masters* (1901), W. C. Brownell began by trying to account for 'one of the most curious of current literary phenomena': the neglect into which 'so little negligible a writer ... has indubitably fallen'. *Middlemarch* was, after all, a novel 'anyone can praise'. In fact, it was 'probably the "favourite novel" of most "intellectual" readers among us – at least those who are old enough to remember its serial appearance'. The reason seemed to be that, while Eliot stood 'at the head of the psychological novelists', the novelty of the psychological form had worn off, revealing her limitations and defects. Her intellectual preoccupations were 'fatal to action'. Very little happened in her novels, certainly less 'than in the world of any other writer of fiction of the first rank'. Her characters tended to be products of intellect, not of imagination, 'the result of the travail of the mind, the incarnation of an idea, not the image of a vision'. They consequently had less vitality and less reality than they would otherwise have had. As for her style, one spoke of it 'as of the snakes of Ireland. She has no style ... No one will ever read her for the sensuous pleasure of the process.'[13] Eliot's intellectual preoccupations were also seen as a limitation by two other sympathetic commentators, both of whom felt that *Middlemarch* somehow fell short of real greatness. For Leslie Stephen, whose English Men of Letters volume on Eliot came out in 1902, the reason was that

> she seems to be a little out of touch with the actual world, and to speak from a position of philosophical detachment which somehow exhibits her characters in a rather distorting light. For that reason *Middlemarch* seems to fall short of the great masterpieces which imply a closer contact with the world of realities and less preoccupation with certain speculative doctrines. Yet it is clearly a work of extraordinary power, full of subtle and accurate observation; and gives, if a melancholy, yet an undeniably truthful portraiture of the impression made by the society of the time upon one of the keenest observers, though upon an observer looking at the world from a certain distance, and rather too much impressed by the importance of philosophers and theorists.[14]

The same note was later struck by Oliver Elton in his *Survey of English Literature, 1830–1880* (1920). For Elton the novel was 'almost one of the great novels of the language. A little more ease and play and simplicity, a little less of the anxious idealism which ends in going beyond nature, and it might have been one of the greatest ... There is no plan, but there is no confusion ... *Middlemarch* is a precious document for the provincial life of that time, vaguely astir with ideas, but promptly sinking back into its beehive routine.'[15]

In 1922, Edmund Gosse published a collection of *Aspects and*

Impressions. The first was of George Eliot and may be regarded as the swansong of the turn-of-the-century depreciations of her work. Gosse began less than gallantly by recalling the glimpses he had caught of the novelist during the late 1870s: 'a large, thickset sybil [sic], dreamy and immobile, whose massive features, somewhat grim when seen in profile, were incongruously bordered' by a fashionable Parisian hat, a contrast that had 'something pathetic and provincial about it'. He went on to assert that Eliot's fame during the last decades of her life had been 'a solemn ... portentous thing ... supported by the serious thinkers of the day, by the people who despised mere novels, but regarded her writings as contributions to philosophical literature'. Gosse's contemporaries, however, were 'sheep that look up to George Eliot and are not fed by her ponderous moral aphorisms and didactic ethical influence'. The predictable discrimination between the early and the later novels was made: 'her failure ... began when she turned from passive acts of memory to a strenuous exercise of intellect'. As for *Middlemarch*, it was

> constructed with unfailing power, and the picture of commonplace English country life which it gives is vivacious after a mechanical fashion, but all the charm of the early stories has evaporated, and has left behind it merely a residuum of unimaginative satire. The novel is a very remarkable instance of elaborate mental resources misapplied, and genius revolving, with tremendous machinery, like some great water-wheel, while no water is flowing underneath it.[16]

It was not until 1919, the centenary of her birth, that the qualitative distinction between George Eliot's early novels and her later ones, and the consequent devaluation of *Middlemarch*, which had been reiterated by critics ever since Leslie Stephen's obituary article, was finally challenged by a critic of distinction and authority. Virginia Woolf, the daughter of Leslie Stephen, had agreed to do a centenary article on George Eliot for *The Times Literary Supplement* and for that purpose had undertaken a reading of all the novels. The doyenne of Bloomsbury was surprised by what she found. 'Do you ever read George Eliot?' she asked a correspondent in October. 'Whatever one may say about the Victorians, there's no doubt they had twice our – not exactly brains – perhaps hearts. I don't know quite what it is; but I'm a good deal impressed.' In her splendid essay, which appeared the following month, Virginia Woolf had high praise for the early novels: 'Over them all broods a certain romance, the only romance that George Eliot allowed herself – the romance of the past. These books are astonishingly readable and have no trace of pomposity or pretense.' But, while the early books had a 'ruddy light', the later ones had a 'searching power and reflective richness':

> to the reader who holds a large stretch of her early work in view it will become obvious that the mist of recollection gradually withdraws. It is not that her power diminishes, for, to our thinking, it is at its highest in the mature *Middlemarch*, the magnificent book which with all its imperfections is one of the few English novels written for grown-up people.[17]

Despite this encomium, Eliot's reputation, and that of her principal novel, remained in eclipse during the 1920s and 1930s. As David Cecil observed in his 1934 study, *Early Victorian Novelists: Essays in Revaluation*:

> she is not admired so much as Charlotte Brontë; she is not even admired so much as Trollope. In spite of the variety of her talents and the width of her scope, in spite of the fact that she is the only novelist of her time who writes on the scale of the great continental novelists, the only novelist who holds the same conception of her art which is held to-day, her reputation has sustained a more catastrophic slump than that of any of her contemporaries. It is not just that she is not read, that her books stand on the shelves unopened. If people do read her they do not enjoy her. It certainly is odd.

The reason for this oddity was said to be Eliot's too 'exclusively moral point of view', which made her 'confront human nature a little like a schoolteacher; kindly but just, calm but censorious ... Victorian ethical rationalism is the least inspiriting of creeds.' As this suggests, Cecil's discussion of Eliot was not only a diagnosis of her diminished reputation; it was also a symptom of it. Cecil did praise *Middlemarch* warmly: it was George Eliot's 'masterpiece' and had

> the biggest subject of any English classical novel. Like Tolstoy in *War and Peace*, she shows us the cosmic process, not just in a single drama but in several; not only in an individual but in a whole society. The principles of moral strength and weakness which in her view are the determining forces of life, exhibit themselves at their work in the lives of four diverse and typical representatives of the human race.

None the less, he did not think that Eliot's 'loss of reputation was wholly undeserved':

Even if we do strain ourselves to acquiesce in her point of view, we do not feel her the supreme novelist that her contemporaries did. Her books never give us that intense unalloyed pleasure we get from the greatest masters. Though like Tolstoy she is an interesting critic of life, though she constructs well like Jane Austen, though like Dickens she creates a world, yet when we set her achievement in any of these lines beside those of these famous competitors, we feel something lacking. Somehow we are dissatisfied.

It is easy to see why she fails to stand a comparison with Tolstoy. Her vision of life is smaller. She knows about life in provincial nineteenth-century England, life in Middlemarch, the life of merchants and doctors and squires and humble clergymen and small town politicians: she does not know about the savage or sophisticated, about artists and adventurers and the world of fashion and affairs. Even in *Middlemarch*, there are certain things she does not see. Her assiduously intellectual view made her oblivious of the irrational instinctive aspects of human nature. She can enter into its deliberate purposes and its conscientious scruples, but not into its caprices, its passions, its mysticism ... Moreover, like all Victorian rationalists, she is a Philistine. She pays lip-service to art, but like Dorothea Brooke confronted with the statues of the Vatican, she does not really see why people set such a value on it. Constructed within so confined an area of vision, it is inevitable that her criticism of life is inadequate. Compared to Tolstoy's it seems petty, drab, provincial. *Middlemarch* may be the nearest English equivalent to *War and Peace*, but it is a provincial sort of *War and Peace*.[18]

It was not until after the Second World War that Eliot's reputation, and that of *Middlemarch*, began to rise to its present level. The upswing was part of a general return to favour of the Victorians. In 1948, Humphry House cited the 'present popularity' of George Eliot as one of a number of examples of renewed interest in the period. One reason for the revival was said to be that information about the lives of the 'thinkers, artists, poets, novelists, architects, churchmen' of the period was finally becoming available. Such knowledge was 'necessary for understanding a whole personality; and with the Victorians ... the whole personality does need understanding before the work can be properly understood'.[19] In the case of George Eliot, however, substantial new information about the person behind the work only became available in 1954–5 with the publication of seven volumes of Gordon S. Haight's monumental edition of *The George Eliot Letters*.

A more specialised reason for the increased interest in Eliot and her novels was the recognition of their usefulness to historians, both historians of ideas and social historians. In his *Nineteenth-Century Studies: Coleridge to Matthew Arnold* (1949), Basil Willey included two substantial chapters on Eliot's intellectual development. The first began with a sketch of her exemplary status:

Probably no English writer of the time, and certainly no novelist, more fully epitomizes the century; her development is a paradigm, her intellectual biography a graph, of its most decided trend. Starting from evangelical Christianity, the curve passes through doubt to a reinterpreted Christ and a religion of humanity: beginning with God, it ends in Duty. George Eliot's representative quality is due largely to her unique position, amongst imaginative writers, as a focus for the best (and the worst) that was being said and thought in her time, in Europe as well as at home. No one was more thoroughly abreast of the newest thought, the latest French or German theory, the last interpretations of dogma, the most up-to-date results in anthropology, medicine, biology, or sociology.[20]

On the social history side, Asa Briggs's important article on '*Middlemarch* and the doctors' (1948) argued that there were cogent reasons for the serious examination of Eliot's novel by students of nineteenth-century society. Eliot had 'the gifts of an historian. Her return to sources was followed by a faithful reconstruction.' For a proper understanding of the 'vital forces in the making of Victorian society ... the historian will find George Eliot's novels of far more value than many other well-established sources'. The treatment of 'the effect of our "imperfect social state" on young and noble impulses makes *Middlemarch* the great novel that it is'; 'in exploring *Middlemarch*, we [social historians] shall be learning how to explore England as well'.[21]
with V. S. Pritchett's essay on George Eliot in *The Living Novel* (1946). For Pritchett, 'no Victorian novel approaches *Middlemarch* in its width of reference, its intellectual power, or the imperturbable spaciousness of its narrative'. Its great scenes were 'exquisite, living transpositions of real moral dilemmas ... there is a humane breadth and resolution in this novel which offers neither hope nor despair to mankind, but simply the necessity of fashioning the moral life'.[22] A more decisive critical event was the publication in 1948 of F. R. Leavis's famous revaluation, *The Great Tradition*, which identified Jane Austen, George Eliot, Henry James, Joseph Conrad and D. H. Lawrence as the great novelists in English. A

good part of Leavis's section on George Eliot was devoted to *Middlemarch*. The keynote was Eliot's 'genius' as manifested 'in a profound analysis of the individual'. The treatment of Casaubon, for example, was 'wholly strong' and 'could have been done only by someone who knew the intellectual life from the inside'. The same was true of the treatment of Lydgate, another 'complete success'. In praising the character of Rosamond, it was 'tribute enough to George Eliot to say that the destructive and demoralizing power of [her] triviality wouldn't have seemed so appalling to us if there had been any animus in the presentment'. As for Bulstrode, his treatment involved 'some of the finest analysis any novel can show; [it] is a creative process; it is penetrating imagination, masterly and vivid in understanding, bringing the concrete before us in all its reality'. But Leavis's panegyric ceased abruptly when he turned to the treatment of Dorothea Brooke, the 'weakness' in *Middlemarch*. The problem was a certain residual immaturity in George Eliot that led to her 'unqualified self-identification' with her heroine, who was 'a product of George Eliot's own "soul-hunger" – another day-dream ideal self'. This complaisant indulgence was 'disconcerting in the extreme. We have an alternation between the poised impersonal insight of a finely tempered wisdom and something like the emotional confusions and self-importances of adolescence.'[23]

In his 1951 *Introduction to the English Novel*, Arnold Kettle disagreed with Leavis's analysis: 'in spite of all our reservations it is Dorothea who, of all the characters in the novel, most deeply captures our imagination'. The reason was that it is she 'alone who, with Ladislaw, successfully rebels against the Middlemarch values'. The remark indicates Kettle's Marxist perspective and points towards his principal reservation about *Middlemarch*: 'though in some respects the most impressive novel in our language and one which it is not ridiculous to compare with the novels of Tolstoy, [it] is not in any sense a revolutionary work'. There was in addition 'a contradiction at the heart of *Middlemarch*, a contradiction between the success of the parts and the relative failure of the whole ... The total effect is immensely impressive but not immensely compelling. Our consciousness is modified and enriched but not much changed.' *Middlemarch* ultimately lacked 'the most important thing of all, that final vibrant intensity of the living organism'. This deficiency was said to have the same root as the novel's lack of a revolutionary dimension: in Eliot's 'philosophy, her consciously formulated outlook, there is no place for the inner contradiction'. She had 'an absorbing sense of the power of society but very little sense of the way it changes. Hence her moral attitudes, like her social vision, tend to be static.' Eliot's 'high-minded moral seriousness ... does have an unfortunate effect on the novel, not because it is moral or serious, but because it is mechanistic and undialectical'.[24]

Kettle's provocative reading appeared three years after Joan Bennett's *George Eliot: Her Mind and Her Art* (1948). Given the priorities indicated in the subtitle, it was not surprising to find her claiming that Eliot's later works appealed to 'the modern reader' more than the early ones, nor to find her endorsing the 'opinion ... shared by most modern critics': that *Middlemarch* was the author's masterpiece. But Joan Bennett became vaguely assertive when she attempted to explain why the novel was Eliot's 'supreme achievement':

> while its characters are at least as various and as deeply studied as any she has created, they are more perfectly combined into a single whole than those in any other of her novels. Nothing here is irrelevant or over-elaborated. Each character reveals itself in the sequence of events with such consistency with its own nature as wins the reader's complete assent. The imagination of the author seems to be wholly engaged in discovering what each one would be doing or saying in the special circumstances of each scene or episode. And yet every one of them has a function in the whole design.[25]

Walter Allen was altogether more professional, and more telling, in his judgement of *Middlemarch* in his excellent *The English Novel: A Short Critical History* (1954), though the moral gymnasium reference (borrowed from W. E. Henley) does smack of the genteel impressionism of David Cecil:

> George Eliot is seen at her greatest in *Middlemarch*. Not all her qualities are manifest in it; it lacks the charm of the first part of *The Mill on the Floss* and *Silas Marner*, and the humour is much more severely controlled. But it expresses, as the earlier books do not, a complete experience of life, experience in the widest sense, imaginative and intellectual alike. The view of life expressed is a sombre one, and one that cannot be wholly accepted: much of value is lost if, as George Eliot seems to conceive it, life is seen as primarily a gymnasium for the exercise of the moral faculties.

Perhaps this is not much more than to say that George Eliot has to pay the price of her earnestness. One says it is excessive, yet, fused with her remarkable imagination and her intellectual power, it made her the great novelist she is. It meant that she had a comprehensive view of life, a view that could take in every variety of experience that she knew.

And, like an ardently held religious belief, it made every action of her characters important. Agnostic though she was, it isn't going too far to say that in this sense she is a religious novelist, as Bunyan is, or Mauriac today. In consequence, the characters themselves achieve a new importance in her novels, almost as though their eternal well-being is constantly in the balance. And one of the signs of this new importance of the characters is her relentless and scrupulous analysis of them: when we meet Dorothea, Casaubon, and Lydgate we realize that it is the very thoroughness and intensity of her analysis that creates them. This is something new in English fiction, which later novelists, such as Gissing and Henry James, Conrad and Lawrence, were to take up. It is indeed precisely here that her essential modernity lies.[26]

At the end of the 1950s two complementary studies of George Eliot's art appeared: Barbara Hardy's *The Novels of George Eliot: A Study in Form* (1959) and W. J. Harvey's *The Art of George Eliot* (1961). The aim of both was to make a case for seeing Eliot as a 'great formal artist'. As Barbara Hardy explained in her introduction, modernist notions of narrative form derived from the dicta and examples of Flaubert and Henry James (which emphasised 'showing' as opposed to 'telling'). This aesthetic had been in the ascendant for the past thirty years; Percy Lubbock's influential *The Craft of Fiction* (1921), for example, did not even mention George Eliot. The time had come to show that Eliot was not a writer of what Henry James called 'large loose baggy monsters', but a sophisticated and accomplished artist whose composition, for example, 'is usually as complex and as subtle as the composition of Henry James or Proust or Joyce, but it is very much less conspicuous because of the engrossing realistic interest of her human and social delineation'.[27] Hardy's and Harvey's influential books, both of which had much to say about *Middlemarch*, were part of a new climate of critical opinion that regarded the novel not only as George Eliot's masterpiece, but also as more than any other text the great English novel. In 1958, for example, Angus Wilson began an important analysis of the state of postwar English fiction by observing:

> if English critics of the novel and English novelists to-day were asked to list in order of excellence the English novels of the past, I imagine that, although *Middlemarch* might not appear at the top of every list, it would secure a high place in all entries. Thirty years ago, of course, it might well have been entirely omitted ... there is a quality about *Middlemarch* which permits it alone of great English novels to pass all but very few

contemporary tests, and this despite its obvious and widely recognized weaknesses.[28]

Four years later, David Daiches spoke of George Eliot as 'one of the very greatest of English novelists and *Middlemarch* in particular as one of the supreme classics of European fiction'.[29] And, in 1967, Barbara Hardy echoed Angus Wilson when she observed in the introduction to a collection of essays on the novel: 'if a poll were held for the greatest English novel there would probably be more votes for *Middlemarch* than for any other work'. One of her contributors reflected that given 'our present-day enthusiasm for the work[,] it is not without reason that we are reproached, as a modern critic has said, for thinking that every novel would be *Middlemarch* if it could'.[30] And, in 1970, Raymond Williams could find little to add to the chorus of critical praise: '*Middlemarch* as a whole is a superb presentation, a superb analysis ... As a way of seeing, it is so powerfully composed that it creates its own conditions, enacts and re-enacts its own kind of achievement. It has been praised so often in just that sense that I don't need to add any other tributary adjectives.'[31]

Barbara Hardy's collection may be taken to mark the high point of the modern reputation of *Middlemarch*. But the novel still continues to have exalted and exemplary status. As David Lodge remarked in 1981:

> *Middlemarch* has achieved a unique status as both paradigm and paragon in discussion of the novel as a literary form. If a teacher or critic wishes to cite a representative example of the nineteenth-century English novel at its best, the chances are that it will be *Middlemarch*. Indeed it is scarcely an exaggeration to say that, for many critics, *Middlemarch* is the only truly representative, truly great Victorian novel – all other candidates, including the rest of George Eliot's fiction, being either too idiosyncratic or too flawed.[32]

Lodge made these observations in an essay in which he took issue with Colin MacCabe's description of the novel (in his *James Joyce and the Revolution of the Word*, 1978) as a 'classic realist text' which purports to represent experience through language. In such a text there is 'a specific hierarchy of discourses which places the reader in a position of dominance with regard to the stories and characters'. At the apex of discourses is a narrative 'meta-language', which interprets and controls the other discourses, ensures that interpretations are not illimitable, and creates the illusion that it is providing 'a window on reality'.[33] The point of Lodge's essay was to show that the surface of *Middlemarch* is a good deal less controlled and unproblematic than MacCabe suggested. In his conclusion, in an idiom borrowed from reader-response criticism, Lodge adumbrated another way in which the greatness of Eliot's novel could be accounted for: 'it is precisely because the narrator's discourse is never entirely unambiguous, predictable, and in total interpretative control of the other discourses in *Middlemarch* that the novel survives, to be read and re-read, without ever being finally closed or exhausted'.[34]

In recent years *Middlemarch* has begun to draw the fire of some of the loudest guns on the contemporary critical front: feminist criticism on the one hand; post-structuralist and deconstructive criticism on the other. Since neither battery has ceased fire it would be premature to attempt an assessment of the damage. But the pyrotechnics have been dazzling and in their light long-familiar features of Eliot's novel have looked very different. I shall take the feminist criticism first. In her provocative 1970 study, *Sexual Politics*, Kate Millett had dismissed George Eliot as one who had lived the feminist revolution but had not written about it: 'Dorothea's predicament in *Middlemarch* is an eloquent plea that a fine mind be allowed an occupation; but it goes no further than petition. She married Will Ladislaw and can expect no more of life than the discovery of a good companion whom she can serve as secretary.'[35] Two years later, in a critical *cri de coeur*, Lee R. Edwards announced that Eliot's novel 'can no longer be one of the books of my life'. When she had read the novel as an adolescent she had thought its ending offered the hopeful possibility of 'combining marriage with intellectual aspiration'. But she subsequently came to see matters in a different light:

> The objection is not that Dorothea should have married Will but that she should have married anybody at all, that she should ultimately be denied the opportunity given Will to find her own paths and forge her energies into some new mold ... We could perhaps have had this vision [of a new and bigger world] if the author had held the mirror to reflect not only the world both she and Dorothea knew and left behind but also that one she forced into existence when she stopped being Mary Ann Evans and became George Eliot instead. In *Middlemarch*, however, George Eliot refuses this option and accepts a safety not entirely celebrated but rather tinged with resignation, ambivalently regarded.[36]

In 1976, in an article entitled 'Why feminist critics are angry with George Eliot', Zelda Austen cast a cool eye on the complaints of Millett and Edwards. The source of their anger was obvious: Eliot's 'failure to allow her heroines any happy fulfillment other than marriage' – for example, the freedom that she had herself achieved. When Eliot depicted 'the misery of the unconventional heroine and the placidity of conventional wives and mothers, she was also sanctioning the norm and making it normative'. Nevertheless, 'to reject *Middlemarch* out of hand because it does not portray the possibility of an independent life for women is absurd'. The feminist critics 'who reject George Eliot have defined liberation for women in terms of intellectual and economic independence – in other words separate self-fulfillment'. But this was too limited a vision in itself as well as being foreign to Eliot's view of human existence.[37]

As these examples suggest, for some feminist commentators *Middlemarch* can be more a pretext for the airing of their own passionately intense convictions and aspirations than a text to be rigorously analysed from a fresh methodological perspective. This is not true of the copious interpretative discourse of Sandra M. Gilbert and Susan Gubar, whose enormous study, *The Madwoman in the Attic: The Woman Writer and the Nineteenth-Century Literary Imagination* (1979), includes an extremely fresh and interesting reading of *Middlemarch*. For Gilbert and Gubar, the novel is 'fundamentally concerned with the potential for violence in the two conflicting sides of [George Eliot] that she identifies as the masculine mind and the feminine heart ... the novel is centrally concerned with the tragic complicity and resulting violence of men and women inhabiting a culture defined as masculine'. Dorothea Brooke's first husband was Casaubon, in whom is said to be found a demonstration of 'the inextricable link between male culture and misogyny'. Similar links are discovered in the other male characters in the novel, even Mr Brooke: 'with his smattering of unconnected information, his useless classicism, and his misogynistic belief in the biological inferiority of Dorothea's brain, Brooke is a dark parody of Casaubon'. As for Dorothea's 'female renunciation', George Eliot 'does not countenance [it] because she believes it to be appropriately feminine, but because she is intensely aware of the destructive potential of female rage'. Eliot knew there was 'bad faith involved in Christian resignation' and emphasised the point through Bulstrode, who is 'a demonic parody of Dorothea, one who reveals both the deathly implications and the potential bad faith of this heroine's saintly renunciation'. As for Rosamond, 'in spite of the narrator's condemnation of her narrow narcissism ... it is clear that [she] enacts Dorothea's silent anger against a marriage of death'. Rosamond is the 'demonic center' of *Middlemarch* and the climax of the novel occurs neither in chapter 80 (Dorothea's night of sorrow and her morning epiphany) nor in chapter 83 (the union of Dorothea and Will). It rather comes in the meeting between Dorothea and Rosamond in chapter 81: this 'brief moment of sisterhood' was the showing forth of 'the heroism of sisterhood within patriarchy'. As for Dorothea's second husband: Ladislaw was 'Eliot's radically anti-patriarchal attempt to create an image of masculinity attractive to women ... in his romance with Dorothea, Eliot substitutes the equality of a brother/sister model for the hierarchical inadequacy of father/daughter relationships'.[38]

J. Hillis Miller was perhaps the first, and is certainly the best known, critic to analyse *Middlemarch* from a deconstructive point of view. In his 1974 article 'Narrative and history' he began by noting the 'curious tradition, present in the middle-class novel from its sixteenth-century beginnings on, whereby a work of fiction is conventionally presented not as a work of fiction but as some other form of language'. The most common displacement was for the novelist to present his work as a form of history. By doing so he avoided the connotations of gratuitousness and mendacity involved in the word 'fiction' and at the same time affirmed 'that verisimilitude, that solid basis in pre-existing fact which is associated with the idea of history'. *Middlemarch* was solidly within this tradition 'and in fact might be taken as the English masterpiece' of the genre of realistic fiction. But within the realistic tradition there was an inherent tendency for the text to undermine its own ground and deconstruct the very assumptions on which it was built. *Middlemarch* itself was an example: 'for those who have eyes to see it', the novel 'pulls the rug out from under itself and ... deprives itself of its ground in history by demonstrating that ground to be a fiction too'. *Middlemarch* 'elaborately deconstruct[ed]' not only the belief that history is 'progressive, teleological', but also the notion that 'a human life gradually reveals its destined meaning', and even the concept of the work of art as 'an organic unity'.[39] In a second article, which studies the novel's metaphors and imagery, Miller found further evidence of subsidence: 'a pervasive figure for the human situation in *Middlemarch* is that of the seer who must try to identify clearly what is present before him. This metaphor contaminates the apparently clear-cut objectivist implications of the metaphor of the flowing web.' So does 'the metaphor of vision'. And the pluralist and relativist view of signs and interpretation, which runs 'like Ariadne's thread through the labyrinthine verbal complexity' of *Middlemarch*, 'contaminates and ultimately subverts the optical model in the same way that the optical model contaminates and makes more problematic the images of the web or of the current'.[40]

One might observe of the dazzling discourse of Miller and the authors of *The Madwoman in the Attic* that it is excessively *engagé* and ideological, too concerned with its own premises, methods and self-delighting excruciations, and insufficiently disinterested in Eliot's novel. But to suggest this is of course to reveal something of my own critical premises and predispositions, and who is to say that in its more mild-mannered way my own discourse is not as *parti pris* as more aggressive and revisionist discourses? There are, however, two points on which all commentators can surely agree. One is the central and exemplary status of *Middlemarch* in literary history – both the history of the novel and the history of nineteenth-century English literature. It is as big a literary landmark as *The Prelude* or *Madame Bovary, In Memoriam* or *Ulysses*. The other area of unanimous agreement, to which the very diversity of contemporary critical commentary attests, would be the extraordinary richness of George Eliot's study of the way it was in a part of provincial England in the early nineteenth century.

NOTES

CHAPTER 1

1 Unsigned review, *Galaxy* (March 1873); reprinted in David Carroll (ed.), *George Eliot: The Critical Heritage*, p. 357. (Hereafter cited as *CH*.)
2 T. H. Johnson (ed.), *The Letters of Emily Dickinson* (Cambridge, Mass.: Harvard University Press, 1958), Vol. 2, p. 506.
3 *CH*, p. 323.
4 ibid., pp. 461–2.
5 Quoted in W. J. Harvey, 'Criticism of the novel: contemporary reception', in Barbara Hardy (ed.), *'Middlemarch': Critical Approaches to the Novel*, p. 145.
6 F. W. H. Myers, 'George Eliot', *Essays Classical and Modern* (London: Macmillan, 1921), p. 489; Richard Ellmann, 'Dorothea's husbands', in his *Golden Codgers: Some Biographical Speculations*, pp. 27, 31.
7 Gordon S. Haight (ed.), *The George Eliot Letters* (London: Oxford University Press/New Haven, Conn.: Yale University Press, 1954–5), Vol. 4, p. 355. (Hereafter cited as *Letters*.)
8 *Letters*, Vol. 5, pp. 3, 16.
9 See Jerome Beaty, *'Middlemarch' from Notebook to Novel: A Study of George Eliot's Creative Method*, pp. 3, 39.
10 See 'Appendix: a checklist of George Eliot's reading January 1868 to December 1871', in John Clark Pratt and Victor A. Neufeldt (eds), *George Eliot's 'Middlemarch' Notebooks: A Transcription*, pp. 279–88.
11 ibid., p. xxviii.
12 *Letters*, Vol. 5, p. 322.
13 ibid., pp. 124, 127.
14 ibid., p. 137.
15 ibid., p. 237.
16 Beaty, *'Middlemarch' from Notebook to Novel*, pp. 9–11.
17 Anna Theresa Kitchel (ed.), *Quarry for 'Middlemarch'*.
18 Stanton Millet, 'The union of "Miss Brooke" and "Middlemarch": a study of the manuscript', *Journal of English and Germanic Philology*, vol. 79, no. 1 (1980), pp. 33, 57.
19 *Letters*, Vol. 5, pp. 145–6.
20 J. H. Sutherland, *Victorian Novelists and Publishers*, p. 204.
21 This remark is made about the chapter epigraphs in Eliot's next novel by one of the speakers in James's 'Daniel Deronda: a conversation', p. 427.
22 ibid.
23 For a different opinion, see David Leon Higdon, 'George Eliot and the art of the epigraph', *Nineteenth-Century Fiction*, vol. 25, no. 2 (1970), pp. 127–51.
24 *Letters*, Vol. 5, pp. 357, 374.
25 *CH*, pp. 319, 332.
26 ibid., p. 339.
27 Quoted in Harvey, 'Criticism of the novel: contemporary reception', p. 133.
28 *CH*, p. 313.
29 ibid., pp. 353–9.

CHAPTER 2

1 'Art and belles lettres'; reprinted in Joseph Wiesenfarth (ed.), *George Eliot: A Writer's Notebook 1854–1879 and Uncollected Writings*, p. 273.

2   Thomas Pinney (ed.), *Essays of George Eliot*, pp. 304, 318, 319, 310, 323. (Hereafter cited as *Essays*.)

3   *Essays*, pp. 366, 367, 371, 385.

4   ibid., pp. 270–1.

5   *Letters*, Vol. 3, p. 111.

6   ibid., Vol. 1, p. 34.

7   Gordon S. Haight, *George Eliot: A Biography*, p. 421.

8   '[Three Novels]', *Essays*, p. 331.

9   See especially David Daiches, *George Eliot: 'Middlemarch'*, pp. 47, 54, 56–7.

10 *Letters*, Vol. 4, p. 300.

11 Thomas Pinney, 'More leaves from George Eliot's notebook', *Huntington Library Quarterly*, vol. 29, no. 4 (1966), p. 360. And see Pinney's 'The authority of the past in George Eliot's novels', *Nineteenth-Century Fiction*, vol. 21, no. 2 (1966); reprinted in George R. Creeger (ed.), *George Eliot: A Collection of Critical Essays*, p. 49.

12 This summary account draws on John Stuart Mill, *Auguste Comte and Positivism* (Ann Arbor, Mich.: University of Michigan Press, 1961; reprint).

13 See Michael York Mason, '*Middlemarch* and science: problems of life and mind', *Review of English Studies*, vol. 22, no. 86 (1971), pp. 154, 157.

14 See Robert A. Greenberg, 'Plexuses and ganglia: scientific allusions in *Middlemarch*', *Nineteenth-Century Fiction*, vol. 30, no. 1 (1975), pp. 33–51.

15 *Letters*, Vol. 4, pp. 287–8. See James F. Scott, 'George Eliot, Positivism, and the social vision of *Middlemarch*', *Victorian Studies*, vol. 16, no. 1 (1972), pp. 59–76.

16 Basil Willey, *Nineteenth-Century Studies: Coleridge to Matthew Arnold*, p. 238.

17 *Letters*, Vol. 1, p. 9.

18 ibid., p. 12.

19 ibid., p. 28.

20 Quoted in Willey, *Nineteenth-Century Studies*, p. 242.

21 *Letters*, Vol. 2, p. 82.

22 ibid., Vol. 3, p. 231.

23 ibid., Vol. 6, p. 98.

24 ibid., Vol. 1, p. 162.

25 *CH*, pp. 318–19.

26 *Letters*, Vol. 4, pp. 300–1. Eliot made the same point to another correspondent twelve years later: 'My function is that of the *aesthetic*, not the doctrinal teacher – the rousing of the nobler emotions, which make mankind desire the social right, not the prescribing of special measures, concerning which the artistic mind, however strongly moved by social sympathy, is often not the best judge. It is one thing to feel keenly for one's fellow-beings; another to say, "This step, and this alone, will be the best to take for the removal of particular calamities"' (ibid., Vol. 7, p. 44).

27 For a different view, see Joseph Wiesenfarth, '*Middlemarch*: the language of art', *PMLA*, vol. 97, no. 3 (1982), pp. 363–77.

28 See D. A. Miller, *Narrative and Its Discontents: Problems of Closure in the Traditional Novel*, pp. 130–5.

29 Review in the *Spectator*, 8 February 1879; quoted in Jeannette King, *Tragedy in the Victorian Novel: Theory and Practice in the Novels of George Eliot, Thomas Hardy and Henry James*, p. 9. My generalisations about common attitudes to modern tragedy in Victorian critics are indebted to King's opening chapter.

30 George Henry Lewes, 'Recent tragedies', *Westminster Review*, vol. 37 (1842), p. 338.

CHAPTER 3

1   Henry James, *Partial Portraits* (London: Macmillan, 1888), pp. 116–17.

2   For the identification of Middlemarch as Coventry, see John Prest, *The Industrial Revolution in Coventry* (London: Oxford University Press, 1960), pp. 143–5. For the

precise dating of the action see Jerome Beaty, 'History by indirection: the era of Reform in *Middlemarch*', *Victorian Studies*, vol. 1, no. 2 (1957), pp. 173–9; reprinted in Gordon S. Haight (ed.), *A Century of George Eliot Criticism.*

3 See Prest, *Industrial Revolution in Coventry*; Beaty, 'History by indirection'; and Asa Briggs, '*Middlemarch* and the doctors', *Cambridge Journal*, vol. 1, no. 12 (1948), pp. 749–62. For a more specialised example of scholarly witness to the historical fidelity of *Middlemarch*, see Elizabeth Jay, *The Religion of the Heart: Anglican Evangelicalism in the Nineteenth-Century Novel* (Oxford: Clarendon Press, 1979).

4 See C. L. Cline, 'Qualifications of the medical practitioners in *Middlemarch*', in Clyde de L. Ryals (ed.), *Nineteenth-Century Literary Perspectives: Essays in Honor of Lionel Stevenson* (Durham, NC: Duke University Press, 1974), pp. 277–8.

5 J. H. Plumb, *The Death of the Past* (London: Macmillan, 1964), pp. 105–6.

6 *Essays*, pp. 446–7.

7 Beaty, 'History by indirection', pp. 306–13.

8 Frank Kermode, 'D. H. Lawrence and the apocalyptic types', *Continuities* (London: Routledge & Kegan Paul, 1968), pp. 137, 139, 142.

9 For the distinction between uniformitarianism and catastrophism, see Charles Coulston Gillispie, *Genesis and Geology: A Study of the Relations of Scientific Thought, Natural Theology, and Social Opinion in Great Britain, 1790–1850* (Cambridge, Mass.: Harvard University Press, 1951). On the usefulness of the distinction to the study of nineteenth-century literature see A. Dwight Culler, *The Poetry of Tennyson* (New Haven, Conn./London: Yale University Press, 1977), p. 15.

10 *Letters*, Vol. 5, p. 168.

11 J. S. Mill, *On Liberty*, ed. Curran V. Shields (Indianapolis, Ind.: Bobbs-Merrill, 1956), pp. 3, 7, 68, 85, 73, 81.

12 Q. D. Leavis, 'The symbolic function of the doctor in Victorian novels', in F. R. Leavis and Q. D. Leavis, *Dickens the Novelist* (London: Chatto & Windus, 1970), pp. 179–83.

13 Quoted in Pinney, 'More leaves from George Eliot's notebook', pp. 371–2.

14 Thomas Carlyle, *Sartor Resartus*, ed. Charles Frederick Harrold (New York: Odyssey, 1937), p. 119. In 1855, Eliot observed that 'there is hardly a superior or active mind of this generation that has not been modified by Carlyle's writings; there has hardly been an English book written for the last ten or twelve years that would not have been different if Carlyle had not lived. The character of his influence is best seen in the fact that many of the men who have the least agreement with his opinions are those to whom the reading of *Sartor Resartus* was an epoch in the history of their minds. The extent of his influence may best be seen in the fact that ideas which were startling novelties when he first wrote them are now become common-places' (*Essays*, pp. 213–14). On the importance of vocation in *Middlemarch* see Alan Mintz, *George Eliot and the Novel of Vocation.*

15 *CH*, p. 307.

16 See especially Kathleen Blake, '*Middlemarch* and the Woman Question', *Nineteenth-Century Fiction*, vol. 31, no. 3 (1976), pp. 285–312.

CHAPTER 4

1 J. Hillis Miller, *The Form of Victorian Fiction* (Notre Dame/London: University of Notre Dame Press, 1968), pp. 63–6.

2 Daiches, *George Eliot: 'Middlemarch'*, pp. 12–13, was the first to apply this useful threefold distinction to the novel.

3 Steven Marcus, 'Literature and social theory: starting with George Eliot', in his *Representations: Essays on Literature and Society*, p. 186.

4 *Letters*, Vol. 4, p. 97.

5 Quoted in Miriam Allott (ed.), *Novelists on the Novel* (London: Routledge & Kegan Paul, 1959), p. 271.
6 James, *Partial Portraits*, pp. 378–9.
7 Preface to *The Golden Bowl*, The New York Edition of the Novels and Tales of Henry James (New York: Scribner's, 1907–9), Vol. 23, pp. vi, v.
8 *CH*, p. 304.
9 F. R. Leavis, *The Great Tradition: George Eliot, Henry James, Joseph Conrad*, p. 67.
10 Walter Allen, *George Eliot* (London: Weidenfeld & Nicolson, 1964), pp. 83–4.
11 *CH*, p. 321. And see Quentin Anderson's description of 'the voice of the wise woman' in the novel; 'George Eliot in *Middlemarch*', in Boris Ford (ed.), *The Pelican Guide to English Literature*, Vol. 6, *From Dickens to Hardy*, revised edn, pp. 274–93; reprinted in Creeger, *George Eliot: A Collection of Critical Essays*, pp. 141–60.
12 Isobel Armstrong, '*Middlemarch*: a note on George Eliot's wisdom', in Barbara Hardy (ed.), *Critical Essays on George Eliot*, pp. 116–32.
13 ibid., pp. 118, 126.
14 Peter Jones, *Philosophy and the Novel* (Oxford: Clarendon Press, 1975), p. 27.
15 The quoted phrases are from Culler's discussion of *In Memoriam* in his *Poetry of Tennyson*, pp. 185–6.

CHAPTER 5

1 J. Hillis Miller, 'Character in the novel: a real illusion', in Samuel T. Mintz and others (eds), *From Smollett to James: Studies in the Novel and Other Essays Presented to Edgar Johnson* (Charlottesville, Va: University Press of Virginia, 1981), pp. 279, 278.
2 *CH*, p. 358.
3 A. O. J. Cockshut, '*Middlemarch*', pp. 40–2.
4 Quoted in Rochelle Girson, 'Asphalt is bitter soil', *Saturday Review*, 13 October 1962, p. 20.
5 *CH*, p. 356.
6 ibid., p. 356.
7 ibid., p. 302.
8 Roy Pascal, *The Dual Voice: Free Indirect Speech and Its Functioning in the Nineteenth-Century European Novel* (Manchester: Manchester University Press, 1977), p. 79.
9 *CH*, p. 358.
10 David Carroll, '*Middlemarch* and the externality of fact', in Ian Adam (ed.), *This Particular Web: Essays on 'Middlemarch'*, p. 82.
11 See Myers, *Essays Classical and Modern*, p. 495.
12 See Graham Martin, '*The Mill on the Floss* and the unreliable narrator', in Anne Smith (ed.), *George Eliot: Centenary Essays and an Unpublished Fragment*, p. 39: 'Hetty is the character, as most readers now agree, who radically questions the author's claims to impartiality. What else could account for the judicial savagery of that "rancored poisoned garment" ...'
13 J. W. Cross, *George Eliot's Life as Related in Her Letters and Journals* (Edinburgh/London: Blackwood, 1885), Vol. 3, p. 425.

CHAPTER 6

1 Margaret Doody, 'George Eliot and the eighteenth-century novel', in U. C. Knoepflmacher and George Levine (eds), *Nineteenth-Century Fiction* (special issue: *George Eliot, 1880–1980*), vol. 35, no. 1 (1980), p. 268.
2 Carlyle, *Sartor Resartus*, pp. 189, 191, 196.
3 Marcus, 'Literature and social theory: starting with George Eliot', pp. 210–12. Milly Barton's last words come in ch. 8.

4 Juliet McMaster, 'George Eliot's language of the sense', in Gordon S. Haight and Rosemary T. VanArsdel (eds), *George Eliot: A Centenary Tribute*, pp. 13, 25.

5 Ellmann, *Golden Codgers*, p. 20.

6 Gordon S. Haight notes that, in 1860, George Eliot had been in Rome during Holy Week, 'and may have assumed that the red draperies symbolizing the Passion would also be used at Christmas. But such a mistake is unusual in her books.' See his 'Poor Mr Casaubon', in Ryals (ed.), *Nineteenth-Century Literary Perspectives*, pp. 259–60. Of the whole passage, Q. D. Leavis observed: it is 'impossible to paraphrase [it] without changing and diminishing its meanings, for it is a complex kind of poetry, working on several different planes at once' ('A note on literary indebtedness: Dickens, George Eliot, Henry James', *Hudson Review*, vol. 8, no. 3 (1955), p. 426).

7 A. L. French, who was perhaps the first to call attention to the sexual substratum in Dorothea's reverie, also finds the paragraph weak and unsatisfactory; see his 'A note on *Middlemarch*', *Nineteenth-Century Fiction*, vol. 26, no. 3 (1971), pp. 339–47. And see Neil Hertz, 'Recognizing Casaubon', *Glyph: Textual Studies*, vol. 6 (1979), pp. 35–8.

8 Haight, 'Poor Mr Casaubon', p. 260.

9 Juliet McMaster has even found suggestions in the novel's imagery of 'abnormal sexual relations' and the combination of 'deprivation and exploitation': 'we are presented with the almost monstrous, a copulation of pen and ink with living human flesh to produce an inhuman offspring. Mr Casaubon's blood, as Mrs Cadwallader reports, examined under a microscope, turns out to be "all semicolons and parentheses" (ch. 8). As a conscientious husband he recognizes his duty to leave after him "a copy of himself"; but the copy he has in mind is "of his mythological key" (ch. 29). By feverish midnight activity in the bedroom he does what he can to impregnate his wife with his key, working with "bird-like speed" (ch. 48) like a lecherous sparrow. The posthumous offspring of this coupling, an "embryo of truth" (ch. 48), will result for Dorothea in "a ghastly labour producing what would never see the light" (ch. 48), "a theory which was already withered in the birth like an elfin child"' (ch. 48). McMaster does, however, go on to say that 'the imagery of coition, labour and parturition here suggests something more than the literal and the physical, evoking the terrified fantasies of a tormented psyche' ('George Eliot's language of the sense', p. 25).

10 Barbara Hardy, 'Implication and incompleteness: George Eliot's *Middlemarch*', in her *The Appropriate Form*, pp. 106, 107, 108, 121, 128.

11 Pinney, 'More leaves from George Eliot's notebook', p. 364.

12 Kermode, 'D. H. Lawrence and the apocalyptic types', p. 146.

13 Martin Price, 'The sublime poet: pictures and powers', *Yale Review*, Vol. 58, no. 2 (1969), p. 213.

CHAPTER 7

1 Leon Edel (ed.), *Henry James Letters*, Vol. 1, *1843–1875* (London: Macmillan, 1974), p. 351.

2 The New York Edition of the Novels and Tales of Henry James, Vol. 3, pp. 68, 66, xii.

3 Leon Edel, *Henry James: The Conquest of London, 1870–1883* (London: Rupert Hart-Davis, 1962), p. 373.

4 The New York Edition, Vol. 7, pp. ix–x.

5 Thomas Pinney, headnote to 'Notes on Form in Art', *Essays*, p. 431.

6 ibid., pp. 432–6.

7 *Letters*, Vol. 5, pp. 168–9, 324, 374, 458–9.

8 John Bayley, *The Uses of Division: Unity and Disharmony in Literature* (London: Chatto & Windus, 1976), p. 11.

9 *Middlemarch*, ed. W. J. Harvey (Harmondsworth: Penguin Books, 1965), p. 9.

10 U. C. Knoepflmacher, *Religious Humanism and the Victorian Novel*, pp. 72–4.

11 E. M. Forster, *Aspects of the Novel* (London: Edward Arnold, 1927), pp. 206–7, 209, 210.

12 For a quite different analysis of this passage, see Kermode, 'D. H. Lawrence and the apocalyptic types', pp. 139–41.

13 Austin M. Wright, *The Formal Principle in the Novel* (Ithaca, NY: Cornell University Press, 1982), pp. 19–21.

14 David Carroll, 'Unity through analogy: an interpretation of *Middlemarch*', *Victorian Studies*, vol. 2, no. 4 (1959), pp. 305–16.

15 Mark Schorer, 'Fiction and the "matrix of analogy"', *Kenyon Review*, vol. 11, no. 4 (1949), pp. 550–9; 'The structure of the novel: method, metaphor and mind', in Hardy (ed.), *'Middlemarch': Critical Approaches to the Novel*, pp. 12–24.

16 *Letters*, Vol. 4, pp. 300–1.

CHAPTER 8

1 *Letters*, Vol. 2, p. 349.

2 Anthony Trollope, *An Autobiography*, ed. Frederick Page (London: Oxford University Press), pp. 245–7.

3 *CH*, pp. 479, 481–2; cf. Mrs Oliphant and F. R. Oliphant, *The Victorian Age of English Literature* (London: Percival, 1892), Vol. 2, p. 172: 'The works of this great writer divide themselves naturally into sections: The first containing the *Scenes of Clerical Life*, the *Mill on the Floss*, *Adam Bede*, and *Silas Marner*. This was her first method and it contained, we think, the best of her books, the unaffected, genuine, and natural utterance of her genius.'

4 Gladstone's and White's comments are quoted by Haight in his preface to *The George Eliot Letters*, Vol. 1, pp. xiv–xvi.

5 *Letters between Samuel Butler and Miss E. M. A. Savage, 1871–1885* (London: Cape, 1935), p. 40.

6 *The Letters of W. B. Yeats*, ed. Allan Wade (London: Rupert Hart-Davis, 1954), p. 31.

7 G. B. Shaw, *Collected Letters, 1898–1910*, ed. Dan H. Laurence (London: Max Reinhardt, 1972), p. 77; *Collected Plays with Their Prefaces*, ed. Dan H. Laurence, Vol. 5 (London: Max Reinhardt/Bodley Head, 1972), p. 702.

8 W. E. Henley, *Views and Reviews: Essays in Appreciations* (London: Macmillan, 1921), p. 118.

9 George Moore, *Confessions of a Young Man*, ed. Susan Dick (Montreal: McGill-Queen's University Press, 1972), pp. 54, 41.

10 George Saintsbury, *Corrected Impressions: Essays on Victorian Writers* (London: Heinemann, 1895), p. 166.

11 George Saintsbury, *Short History of English Literature* (London: Macmillan, 1937), p. 753.

12 W. J. Dawson, *The Makers of English Fiction* (London: Hodder & Stoughton, 1905), p. 134.

13 Brownell's discussion of Eliot is reprinted in Gordon S. Haight (ed.), *A Century of George Eliot Criticism*, pp. 170–9.

14 Leslie Stephen, *George Eliot*, p. 184.

15 Oliver Elton, *Survey of English Literature, 1830–1880* (London: Arnold, 1920), Vol. 2, pp. 264–5.

16 Edmund Gosse, *Aspects and Impressions* (London/New York: Cassell, 1922), pp. 1, 2, 15, 4, 14.

17 *The Question of Things Happening: The Letters of Virginia Woolf*, Vol. 2, *1912–1922*, ed. Nigel Nicolson (London: Hogarth Press, 1976), p. 391; 'George Eliot', *The Common Reader*, first series (London: Hogarth Press, 1925), pp. 213, 216, 213. In his 1919 review of Virginia Woolf's *Night and Day*, Ford Madox Ford made an interesting

Notes   157

observation: 'in reading Mrs Woolf ... one seems to hear ... the voice of a George Eliot
who, remaining almost super-educated, has lost the divine rage to be didactic'; quoted
in David Dow Harvey (ed.), *Ford Madox Ford, 1873-1939: A Bibliography of Works
and Criticism* (Princeton, NJ: Princeton University Press, 1962), p. 217.

18 David Cecil, *Early Victorian Novelists: Essays in Revaluation* (London: Constable,
1934), pp. 318-19, 304, 321-2.

19 Humphry House, 'Are the Victorians coming back?', in his *All in Due Time* (London:
Rupert Hart-Davis, 1955), pp. 79, 78.

20 Willey, *Nineteenth-Century Studies*, pp. 204-5.

21 Briggs, '*Middlemarch* and the doctors', pp. 750-1, 762, 758.

22 V. S. Pritchett, 'George Eliot', in his *The Living Novel* (London: Chatto & Windus,
1946), pp. 88, 92, 94.

23 Leavis, *The Great Tradition*, pp. 61, 65, 67, 69, 72, 74, 75.

24 Arnold Kettle, *An Introduction to the English Novel* (London: Hutchinson, 1951), Vol.
1, pp. 188, 171, 180, 183, 185, 187.

25 Joan Bennett, *George Eliot: Her Mind and Art*, pp. xi, 160, 174.

26 *The English Novel: A Short Critical History*, p. 223. Henley (*Views and Reviews*, p. 118)
imagined a reader who went to Eliot's novels 'in much the same spirit and to much the
same purpose that he went to the gymnasium and diverted himself with parallel bars'.

27 Barbara Hardy, *The Novels of George Eliot: A Study in Form*, pp. 1-5. Twenty-three
years later Barbara Hardy reiterated her belief that 'George Eliot's imaginative
achievement shows itself in triumphs of structure and language which can be examined
without constant reference to post-Jamesian models of fictional art'. But she went on to
note that 'the fact of artistry can now be taken for granted' and further observed that
'like many critics I have moved away from concepts of realism; rather, my emphasis
would be placed on the novelist's investigation of life, made through the particularities
of a literary genre'; introduction to *Particularities: Readings in George Eliot*, p. 10.

28 Angus Wilson, 'Diversity and depth', *The Times Literary Supplement*, 15 August 1958,
p. viii.

29 David Daiches, 'The return of George Eliot', *Nation*, 9 June 1962, p. 518.

30 Hardy (ed.), '*Middlemarch*': *Critical Approaches to the Novel*, pp. 3, 94-5.

31 Raymond Williams, *The English Novel from Dickens to Lawrence*, pp. 90-1.

32 David Lodge, '*Middlemarch* and the idea of the classic realist text', in Arnold Kettle
(ed.), *The Nineteenth-Century Novel: Critical Essays and Documents*, revised edn, p.
218.

33 Colin MacCabe, *James Joyce and the Revolution of the Word* (London: Macmillan,
1978), pp. 15-16.

34 Lodge, '*Middlemarch* and the idea of the classic realist text', p. 236.

35 Kate Millett, *Sexual Politics* (New York: Doubleday, 1970), p. 139.

36 Lee R. Edwards, 'Women, energy and *Middlemarch*', *Massachusetts Review*, vol. 13,
nos 1-2 (1972); reprinted in Hornbeck (ed), *Middlemarch*, Norton Critical Edition, pp.
692, 685, 690.

37 Zelda Austen, 'Why feminist critics are angry with George Eliot', *College English*, vol.
37, no. 6 (1976), pp. 550, 555, 561.

38 Sandra M. Gilbert and Susan Gubar, *The Madwoman in the Attic*, 500, 501, 507, 513,
514, 516, 520, 519, 517, 528-9.

39 J. Hillis Miller, 'Narrative and history', *ELH*, vol. 41, no. 3 (1974), pp. 455-73.

40 J. Hillis Miller, 'Optic and semiotic in *Middlemarch*', in Jerome H. Buckley (ed.), *The
Worlds of Victorian Fiction*, pp. 136-7, 143. For another deconstructive reading that
follows along the lines laid down by Miller, see Jan Gordon's 'Origins, *Middlemarch*,
endings: George Eliot's crisis of the antecedent', in Smith (ed.), *George Eliot:
Centenary Essays*, pp. 124-51. Jan Gordon argues that during the course of
Middlemarch 'an ardent willingness to believe in some pure Origin of events prior to the
corruption by "circumstances"' gradually gives way to the emergence of 'the awful

truth'; that 'Origins, "Keys", primitive tissues, sources, historical "background" – the
Ur-texts of an epoch – are arbitrary and fictional rather than real, mere attempts to
individually appropriate that metaphysical absence which is every Origin' (pp. 124–5).

BIBLIOGRAPHY

(1) TEXTS OF *MIDDLEMARCH*

Middlemarch was first published in eight book-length instalments between December 1871 and December 1872. The text was set from the manuscript in Eliot's hand which is now in the British Library. Two other editions from the same sheets were issued in four volumes in 1872 and 1873. A one-volume edition, the last to be corrected by the author, was published in 1874. Good modern editions of *Middlemarch* (all based on the 1874 edition) include the following:

Gordon S. Haight's Riverside edition (Boston, Mass.: Houghton Mifflin, 1956)
W. J. Harvey's Penguin English Library edition (Harmondsworth: Penguin Books, 1965)
Bert G. Hornback's Norton Critical Edition (New York: Norton, 1977).

For scholarly purposes these editions will be superseded by that being prepared by David Carroll for the Clarendon Edition of the Novels of George Eliot. Carroll's copy-text will be the one-volume edition of 1874; all substantive variants from the manuscript and the first edition will be recorded, as will all of the several thousand decipherable deletions in the manuscript.

The manuscript of *Middlemarch* has been studied by Jerome Beaty, *'Middlemarch' from Notebook to Novel: A Study of George Eliot's Creative Method* (Urbana, Ill.: University of Illinois Press, 1960), and Stanton Millet, 'The union of "Miss Brooke" and "Middlemarch": a study of the manuscript', *Journal of English and Germanic Philology*, vol. 79, no. 1 (1980), pp. 32–57.

(2) OTHER WORKS BY GEORGE ELIOT

Good editions of Eliot's seven novels, and of *Scenes of Clerical Life*, are available in the Penguin English Library. Her two volumes of verse and the *Impressions of Theophrastus Such* are included in various collected editions, for example the Cabinet Edition (Edinburgh/London: Blackwood, [1877–80]) and the Standard Edition (Edinburgh/London: Blackwood, [1895]). So are two pieces of shorter fiction, 'The Lifted Veil' and 'Brother Jacob'.

(A) WORKS PUBLISHED DURING ELIOT'S LIFE

The Life of Jesus Critically Examined by D. F. Strauss. Translated from the fourth German edition [by Marian Evans] (1846). Reprinted, ed. Peter Hodgson (London: SCM, 1972).
The Essence of Christianity by L. Feuerbach. Translated from the second German edition by Marian Evans (1854). Reprinted, introduction by Karl Barth, foreword by H. Richard Niebuhr (New York: Harper Torchbooks, 1957).
Scenes of Clerical Life, 2 vols (1858). The three stories were originally published separately in *Blackwood's Magazine* in 1857.
Adam Bede, 3 vols (1859).

The Mill on the Floss, 3 vols (1860).
Silas Marner: The Weaver of Raveloe (1861).
Romola, 3 vols (1863). Originally published in the *Cornhill Magazine*, 1862–3.
Felix Holt, the Radical, 3 vols (1866).
The Spanish Gypsy: A Poem (1868).
Middlemarch: A Study of Provincial Life, 4 vols (1872). Originally published in eight instalments, 1871–2.
The Legend of Jubal and Other Poems (1874).
Daniel Deronda, 4 vols (1876). Originally published in eight monthly parts in 1876.
Impressions of Theophrastus Such (1879). Essays.

(B) OTHER WRITINGS

Haight, Gordon S. (ed.), *The George Eliot Letters*, Vols 1–7 (London: Oxford University Press/New Haven, Conn.: Yale University Press, 1954–5); Vols 8–9 (New Haven, Conn./London: Yale University Press, 1978).

Kitchel, Anna Theresa (ed.), *Quarry for 'Middlemarch'* (Berkeley, Calif.: University of California Press, 1950).

Pinion, F. B. (ed.), *A George Eliot Miscellany: A Supplement to Her Novels* (London: Macmillan, 1982). Reprints selections from the essays and some poems, plus 'The Lifted Veil' and 'Brother Jacob'.

Pinney, Thomas (ed.), *Essays of George Eliot* (London: Routledge & Kegan Paul/New York: Columbia University Press, 1963). An appendix lists all of Eliot's periodical essays and reviews.

Pinney, Thomas (ed.), 'More leaves from George Eliot's notebook', *Huntington Library Quarterly*, vol. 29, no. 4 (1966), pp. 353–76.

Pratt, John Clark, and Neufeldt, Victor A. (eds), *George Eliot's 'Middlemarch' Notebooks: A Transcription* (Berkeley, Calif.: University of California Press, 1979).

Wiesenfarth, Joseph (ed.), *George Eliot: A Writer's Notebook 1854–1879 and Uncollected Writings* (Charlottesville, Va: University Press of Virginia, 1981). Includes a number of essays not in Pinney's edition.

(3) BIOGRAPHICAL

Cross, J. W., *George Eliot's Life as Related in Her Letters and Journals*, 3 vols (Edinburgh/London: Blackwood, 1885). Act of piety by Eliot's second husband.

Haight, Gordon S., *George Eliot: A Biography* (Oxford: Clarendon Press, 1968). The standard life.

Laski, Marghanita, *George Eliot and Her World* (London: Thames & Hudson/New York: Scribner's, 1973). Good short account of the life, with many illustrations.

Redinger, Ruby V., *George Eliot: The Emergent Self* (New York: Knopf, 1975/London: Bodley Head, 1976).

Stephen, Leslie, *George Eliot*, English Men of Letters (London: Macmillan, 1902). Biographical–critical study.

(4) CRITICISM

For an annotated list of published critical material from 1858 to 1971, see Constance Marie Fulmer, *George Eliot: A Reference Guide* (Boston, Mass.: G. K. Hall, 1977). More recent work is listed in David Leon Higdon, 'A bibliography of George Eliot criticism 1971–1977', *Bulletin of Bibliography*, vol. 37, no. 2 (1980), pp. 90–103, and in the annual listings in the Modern Language Association's *International Bibliography* and in *Victorian Studies*. For guides through this material, see Jerome Beaty, 'George Eliot', in A. E. Dyson (ed.), *The English Novel: Select Bibliographical Guides* (London: Oxford University Press, 1974), pp. 246–63; and U. C. Knoepflmacher, 'George Eliot', in George H. Ford (ed.), *Victorian Fiction: A Second Guide to Research* (New York: Modern Language Association, 1978), pp. 234–73.

(A) GENERAL STUDIES

Allen, Walter, *The English Novel: A Short Critical History* (London: Phoenix House, 1954).

Ashton, Rosemary, *George Eliot*, Past Masters (Oxford: Oxford University Press, 1983).

Bedient, Calvin, *Architects of the Self: George Eliot, D. H. Lawrence, E. M. Forster* (Berkeley, Calif.: University of California Press, 1972).

Bennett, Joan, *George Eliot: Her Mind and Art* (Cambridge: Cambridge University Press, 1948).

Carroll, David (ed.), *George Eliot: The Critical Heritage* (London: Routledge & Kegan Paul, 1971). Includes seven contemporary reviews of *Middlemarch*.

Cecil, David, *Early Victorian Novelists: Essays in Revaluation* (London: Constable, 1934).

Cox, C. B., *The Free Spirit: A Study of Liberal Humanism in the Novels of George Eliot, Henry James, E. M. Forster, Virginia Woolf and Angus Wilson* (London: Oxford University Press, 1963).

Creeger, George R. (ed.), *George Eliot: A Collection of Critical Essays* (Englewood Cliffs, NJ: Prentice-Hall, 1970). Reprints ten essays, including Thomas Pinney's 'The authority of the past in George Eliot's novels' and Darrel Mansell's 'George Eliot's conception of "form".'

Emery, Laura Comer, *George Eliot's Creative Conflict: The Other Side of Silence* (Berkeley, Calif.: University of California Press, 1976). A psychoanalytic perspective.

Gilbert, Sandra M., and Gubar, Susan, *The Madwoman in the Attic: The Woman Writer and the Nineteenth-Century Literary Imagination* (New Haven, Conn./ London: Yale University Press, 1979).

Haight, Gordon S. (ed.), *A Century of George Eliot Criticism* (Boston, Mass.: Houghton Mifflin, 1970). Wide-ranging selections, from contemporary reviews to the early 1960s.

Haight, Gordon S., and VanArsdel, Rosemary T. (eds), *George Eliot: A Centenary Tribute* (London: Macmillan, 1982). Thirteen original essays.

Hardy, Barbara (ed.), *Critical Essays on George Eliot* (London: Routledge & Kegan Paul, 1970).

Hardy, Barbara, *The Novels of George Eliot: A Study in Form* (London: Athlone Press, 1959).

Hardy, Barbara, *Particularities: Readings in George Eliot* (London: Peter Owen, 1982). Reprints ten essays, five of them on *Middlemarch*.

Harvey, W. J., *The Art of George Eliot* (London: Chatto & Windus, 1961).

Holloway, John, *The Victorian Sage: Studies in Argument* (London: Macmillan, 1953).

Holmstrom, John, and Lerner, Laurence (eds), *George Eliot and Her Readers: A Selection of Contemporary Reviews* (London: Bodley Head, 1966).

Jones, R. T., *George Eliot* (Cambridge: Cambridge University Press, 1970).

King, Jeannette, *Tragedy in the Victorian Novel: Theory and Practice in the Novels of George Eliot, Thomas Hardy and Henry James* (Cambridge: Cambridge University Press, 1978).

Knoepflmacher, U. C., *Religious Humanism and the Victorian Novel: George Eliot, Walter Pater and Samuel Butler* (Princeton, NJ: Princeton University Press, 1965).

Knoepflmacher, U. C., and Levine, George (eds), *Nineteenth-Century Fiction* (special issue: *George Eliot, 1880–1980*), vol. 35, no. 3 (1980), pp. 253–455.

Kroeber, Karl, *Studies in Fictional Structure: The Art of Jane Austen, Charlotte Brontë and George Eliot* (Princeton, NJ: Princeton University Press, 1971). Interesting statistical data.

Leavis, F. R., *The Great Tradition: George Eliot, Henry James, Joseph Conrad* (London: Chatto & Windus, 1948).

Lerner, Laurence, *The Truthtellers: Jane Austen, George Eliot, D. H. Lawrence* (London: Chatto & Windus, 1967).

Marcus, Steven, 'Literature and social theory: starting with George Eliot', in his *Representations: Essays on Literature and Society* (New York: Random House, 1975), pp. 183–213.

Milner, Ian, *The Structure of Values in George Eliot* (Prague: Universita Karlova, 1968). A Marxist perspective.

Mintz, Alan, *George Eliot and the Novel of Vocation* (Cambridge, Mass.: Harvard University Press, 1978).

Newton, K. M., *George Eliot, Romantic Humanist: A Study of the Philosophical Structure of Her Novels* (London: Macmillan, 1981).

Paris, Bernard J., *Experiments in Life: George Eliot's Quest for Values* (Detroit, Mich.: Wayne State University Press, 1965).

Pinion, F. B., *A George Eliot Companion* (London: Macmillan, 1981).

Price, Martin, *Forms of Life: Character and Moral Imagination in the Novel* (New Haven, Conn./London: Yale University Press, 1983).

Roberts, Neil, *George Eliot: Her Beliefs and Her Art* (London: Elek, 1975).

Showalter, Elaine, *A Literature of Their Own: British Women Novelists from Brontë to Lessing* (Princeton, NJ: Princeton University Press, 1977).

Smith, Anne (ed.), *George Eliot: Centenary Essays and an Unpublished Fragment* (London: Vision Press, 1980).

Speaight, Robert, *George Eliot* (London: Arthur Barker, 1954).

Stang, Richard, *The Theory of the Novel in England, 1850–1870* (London: Routledge & Kegan Paul, 1959).

Thale, Jerome, *The Novels of George Eliot* (New York: Columbia University Press, 1959).

Willey, Basil, *Nineteenth-Century Studies: Coleridge to Matthew Arnold* (London: Chatto & Windus, 1949).

Williams, Raymond, *The English Novel from Dickens to Lawrence* (London: Chatto & Windus, 1970).

Witemeyer, Hugh, *George Eliot and the Visual Arts* (New Haven, Conn./London: Yale University Press, 1979).

(B) STUDIES OF *MIDDLEMARCH*

Adam, Ian (ed.), *This Particular Web: Essays on 'Middlemarch'* (Toronto: University of Toronto Press, 1975). Five original essays.

Anderson, Quentin, 'George Eliot in *Middlemarch*', in Boris Ford (ed.), *The Pelican Guide to English Literature*, Vol. 6, *From Dickens to Hardy*, revised edn (Harmondsworth/New York: Penguin Books, 1966), pp. 274–93. Reprinted in George R. Creeger (ed.), *George Eliot: A Collection of Critical Essays*, pp. 141–60.

Armstrong, Isobel, '*Middlemarch*: a note on George Eliot's wisdom', in Barbara Hardy (ed.), *Critical Essays on George Eliot*, pp. 116–32.

Ashton, Rosemary D., 'The intellectual "medium" of *Middlemarch*', *Review of English Studies*, vol. 30, no. 118 (1979), pp. 154–68.

Austen, Zelda, 'Why feminist critics are angry with George Eliot', *College English*, vol. 37, no. 6 (1976), pp. 549–61.

Beaty, Jerome, 'History by indirection: the era of Reform in *Middlemarch*, *Victorian Studies*, vol. 1, no. 2 (1957), pp. 173–9. Reprinted in Gordon S. Haight (ed.), *A Century of George Eliot Criticism*, pp. 306–13, and in Bert G. Hornback's Norton Critical Edition, pp. 700–6.

Blake, Kathleen, '*Middlemarch* and the Woman Question', *Nineteenth-Century Fiction*, vol. 31, no. 3 (1976), pp. 285–312.

Briggs, Asa, '*Middlemarch* and the doctors', *Cambridge Journal*, vol. 1, no. 12 (1948), pp. 749–62.

Carroll, David, 'Unity through analogy: an interpretation of *Middlemarch*', *Victorian Studies*, vol. 2, no. 4 (1959), pp. 305–16.

Cockshut, A. O. J., '*Middlemarch*', Notes on English Literature (Oxford: Basil Blackwell, 1966).

Daiches, David, *George Eliot: 'Middlemarch'*, Studies in English Literature (London: Edward Arnold, 1963).

Edwards, Lee R., 'Woman, energy and *Middlemarch*', *Massachusetts Review*, vol. 13, nos 1–2 (1972), pp. 223–38. Reprinted in Bert G. Hornback's Norton Critical Edition, pp. 683–93.

Ellmann, Richard, 'Dorothea's husbands', in his *Golden Codgers: Some Biographical Speculations* (London/New York: Oxford University Press, 1973), pp. 17–38.

French, A. L., 'A note on *Middlemarch*', *Nineteenth-Century Fiction*, vol. 26, no. 3 (1971), pp. 339–47.

Gordon, Jan, 'Origins, *Middlemarch*, endings: George Eliot's crisis of the antecedent', in Anne Smith (ed.), *George Eliot: Centenary Essays*, pp. 124–51.

Hardy, Barbara, 'Implication and incompleteness: George Eliot's *Middlemarch*', in her *The Appropriate Form* (London: Athlone Press, 1964), pp. 105–31.

Hardy, Barbara (ed.), '*Middlemarch*': Critical Approaches to the Novel* (London: Athlone Press, 1967). Eight original essays, including Mark Schorer's 'The structure of the novel: method, metaphor and mind'.

Hertz, Neil, 'Recognizing Casaubon', in *Glyph: Textual Studies*, vol. 6,

(Baltimore, Ma/London: The Johns Hopkins University Press, 1979), pp. 22–41.

Hornback, Bert G. (ed.), *Middlemarch*, Norton Critical Edition (New York: Norton, 1977). Includes reprints of nine pieces of modern criticism.

Jones, Peter, 'Imagination and egoism in *Middlemarch*', in his *Philosophy and the Novel* (Oxford: Clarendon Press, 1975), pp. 9–69.

Kettle, Arnold, 'George Eliot: *Middlemarch*', in his *An Introduction to the English Novel* (London: Hutchinson, 1951), Vol. I, pp. 171–90.

Kiely, Robert, 'The limits of dialogue in *Middlemarch*', in Jerome H. Buckley (ed.), *The Worlds of Victorian Fiction* (Cambridge, Mass./London: Harvard University Press, 1975), pp. 103–23.

Knoepflmacher, U. C., '*Middlemarch*: affirmation through compromise', in his *Laughter and Despair: Readings in Ten Novels of the Victorian Period* (Berkeley, Calif.: University of California Press, 1971), pp. 168–201.

Knoepflmacher, U. C., '*Middlemarch*: an avuncular view', *Nineteenth-Century Fiction*, vol. 30, no. 1 (1975), pp. 53–81.

Leavis, Q. D., 'A note on literary indebtedness: Dickens, George Eliot, Henry James', *Hudson Review*, vol. 8, no. 3 (1955), pp. 423–8.

Lodge, David, '*Middlemarch* and the idea of the classic realist text', in Arnold Kettle (ed.), *The Nineteenth-Century Novel: Critical Essays and Documents*, revised edn (London: Heinemann, 1981), pp. 218–36.

Mason, Michael York, '*Middlemarch* and history', *Nineteenth-Century Fiction*, vol. 25, no. 4 (1971), pp. 417–31.

Mason, Michael York, '*Middlemarch* and science: problems of life and mind', *Review of English Studies*, vol. 22, no. 86 (1971), pp. 151–69.

Miller, D. A., 'George Eliot: "the wisdom of balancing claims"', in his *Narrative and Its Discontents: Problems of Closure in the Traditional Novel* (Princeton, NJ: Princeton University Press, 1981), pp. 107–94.

Miller, J. Hillis, 'Narrative and history', *ELH*, vol. 41, no. 3 (1974), pp. 455–73.

Miller, J. Hillis, 'Optic and semiotic in *Middlemarch*', in Jerome H. Buckley (ed.), *The Worlds of Victorian Fiction* (Cambridge, Mass./London: Harvard University Press, 1975), pp. 125–45.

Schorer, Mark, 'Fiction and the matrix of analogy', *Kenyon Review*, vol. 11, no. 4 (1949), pp. 539–60.

Scott, James F., 'George Eliot, Positivism, and the social vision of *Middlemarch*', *Victorian Studies*, vol. 16, no. 1 (1972), pp. 59–76.

Sutherland, J. H., 'Marketing *Middlemarch*', in his *Victorian Novelists and Publishers* (London: Athlone Press, 1976), pp. 188–205.

Swindon, Patrick (ed.), *George Eliot: 'Middlemarch'*, Casebook Series (London: Macmillan, 1972). Reprints selections from contemporary reviews, 'some opinions and criticism 1874–1968', and five modern critical essays.

Wiesenfarth, Joseph, '*Middlemarch*: the language of art', *MPLA*, vol. 97, no. 3 (1982), pp. 363–77.

INDEX

Acton, Lord 2
Adam Bede 3, 11, 17, 18, 27, 90, 133, 134, 137
Allen, Walter 69, 144
Aristotle 22; *Poetics* 122
Armstrong, Isobel 71, 72
Arnold, Matthew, 'Resignation' 103
Austen, Jane 141, 142; *Emma* 98; *Mansfield Park* 98
Austen, Zelda 147-8

Balzac, Honoré de 2
Bayley, John 123
Beaty, Jerome 7, 51
Bennett, Joan 144
Bentham, Jeremy 22
Bichat, Marie-François 23
Blackwood, John 4, 6, 9
Book of Tobit 10
Briggs, Asa 141
Brontë, Charlotte 140; *Jayne Eyre* 98; *Villete* 98
'Brother and Sister' 18
Brown, Ford Madox 78
Brown, Robert, *Microscopic Observations on the Particles Contained in the Pollen of Plants* 23
Brownell, W. C. 137
Browning, Robert, *The Ring and the Book* 98
Bunyan, John 145
Burke, Edmund 83
Butler, Samuel 136

Carlyle, Thomas 54, 124, 153; *Sartor Resartus* 53, 55, 103, 153
Carroll, David 90, 128
Cecil, David 140-1, 144
Cervantes, Miguel de, *Don Quixote* 10
Characters in *Middlemarch*
  Mr Brooke 41, 42, 45, 46, 48-9, 50, 57, 61, 62, 65-6, 67, 76, 77-8, 83, 123, 148
  Celia 26, 41, 76, 99-100, 118
  Bulstrode 8, 14, 27, 45, 46, 47, 49, 61, 63, 65, 66, 70, 81, 82, 85, 88-91, 125, 131, 143, 148
  Bulstrode, Harriet 46, 80-1, 91, 116
  Mr Cadwallader 42-3, 78
  Mrs Cadwallader 42-3, 49, 77, 83, 99, 115, 123
  Casaubon 3, 5-6, 10, 26, 27, 34, 41, 50, 57, 58, 63, 67, 80, 81, 82, 85-8, 105, 106, 108-9, 123, 128, 143, 145, 148

Chettam, Sir James 26, 56, 76, 100
Dorothea 3, 6, 7, 8, 10, 12, 13-14, 21-2, 26, 27, 29, 30-2, 33, 34, 41, 47, 48, 51, 55-6, 57, 58-9, 61, 62, 63, 66, 68, 78, 79, 80, 81, 82, 84, 86, 87, 92, 96, 98-118, 131-2, 141, 143, 145, 147, 148
Farebrother 27, 29, 45, 47, 50, 54, 63, 70, 78, 79-80, 82, 97, 114
Featherstone 4, 43, 45, 49, 63, 123, 125, 126
Garth, Caleb 3, 19-20, 27, 43, 45, 54, 57, 65-6, 67, 78, 100
Garth, Mary 19-20, 27, 29, 45, 46-7, 54-5, 57, 78-9, 84, 126
Garth, Mrs 45, 47
Ladislaw 3, 14, 27, 31-2, 33, 53-4, 55, 58, 66, 81, 82-4, 86, 91, 99, 100, 101, 109, 110-11, 112, 114-15, 117-18, 125, 131, 143, 147, 149
Laure 61, 96, 130-1
Lydgate 4, 7, 8, 14, 21, 27, 29, 33, 36-8, 48, 52-3, 54, 57, 59, 61, 63, 64, 66, 79, 80, 81, 82, 83, 91-7, 100, 101, 102, 121, 128, 130-2, 143, 145
Naumann 21, 31, 105
Raffles 46, 80, 82, 89-91, 125, 131
Trumbull, Borthrop 40, 43, 57, 63, 76-7
Vincy, Fred 4, 8, 19, 20, 26, 28-9, 40, 45, 48, 54-5, 63, 78, 79, 81, 82, 84-5, 126, 131
Vincy, Mr 46, 47-8, 71
Vincy, Mrs 45, 47
Vincy, Rosamond 4, 29, 33, 40, 48, 49, 57-8, 64, 66, 67-8, 78, 80, 81, 82, 83, 91, 93-7, 100, 131, 143, 148
Christian Observer 24
Cockshut, A. O. J. 78
Comte, Auguste 22
Conrad, Joseph 142, 145
Cross, John Walter 3, 135

Daiches, David 146
Daniel Deronda 98, 102, 133, 135, 137
Dante 34
Darwin, Charles 14, 122
Davy, Sir Humphry, *Elements of Agricultural Chemistry* 23
Dawson, W. J. 137
Dicey, A. V. 12
Dickens, Charles 10, 16, 60, 77, 78, 89-90, 91, 133, 141; *Bleak House* 52; *Little Dorrit* 90, 91; *Oliver Twist* 90